Secularity and Nonreligion in North America

BLOOMSBURY RELIGION IN NORTH AMERICA

The articles in this book were first published in the digital collection *Bloomsbury Religion in North America*. Covering North America's diverse religious traditions, this digital collection provides reliable and peer-reviewed articles and eBooks for students and instructors of religious studies, anthropology of religion, sociology of religion, and history. Learn more and get access for your library at www.theologyandreligiononline.com/bloomsbury-religion-in-north-america

BLOOMSBURY
RELIGION IN
NORTH AMERICA

Also available:

Islam in North America, edited by Hussein Rashid,
Huma Mohibullah and Vincent Biondo

Religion and Nature in North America,
edited by Whitney Bauman and Laurel D. Kearns

Christianity in North America,
edited by Dyron B. Daughrity

Religion, Science and Technology in North America,
edited by Whitney Bauman and Lisa Stenmark

Secularity and Nonreligion in North America

An Introduction

EDITED BY
JESSE M. SMITH AND
RYAN T. CRAGUN

BLOOMSBURY ACADEMIC
LONDON • NEW YORK • OXFORD • NEW DELHI • SYDNEY

BLOOMSBURY ACADEMIC
Bloomsbury Publishing Plc
50 Bedford Square, London, WC1B 3DP, UK
1385 Broadway, New York, NY 10018, USA
29 Earlsfort Terrace, Dublin 2, Ireland

BLOOMSBURY, BLOOMSBURY ACADEMIC and the Diana logo are
trademarks of Bloomsbury Publishing Plc

First published online in 2021

This print edition published 2024

Copyright © Bloomsbury Publishing Plc, 2021, 2024

Jesse M. Smith and Ryan T. Cragun have asserted their right
under the Copyright, Designs and Patents Act, 1988, to be identified as Editors of this work.

Cover design: Rebecca Heselton
Cover image © Lisa-Blue/ Getty Images'

All rights reserved. No part of this publication may be reproduced or transmitted
in any form or by any means, electronic or mechanical, including photocopying,
recording, or any information storage or retrieval system, without prior
permission in writing from the publishers.

Bloomsbury Publishing Plc does not have any control over, or responsibility for,
any third-party websites referred to or in this book. All internet addresses given in
this book were correct at the time of going to press. The author and publisher regret
any inconvenience caused if addresses have changed or sites have ceased to exist,
but can accept no responsibility for any such changes.

A catalogue record for this book is available from the British Library.

Library of Congress Cataloging-in-Publication Data
Names: Smith, Jesse M., editor. | Cragun, Ryan T., editor.
Title: Secularity and nonreligion in North America : an introduction /
edited by Jesse M. Smith and Ryan T. Cragun.
Description: London ; New York : Bloomsbury Academic, 2024. |
Series: Bloomsbury religion in North America | First published online in 2021. |
Includes bibliographical references and index.
Identifiers: LCCN 2023040305 | ISBN 9781350407435 (hardback) |
ISBN 9781350407442 (paperback)
Subjects: LCSH: Secularism–North America. | Non-church-affiliated people–North America.
Classification: LCC BL2765.N7 S43 2024 | DDC 211/.6097–dc23/eng/20231010
LC record available at https://lccn.loc.gov/2023040305

ISBN: HB: 978-1-3504-0743-5
        PB: 978-1-3504-0744-2

Series: Bloomsbury Religion in North America

Typeset by Integra Software Services Pvt. Ltd.
Printed and bound in Great Britain

To find out more about our authors and books visit www.bloomsbury.com
and sign up for our newsletters

Contents

List of Figures … vi

List of Tables … xii

1 Secularity and Nonreligion *Jesse M. Smith and Ryan T. Cragun* … 1

2 Demographics of the Nonreligious in the United States *Ariela Keysar* … 29

3 Being Nonreligious in the United States *Caitlin Halligan* … 44

4 Nice, Tolerant, Indifferent Canadians: Religious Nones North of the 49th *Joel Thiessen and Sarah Wilkins-Laflamme* … 63

5 Nonreligious Organizations in North America *Mathieu Colin* … 81

6 The Organizational Dynamics of Local Secular Communities *Amanda Schutz* … 99

7 Minority Nonreligion in North America *Daniel Swann* … 118

8 Morality, Prosociality, and Nonreligion *Luke Galen* … 135

9 The Politics of Nonreligion *Jonathan Simmons* … 152

10 Nonreligion and Health *David Speed* … 171

11 Secular Parenting *Christel Manning* … 194

List of Contributors … 212

Index … 213

List of Figures

1.1 References to the nonreligious in two leading sociology of religion journals, 1975–2018. Journals: Sociology of Religion and Journal for the Scientific Study of Religion. *Source:* created by author 3

1.2 Percentage nonreligious in the United States, Mexico, and Canada—1972–2018. *Source:* created by author from US general social survey, world values survey, Mexican census, Canadian census; with interpolated missing values 4

1.3 Belief in God by religious affiliation in the United States, 2018. *Source:* created by author from general social survey 2018 data 10

1.4 Marital status by belief in God in Mexico, 2012. *Source:* created by author from world values survey 2012 data 11

1.5 Average number of children by belief in God in the United States and Mexico. *Source:* created by author from GSS 2018 for the United States and world values survey 2012 for Mexico 11

1.6 How justifiable is it to claim government benefits to which you are not entitled by country and belief in God. *Source:* created by author from world values survey data—for the United States and Mexico 2010–2014; and Canada 2005–2008 17

2.1 Percentage of people identifying with no religion, 1972–2018. *Source:* created by author from general social survey data 32

2.2 Gender composition of the religiously affiliated, nonreligious, and atheists and agnostics. *Source:* created by author from Pew Research Center (2012) data 33

2.3 Religious and nonreligious by age group. *Source:* created by author from Pew Research Center (2012) data 34

LIST OF FIGURES

2.4 Percentage of each generation identifying as having no religious affiliation. *Source:* created by author from Pew Religious Landscape Survey 2014 data 35

2.5 Religious and nonreligious by educational attainment. *Source:* created by author from Pew Research Center 2012 data 38

2.6 Percentage of nonreligious by state, 2008. *Source:* created by author from ARIS 2008 data 39

3.1 Brother Jed is confronted by students at Indiana University in Bloomington, Indiana, while preaching about religion. *Source:* SOPA Images/Getty Images 46

3.2 An individual holds up a sign telling his mother that he's an atheist. *Source:* Elvert Barnes 49

3.3 Military personnel are able to include atheist on their dog tags. *Source:* darwin.wins 53

3.4 Nonreligious organizations have posted signs and billboards around the world to help other nonreligious individuals realize they are not alone. *Source:* Sandy Huffaker Getty Images 54

4.1 Rates of religious nones, six Canadian census regions, 1971–2016. *Source of data:* 1971 census, 1981 census, 1985–2016 (cycles 1–30) general social surveys, statistics Canada (N British Columbia = 35,497; N Prairies = 78,242; N Ontario = 99,591; N Quebec = 83,299; N Atlantic Canada = 83,093). Missing data for 1987–1988, 1997, 2002 and 2007 replaced by averages from preceding and posterior years. Northern Canada: 1991 census, 2001 census and 2011 nhs. all estimates weighted to be representative of general populations 65

4.2 Demographic composition of those who are religiously affiliated and those with no religion, Canada, 2010–14, averages. *Source of data:* 2010–2014 (cycles 24–28) general social surveys, statistics Canada. estimates weighted to be representative of the general populations. N 15 years and older = 118,763. n 25–44 years old = 31,856 67

4.3 Types of religious nones, among unaffiliated respondents eighteen to thirty-five years old, Canada, 2019. *Source of data:* millennial trends survey 2019. estimates weighted to be representative of the young adult population. N = 687   68

4.4 "On a scale from 0 to 10 (0 indicating very uncomfortable; 10 indicating very comfortable), please indicate what level of comfort you would feel if the following type of person became your relative by marriage (in-law)." Religiously unaffiliated respondents eighteen to thirty-five years old, Canada and the United States, 2019. *Source of the data:* millennial trends survey 2019. N Canada = 683; N USA = 420. estimates weighted to be representative of young adult populations   72

4.5 Predicted probabilities of left-leaning sociopolitical attitudes among religious none adults, United States, 2014, with CI (95 per cent). *Source:* created by author   73

4.6 Predicted probabilities of left-leaning sociopolitical attitudes among adults, Canada, 2011 and 2015, with CI (95 per cent). *Source:* created by author   74

5.1 April 18, 1987; Madalyn Murray O'hair at the atheists convention at the Radisson Hotel. *Source:* photograph by Dave Buresh/The Denver Post via Getty Images   83

5.2 Abortion activist Dr. Henry Morgentaler celebrating the Canadian supreme court ruling on the abortion law, January 28, 1988. *Source:* David Cooper/Toronto Star via Getty Images   86

5.3 Comedy writer Ariane Sherine (l), professor Richard Dawkins (c), and guardian writer Polly Toynbee (r) pose for pictures beside a London bus displaying an advertising campaign with the words: "there's probably no god. Now stop worrying and enjoy your life," London, January 6, 2009. *Source:* Leon Neal/AFP via Getty Images   88

5.4 Salem, MA—July 25: lucien greaves, spokesman for the satanic temple, is photographed outside a Salem courthouse, a group of

LIST OF FIGURES

political activists who identify themselves as a religious sect, are seeking to establish after-school satan clubs as a counterpart to fundamentalist christian good news clubs, which they see as the religious right trying to infiltrate public education and erode the separation of church and state. *Source:* photograph by Josh Reynolds for the Washington Post via Getty Images 90

5.5 The baphomet statue is seen in the conversion room at the satanic temple where a "hell house" is being held in Salem, Massachusetts, on October 8, 2019. the hell house was a parody on a christian conversion center meant to scare atheists and other satanic church members. *Source:* photograph by Joseph Prezioso/AFP via Getty Images 92

6.1 National secular organization American Atheists advertises its holiday message in Times Square. *Source:* Richard Levine/Alamy Stock Photo 100

6.2 Greater Houston is home to some of the largest megachurches in the United States, including Woodland Church, Second Baptist Church, and Lakewood Church (pictured here). Attendance at Lakewood Church averages about 43,000 every week. *Source:* Timothy Fadek / Getty Images 102

6.3 A local secular organization participates in their city's LGBTQ Pride Parade. *Source:* 400tmax / Getty Images 104

6.4 Attendees sing along to pop songs at the Sunday Assembly, a godless congregation in London that has established local franchises around the world. *Source:* Leon Neal / Getty Images 106

6.5 Nonbelievers, and atheists specifically, are often associated with other groups that are perceived as lacking morality. *Source:* Education Images/Getty 111

7.1 Map of Canada, the United States, and Mexico. *Source:* Bergserg/Getty 119

LIST OF FIGURES

7.2 Zora Neale Hurston was a prominent member of the Harlem Renaissance. *Source:* Carl Van Vechten. silver geletin print, 1938   122

7.3 A. Philip Randolph was a freethinker and leader of the civil rights movement. *Source:* Science History Images/Alamy Stock Photo   123

7.4 Images from the Mexican Revolution. *Source:* Photo 12 /Alamy Stock Photo   128

7.5 Example of the way in which "visible minority" appears on many forms in Canada. *Source:* Government of Canada   129

8.1 Guidance on questions of right and wrong (Pew Research Center 2015). Percentage of Americans who say they "look to ___ for guidance on questions of right and wrong." *Source:* created by author from Pew 2015 data   138

8.2 Curvilinear model of morality and prosociality by strength of worldview conviction. *Source:* created by author   140

9.1 The nonreligious have historically been disproportionately white and male, but that is changing in North America. *Source:* SOPA Images / Getty Images   154

9.2 The sign in this photograph with the suggestion, "Get religion out of my underwear," illustrates that the nonreligious are increasingly organized and pushing against religious intrusions into secular spheres. *Source:* Brendan Smialowski / Getty images   155

9.3 Nonreligious individuals have taken to debating religious fundamentalists when fundamentalists attempt to proselytize in public. *Source:* Brendan Smialowski / Getty images   156

9.4 Evangelical Americans have been among the most reliable of President Donald Trump's supporters. *Source:* Mark Wallheiser/Stringer/Getty   157

10.1 Projected growth of the religiously unaffiliated populations in Canada, Mexico, and the United States. *Source:* created by author from Pew Research Center (2015) data   172

LIST OF FIGURES

10.2 How belief in God is associated with beliefs about teenagers' access to birth control (with linearized error bars). *Source:* created by author from general social survey data for 2012, 2014, 2016, and 2018 177

10.3 Self-reported health data from the 2011 and 2012 Canadian Community Health Survey by religious affiliation (with standard error bars) 179

10.4 Church attendance predicting self-rated health and satisfaction with life in the combined 2011 and 2012 Canadian Community Health Survey (with standard error bars) 180

10.5 Confidence in God's existence predicting happiness category in the 2018 General Social Survey (with standard error bars) 181

10.6 Simulated curvilinear relationship between religion/spirituality and health 183

11.1 People starting families now are more likely to be nonreligious. *Source:* Pew, 2014 195

11.2 Many secular individuals find meaning in nature. *Source:* bombuscreative / Getty Images 197

11.3 Some nones have a distinct nonreligious identity. *Source:* castillodominici/Getty/iStock Images Plus 199

11.4 Some nones are better described as spiritual but not religious. *Source:* fizkes / Getty Images 200

11.5 Grandparents may influence the transmission of secular worldviews. *Source:* eclipse_images / Getty Images 202

11.6 Secular parents want to expose their children to diverse worldviews. *Source:* FatCamera / Getty Images 205

11.7 Tolerance of diversity is a core value for many secular parents. *Source:* Mixmike / Getty Images 208

List of Tables

2.1 Percentage of the US Population That Was Atheist, Agnostic, or Nothing in Particular by Time and Data Set 31
2.2 Race and Ethnicity of Affiliated and Unaffiliated Americans, 2007–14 36
2.3 Marital Status of Religiously Affiliated and Unaffiliated Americans, 2007–14 37
3.1 Negative Familial Responses to Coming Out as an Atheist 50
7.1 Racial/Ethnic Composition of Religious Groups in the United States (%) 120
7.2 Religiosity of Asian Americans Compared with the General Public 126
7.3 Racial/Ethnic Minorities in Canada 130
8.1 Moral Foundations Theory 136
8.2 Do Americans Believe It Is Necessary to Believe in God to Be Moral? Percentage of US Adults Who Say It Is Not Necessary to Believe in God to Be Moral and Have Good Values 144
8.3 Summary of Moral, Ethical, and Prosocial Differences Between the Nonreligious and Religious 146

1

Secularity and Nonreligion

Jesse M. Smith and Ryan T. Cragun

The empirical study of secularity and nonreligion is beginning to mature. Although there were a few scholars in the 1960s and 1970s (see Campbell 1971; Demerath 1969; Vernon 1968) who took seriously the project of studying some of the phenomena now included under the rubric of *secularity and nonreligion*, in historical perspective, the subject was largely unrecognized, ignored, or seen as unimportant. This is no longer the case. Studies of those who claim no religion, as well as those who embrace affirmatively secular identities or some version of "religion's other" (Smith and Cragun 2019), has steadily risen. Especially since the early 2000s, social science research on secularism, nonreligion, and atheism has seen impressive growth.

For centuries, philosophers and theologians have contemplated or arm-chair theorized the validity of atheism and its social and moral implications, but *empirical* studies that define, measure, and analyze data collected from the real world on such a topic is a relatively recent occurrence. For their part, sociologists have, for a century and a half, empirically studied *secularization*: the decline of religion in the face of modernization. Indeed, there is substantial evidence the societies of North America have undergone secularization. However, the validity of secularization as an overarching theoretical model that explains the complex role of religion and nonreligion in contemporary society is contested, and few scholars today would claim that modernization will spell the complete demise of religion around the globe, let alone in North America. Even scholars who subscribe to the theory are unlikely to suggest it explains *everything* concerning the rise—and various dimensions of—contemporary secularity and nonreligion in North America. Moreover, the various topics, populations, and processes discussed throughout this volume include perspectives from different academic disciplines (a strength of this project), and some researchers are less concerned with the secularization thesis as such, since there are different versions and adaptations of the thesis to which scholars apply varying importance and credibility (see Berger 1967; Bruce 2002; Stark 1999). Still, general readers and all students of religion and nonreligion alike should be aware of the concept of secularization and consider its relevance to the *Religion in North America* resource as a whole.

The articles in this volume showcase a sampling of the kind of research being conducted today by sociologists, psychologists, and other scholars of nonreligion. We use the phrase *secularity and nonreligion* broadly, as a way to capture disparate but related psychological and sociological processes, and other cultural phenomena. We examine categories including secularism, atheism, humanism, and the nones, and how these intersect with variables such as the family, politics, health, and inequality in the context of North America. It is important to note that scholars across disciplines may recognize and use these terms in slightly different ways, studying their relationships to other variables not covered in our discussion. Finding complete consensus on definitions of all the concepts under the banner of secularity and nonreligion is not possible. Indeed, the same can be said for religion itself, as there exists no single definition that enjoys universal consensus. Our goal here is simply to function as a starting point for introducing, defining, and discussing the major questions, issues, and discoveries in this still-evolving field of inquiry. Given its history and the relative newness of the field, it is also important to note the broader discussion among scholars regarding how best to study and theorize secularity and nonreligion. As one might expect, researchers have applied traditional, tried, and true methods such as quantitative analysis of survey data and qualitative analysis of interview data. Traditional theories too, such as secularization or rational choice theory (discussed below), have been used to help explain the growing presence of secularity and increasing numbers of those who claim no religion. But some scholars are also discussing how, and in what ways, there should be unique methods and theories developed for the study of nonreligion in its own right, apart from those long used to study religion (Lee 2015).

In the present article, we provide a general overview of the topic of secularity and nonreligion in North America. We discuss relevant research questions and terminology, outline significant subtopics, and highlight some of the key social scientific findings. These substantive issues are dealt with in more detail in the articles in this volume. As mentioned, there are a few studies from the second part of the twentieth century relevant to this overview, but our focus is on the proliferation of research that has emerged in the twenty-first century. There is now significant scholarly interest in the field, and a substantial empirical literature to draw from in learning about these phenomena (Cragun 2016). This is evidenced in part by new funded research in the area, an international professional organization called the Nonreligion and Secularity Research Network, and two academic journals devoted exclusively to the topic: *Secularism and Nonreligion* and *Secular Studies*. There are many reasons for the new interest in this area; a primary one being the much-discussed rise in the number

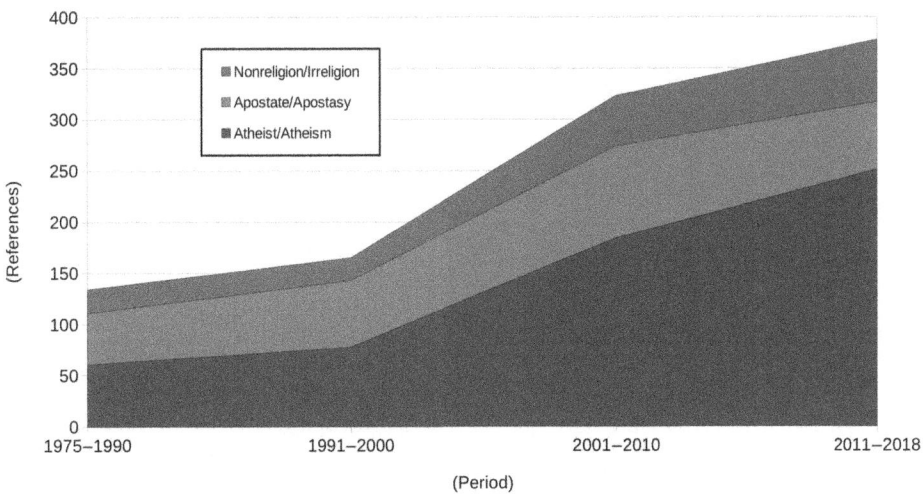

FIGURE 1.1 *References to the nonreligious in two leading sociology of religion journals, 1975–2018. Journals:* Sociology of Religion *and* Journal for the Scientific Study of Religion. Source: *Created by author.*

of those who claim no religion in North America, and especially the United States, where the fastest growing "religious" group is the nones (Baker and Smith 2015; Kosmin and Keysar 2006; Kosmin et al. 2009). In this context, the importance of understanding secularity and nonreligion is clear, as is the need for more research in the area.

Defining Secularity and Nonreligion

All discussions throughout the *Religion in North America* resource require defining relevant terms. Religious ideas, institutions, and the ways in which these are studied necessitate careful scholarly attention. As Lee (2015) and others observe, there is an additional reason for this in the study of nonreligion: the conceptual relationship between religion and "religion's other" is complex (Smith and Cragun 2019). Much about how scholars think about nonreligion and, indeed, how many nonreligious people think of themselves is done in terms of the religious beliefs and behaviors to which they do not subscribe. It is for this reason that we first discuss in some detail the definitions and challenges of studying secularity and nonreligion.

The nonreligious in North America are diverse and comprised of many subgroups with varying ideologies, political preferences, daily practices, and values. Some are indifferent to religion; others positively repudiate it. But one thing the nonreligious have in common, at least in terms of how social scientists study them, is that they

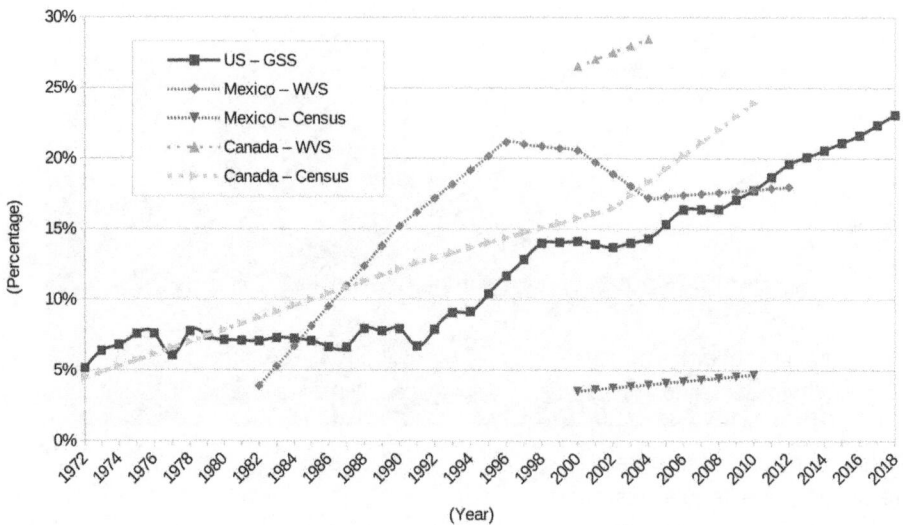

FIGURE 1.2 *Percentage nonreligious in the United States, Mexico, and Canada—1972–2018.* Source: *Created by author from US General Social Survey, World Values Survey, Mexican Census, Canadian Census; with interpolated missing values.*

stand in some kind of relationship to religion. As Quack notes, nonreligion deals with phenomena that are not considered religious but that are in some ways "dependent on religion" (2014: 1). Agreeing that there is much diversity in nonreligion and that it should be studied in its own right, he argues that scholars should nevertheless take into account the various "entanglements" nonreligion (and secularity) has with religion. It is in this context that the definitions of all the terms outlined below should be understood.

Before defining the words that point to various dimensions of secularity and nonreligion, let us first define these two words themselves. *Secularity* is a noun that simply refers to the state of *being* secular. Thus, it is really the adjective "secular" that needs definition. *Secular*, in its broadest sense, refers to all things *not* religious. Its Latin roots signal the idea of the temporal or worldly, and it has been used in this way for nearly seven hundred years. Importantly, secular can refer not only to that which is not religious but also to a wide range of behaviors completely unrelated to religion. Riding a bike or eating a snack are secular activities in this sense. Of course, individuals and groups that *identify* as secular (our concern here) are referring more narrowly to the fact that they are not religious and that they hold secular beliefs and values.

Nonreligion is a much newer term, and it is increasingly used by scholars to refer to that which is not religious (like secular) but *related to* religion in some important way. To examine those who reject a formerly held religious identity and then embrace a secular one is to study nonreligion. An ex-Catholic who becomes an atheist is no longer religious, but this process necessarily entails a relationship to religion. Likewise, the study of secular organizations devoted to the separation of church and state is another instance of nonreligion because of the context of its relationship to religion. In both of these situations, what is under investigation is other to, but also related to, religion (Cragun 2016; Lee 2015; Quack 2014; Smith and Cragun 2019).

Atheism, Agnosticism, Humanism

The most basic definition of *atheism* derives from its two roots, the prefix "a" meaning "not" or "without" and the word "theism," which comes from the Greek "theos," meaning God. Atheism, thus, refers to not believing in God. However, as many scholars will point out, there are various qualifiers to atheism, some with meaningful differences. One regular distinction is between positive and negative atheism. The former implies an awareness of, but disbelief in, a particular god. A person's rejection of the existence of the Greek god Apollo is an instance of positive atheism because the person is aware of the claim about Apollo's existence. Conversely, with negative atheism, one is unaware of the claimed existence of a particular god and therefore cannot actively disbelieve in such a god. Most people are simply unaware of the many gods and deities that have been posited throughout human history. They do not believe in such gods, but not because they have had a chance to learn about them. George Smith (1980) observed another distinction in defining atheism. For him, an atheist is "someone who does not believe in God, not someone who believes God does not exist." The first clause indicates simple absence of belief (negative atheism), whereas the second asserts an *affirmative belief* that there is no God. Smith saw this as a critical difference.

Interestingly, much of the contemporary empirical research on atheists leaves such differences unstated. This is likely due to both the lack of specificity on survey questionnaires and the fact that most people who participate in qualitative studies are doing so based on their positive atheism (i.e., people are unlikely to be questioned about gods they have never heard of). Notwithstanding the commingling of positive and negative atheists, atheists have been the subject of many studies in the area of secularity and nonreligion in North America, in part because of their symbolic and moral relevance and non-normative status, especially in the United States (Hunsberger and Altemeyer 2006).

Agnosticism was coined by Thomas Huxley in the late 1860s. Here again the prefix "a" ("not" or "without") is attached to a Greek word, "gnostic," which refers to knowledge. A literal translation then, is to be "without knowledge." Those who claim no knowledge of God or the supernatural are therefore agnostic. The term is often used today in a way that also implies it may not be possible to know of such things. The philosopher Bertrand Russell (1872–1970) famously opined in a 1953 essay, "I ought to call myself an agnostic; but, for all practical purposes, I am an atheist." In discussing where the burden of proof lies, Russell was suggesting that all atheists are technically agnostics, since they cannot prove the negative, "God does not exist." In contexts where atheism is highly stigmatized, some nonbelievers apply the label agnostic as a more socially accepted alternative to atheist (Smith 2011).

Humanism is a broader concept than either atheism or agnosticism in that it is less a direct statement about the existence of a god than a philosophical position encompassing a wide range of values and principles (indeed, some religious people identify with humanism). Generally, humanism outlines a nontheistic and non-supernaturalist interpretation of human existence. It posits that the major domains of human concern such as ethics and morality, human rights, social equality, and the principles by which societies should organize, are best understood and accomplished through science, reason, and other Enlightenment values. Humanists may identify with humanism alone, or they may also answer to atheist, agnostic, or any number of related terms. Secular is often prefixed to humanist for "secular humanist" to further clarify one's position concerning the role of God and religion in human affairs. Multiple humanist manifestos have been produced by organizations that outline the humanist position in detail.

Secularism, Irreligion, and the Nones

We have already defined "secular," but there is another important variant of the word, and that is s*ecularism*: the set of beliefs around the idea that religion should be kept separate from the state and its institutions. Coined by the English author George Holyoake (1817–1906), leader of the secularist movement in the nineteenth-century Britain, this word has traditionally invoked the political dimension of the secular. Organizations that work to ensure the separation of church and state, for instance, promote a political philosophy that discourages a relationship between government and religion. The United States, despite being somewhat more religious compared to other developed nations, hosts a secular society insofar as its government and citizens respect the first amendment to its constitution. Both Canada and Mexico today have analogous secular laws establishing freedom of and from religion. Some secularists—those who support secularism—in North America seek to redouble the boundary between the church and the state. That is, they do not seek the demise of religion; they simply want to see it kept to the private sphere. Other secularists may promote a form of secularism that intends the erosion of religious worldviews by more widespread acceptance of secular and scientific ones (see the section on secular organizations below).

The word *irreligion* simply applies the prefix "ir," meaning "not" or "no," to religion. Thus, to be irreligious is to be nonreligious or have no religion. Somewhat confusingly, the term also has a history of being used to refer not just to the lack of religion but also to working against or disrespecting religion in some way (Demerath 1969). This may be one reason why the word (along with "areligion"), although it is still occasionally referenced, has not been widely adopted in the contemporary research literature. There were some empirical studies of "irreligion," Colin Campbell's 1971 monograph, *Toward a Sociology of Irreligion*, being foremost among them. Likewise, several studies of the "nones" were conducted in the 1960s (e.g., Vernon 1968), and it is this term that has become much more widely used today. The *nones* are simply those who have no religious preference (the term comes from the "none" option on surveys). Sometimes used interchangeably with the nonreligious or religiously unaffiliated, the nones do not subscribe to any particular religion and may be indifferent to it. Although some nones may also be atheists, agnostic, or embrace some other nonreligious identity, research indicates many nones continue to hold theistic beliefs (Hout and Fischer 2002; Packard and Ferguson 2018; Pew Research Center 2014).

Apostasy and Religious Exiting

One final category needing definition relates to how people leave religion. The concept of apostasy has a long history (Smith 2017b), but a significant part of the growing literature in secularity and nonreligion deals with apostasy and other forms of religious exiting. The word *apostasy* has both Greek and Latin roots. The Greek *apostasia* and Latin *apostasis* refer respectively to "defection" and "revolt." Most standard definitions today include something like "total departure from [one's] religion" (Smith 2017b). Usually this involves an explicit repudiation of former religious beliefs (not just religious inactivity). One can technically depart from any group or ideology (e.g., political beliefs) but its strongest connotation is with religion. One may abandon one religious group in favor of another, but this is referred to as religious switching in the literature, not apostasy.

As Cragun and Hammer (2011) have noted, apostasy is a symbolically loaded term and the label "apostate" is often applied pejoratively. Because of this, they suggest *religious exiting*, or the social and psychological process by which an individual exits a former religious identity or ideology (Brinkerhoff and Mackie 1993). As a more neutral phrase than apostasy, it has the additional advantage of capturing a wider range of activity, "as it reflects only the fact that someone left a religion and implies nothing else about where that person went or whether they are now critical of the religion they left" (Cragun 2016: 305). Cragun and Hammer's point is important, but for most scholars of secularity and nonreligion, the primary focus when studying religious "exiters" has tended to be on those who have not just left religion (Bromley 1998) but adopted in its place some kind of nonreligious identity, a process some call deconversion (Fazzino 2014; Jacobs 1989).

All of the above terms, to varying degrees, have been and continue to be the subject of research in the area of secularity and nonreligion. The articles in this volume explore and explain the relevance of these concepts and point toward the kinds of empirical research being conducted on them in the twenty-first century. As noted earlier, scholars (including the authors of this volume) may vary somewhat in their exact definitions and usage of these words, but the aim of this volume of this introductory article is to sensitize readers to the vocabulary of secularity and nonreligion.

Rise of Research on Secularity and Nonreligion

As suggested earlier, there are several causes for the increased interest, both scholarly and popular, in the nonreligious. One cause of interest was the host of best-selling books in the first decade of the twenty-first century critical of religion, including *The End of Faith* (2004) by Sam Harris, *The God Delusion* (2006) by Richard Dawkins, *Breaking the Spell: Religion as a Natural Phenomenon* (2006) by Daniel Dennett, and *God Is Not Great: How Religion Poisons Everything* (2007) by the late Christopher Hitchens. These books fueled controversy and debate and brought new attention to the public regarding the question of the role of religion and theism in society. This public conversation likely played some role for scholars of nonreligion, but it is the statistical rise of the nones and other nonreligious individuals, particularly in the United States and Canada, that spurred the dramatic increase in research on the nonreligious (as shown in Figure 1.2). Not surprisingly, the bulk of this research has been directed at the American and Canadian contexts, particularly since the early 2000s. To date, there is much less research on the nonreligious in Mexico, although we do have some reliable estimates of the nones, as shown in Figure 1.2. Figure 1.2 also illustrates that how these groups are defined makes a big difference in estimates. In both Canada and Mexico, their censuses include a question about religious affiliation. In the censuses, the early estimates of the nonreligious were quite low. In contrast, the World Values Survey (WVS) asked individuals whether they belonged to a religious denomination or not. Estimates based on that question were historically much higher, but the two estimates are now approaching parity in the two countries.

References to the nonreligious do appear in the literature prior to the turn of the twenty-first century, but it was mostly in the context of the vast research on religion. The nonreligious were generally not studied in their own right. The question "what is the character of nonreligion and the experience of the nonreligious" was left untreated; instead the nonreligious tended to be viewed by scholars as a deviant subset of the religious (Cragun 2016). The term secular regularly appeared in research from decades ago, but mostly in reference to secularization or secularism in senses defined earlier, not in terms of the secularity of individuals, or the practices, beliefs, and lives of those who explicitly claim a secular identity. More dramatically, as Figure 1.1 shows, only a handful of studies prior to the 1960s even mention atheists.

Fast forward to the first decade of the twenty-first century and one will find a great deal more empirical research on all these groups, and a general acknowledgment of the diversity of nonreligion in terms of both behavior and belief (Lim, MacGregor, and Putnam 2010; Smith 2017a, b). Scholars are studying secularity and nonreligion on its own terms both as a subfield of research on religion and as its own area (Smith and Cragun 2019). There have been many dozens of studies of atheists and agnostics, the nones, the spiritual-but-not-religious (SBNR), skeptics, and freethinkers, secularists, religious exiters, those indifferent to religion, and more. The diversity of such studies reflects the actual diversity in the North American nonreligious community at large. Research by sociologists, psychologists, and other scholars has led to greater understanding of this community as well as the nature and character of secularity and nonreligion. The remaining sections of this overview article (excluding the last one on future research) provide a brief outline of the major areas of inquiry and their associated empirical studies, both qualitative and quantitative, primarily over the last fifteen years when research on the nonreligious began to accelerate.

Characteristics of the Nonreligious and Affirmatively Secular

Because of data limitations and issues with survey design (see Cragun 2019), knowing what the true nonreligious population across North America is can be difficult. Fortunately, there is sufficient data for the United States, Canada, and Mexico (there is very limited data in other countries in North America) to offer useful estimates. Taking the average of several major survey estimates (including Pew, Gallop, and WVS), in the United States, which has a total population of 327 million, approximately 25 percent are nonreligious; somewhere between 4 percent and 11 percent are atheists. Of Canada's population of 37 million, around 24 percent are nonreligious; roughly 7 percent of whom are atheists. In Mexico, with 126 million people, roughly 20 percent are nonreligious; around 4 percent of Mexicans are atheists. It is important to note these estimates are based on different types of questions that can be interpreted in different ways (Cragun 2019). For instance, individuals who respond "no" to Gallup's question, "Is religion an important part of your daily life?" are not being assessed on any of their beliefs (or nonbelief). A negative response to this question only implies such respondents do not consider themselves particularly religious. The estimates of the number of atheists are likely more accurate because survey questions tend to be more direct; for example, the WVS simply asks, "Do you believe in God?" to which the respondent can respond "yes," "no," or "I don't know."

With these general estimates in mind, one major focus has been on the social and demographic characteristics of atheists, the nones, and other nonreligious individuals (see Pasquale 2010). As Smith and Cragun (2019) and others note, it would be wrong to assume the nonreligious in North America make up anything resembling a homogeneous community. Those who practice no religion have different personal

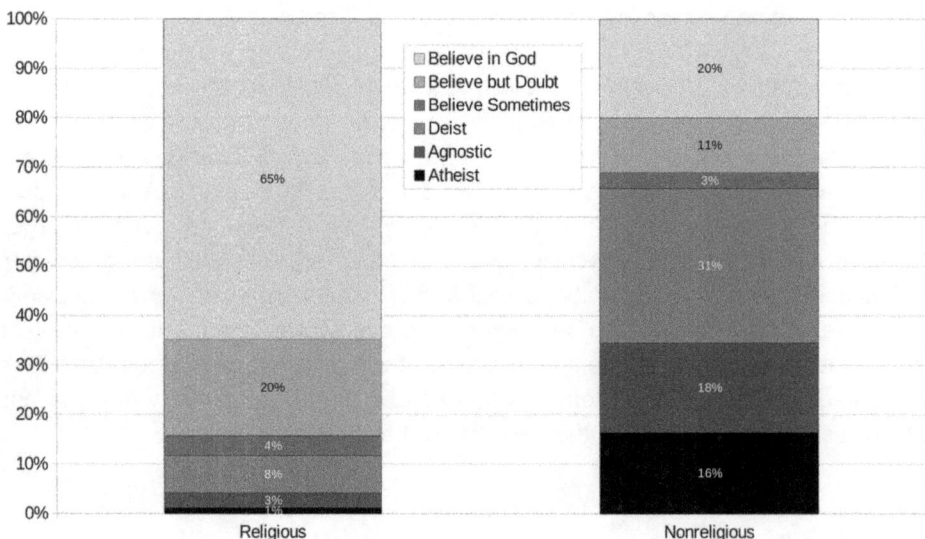

FIGURE 1.3 *Belief in God by religious affiliation in the United States, 2018.* Source: *Created by author from General Social Survey 2018 data.*

beliefs, political attitudes, and even hold disparate worldviews (Beaman and Tomlins 2015; Coleman, Hood, and Streib 2018; Taves, Asprem, and Ihm 2018), some of which include theistic or supernatural beliefs. Clearly, being nonreligious (an identity reference) cannot be equated with being an atheist (a particular view regarding the existence of a deity) although, as expected, the nonreligious are indeed more likely to claim atheism, as Figure 1.3 shows.

Despite these challenges, researchers have identified clear patterns regarding variables such as age, race, class, gender, education, and geography that tell us something about who is more likely to be nonreligious and/or embrace a secular identity. Though there is some evidence challenging the degree to which we can actually predict being nonreligious (see Strawn 2019), compared to their religious counterparts, most survey research to date finds that the nonreligious tend to be disproportionately male, are younger, more highly educated, are less likely to be married, and are more progressive in their political views (Baker and Smith 2015; Kosmin et al. 2009; Sherkat 2016; Williamson and Yancey 2013).

There are also similarities and points of comparison across the United States, Canada, and Mexico. For instance, across all three countries atheists are less likely to be married than theists and tend to have fewer kids (see Figures 1.4 and 1.5). However, American atheists are more likely than both Canadian and Mexican atheists to claim that marriage is still a highly valued institution (Cragun, Hammer, and Smith 2013).

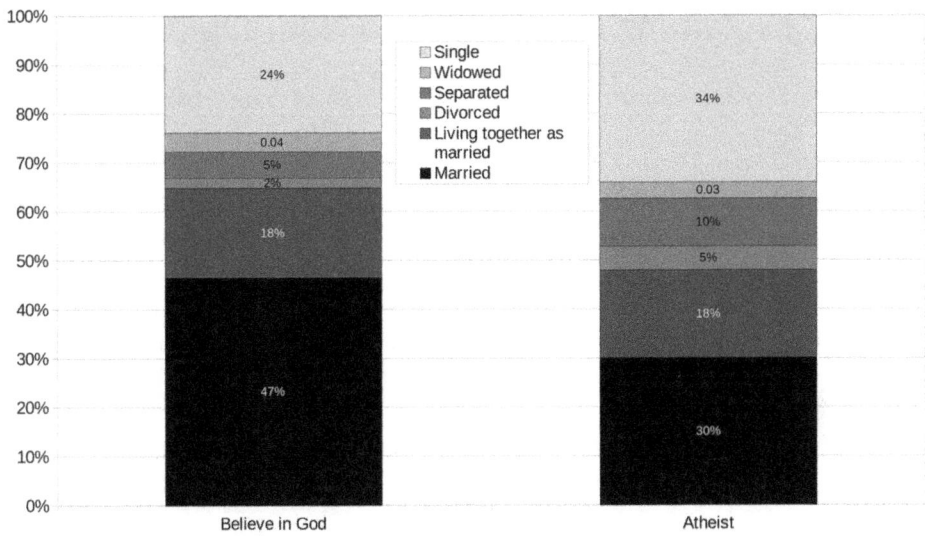

FIGURE 1.4 *Marital status by belief in God in Mexico, 2012.* Source: *Created by author from World Values Survey 2012 data.*

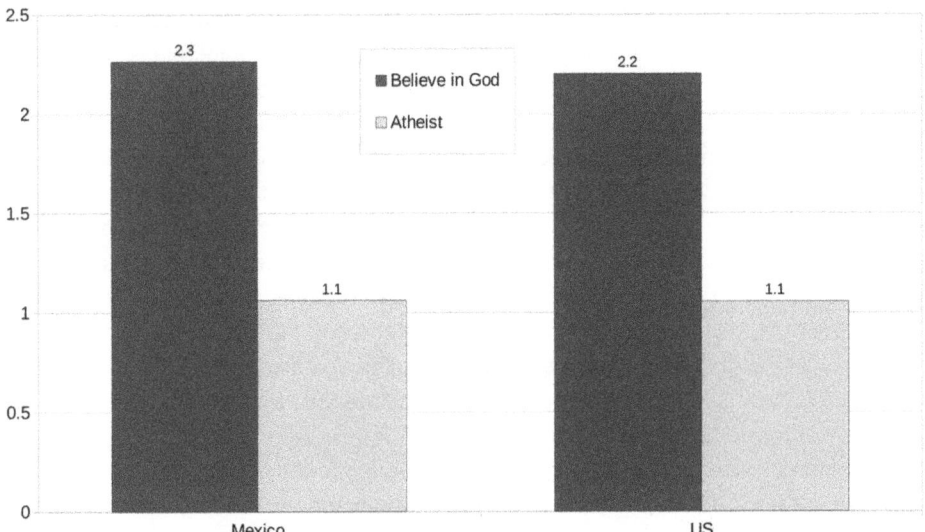

FIGURE 1.5 *Average number of children by belief in God in the United States and Mexico.* Source: *Created by author from GSS 2018 for the United States and World Values Survey 2012 for Mexico.*

Explaining Secularity and Nonreligion

Why are some people indifferent to religion? Why do others leave religion in adulthood despite having been socialized into it from childhood? Why still do others find they cannot believe the claims of religion and actively seek to promote competing secular beliefs about the world? Put succinctly, what are the social, psychological, and historical *sources* of secularity and nonreligion? Such "why" questions are challenging, since any satisfactory answer to them will have to be multilayered. Investigating the "how" of secularity and nonreligion is, in a sense, less challenging because it simply requires close observation and empirical *description* of what is happening. Researchers can, for instance, gather and report data showing that the nonreligious tend to be younger on average than the religious. But explaining why this is the case (and why it is important) is another matter. Similarly, investigating the process of becoming nonreligious requires a deeper understanding of, for example, why individuals would voluntarily adopt a label such as "atheist" despite the social cost of doing so (Abbott and Mollen 2018; Smith 2013).

Though much of the research in this area does indeed concern itself with describing and reporting various facts about the nonreligious, it has also examined different sociological, psychological, and cultural processes in an effort to explain nonreligion theoretically. Two general theories have been predominant in the literature, and are offered as broad explanatory frameworks to help address the role of religion and some of the "why" questions above. The first is *secularization theory*, which was defined earlier as the overall decline of religion because of modernization. What is modernization? This refers to the various institutions, norms and values, and ways of thinking that characterize the modern world. Liberalism, democracy, individualism, science, rationality, education, and the fact of cultural diversity are all features of modernity that have eroded premodern religious belief systems and institutions (Bruce 2013). All of these forces combined have led to the differentiation of society, or the process of religion being removed from the various social spheres in which it previously had authority, such as education and the government. Secularization occurs not only at the societal level but at the organizational and individual levels as well (Dobbelaere 2002). Consequently, the loss of religious authority, according to secularization theory, has also undercut the religious beliefs and practices of ordinary individuals in society (Yamane 1997), thus helping to explain why some have left religion or simply no longer find it relevant to their everyday lives.

The second theory is *rational choice theory*, applied to the domain of religion. Most often this is referred to in the literature as the *religious economies model* because it bases its analysis of religion on the economic model of supply and demand. In line with rational choice theory, which assumes individuals rationally evaluate the relative costs and benefits of their behaviors, people make religious choices based on what is offered in the religious marketplace and most aligned with their individual values and goals. Researchers who take this approach use the language of economics, holding that the demand by "consumers" for religious "goods" such as fellowship and belief in the promise of an afterlife, are offered by religious "firms" such as churches and congregations. The assumption is that religion is a universal need, and so demand for it is always constant. That religion can be found in all cultures throughout history is cited as evidence of this universal need. What explains disinterest in religion (and by implication the rise of the nones) is a problem with the supply of religious goods, namely, religious firms are not offering the right products, or doing so ineffectively. Such supply-side economics of religion (Stark and Finke 2000) suggest that if religious organizations did a better job of offering ideas, rituals, and other products that connected with, and appealed more to, the nonreligious, then such individuals would take up religion.

Both of these theories have limitations, particularly as they are applied to secularity and nonreligion. For example, the religious economies model simply assumes that religion has been and will always be a universal human need. The fear of death, for instance, will always keep religion in demand, as it alone offers answers to this and similar existential questions. Whether this assumption is warranted, however, is questionable, as other research shows that not all peoples and cultures seek religious or metaphysical solutions to the "problem of death" (MacMurray and Fazzino 2017; Zuckerman 2014). The supply-side view of religion is also problematic in explaining the rise of the nones in North America. For proponents of this model, the open, competitive religious marketplace in the United States compared to other advanced Western democracies where competition and enthusiasm for religion is low, explains its high number of believers and churchgoers. But some scholars (Cragun 2016; Sherkat 2016) are doubtful that the source of the sharp rise of nonreligious people in the United States today could be attributed solely to something wrong with its religious supply. Given constant competition, new forms of religion, and its long history of religious opportunity, the United States should be among the *least* likely to have such a large percentage of its population turn away from religion.

This could be a credit to secularization theory, which predicts the rise of the nones given structural differentiation and the weakened authority of religion in a pluralist society. However, though it may help explain in a generic way the declining role of religion in North America, where the forces of modernity are salient, one problem with secularization theory is that it does not itself explain why some nonreligious people adopt overtly secular identities. It is one thing to have no religious preference; it is another to embrace and, for some, actively promote a nonreligious ideology (discussed further in the secular organizations section below). Canadian society, which has some important differences from American culture, has also seen a significant rise of the nones in recent years, and scholars are still working out what this means for the future of religious diversity and theistic belief in that country (see Tomlins 2018). In the end, both secularization theory and religious economies theory should be understood in context. Both can be useful for thinking about the questions outlined above, but neither can fully explain the diversity and complexity of secularity and nonreligion today.

Anticipating the limitations of applying both secularization and rational choice to the study of the nonreligious, much of the contemporary research blends description with more carefully circumscribed "middle-range" theories (Hedstrom and Udehn 2009), which avoid some of the more sweeping claims of secularization and some of the questionable claims of the religious economies model. Such research tends to rely on what nonreligious people themselves say about why they do not adhere to any religion. From the study of apostates and other religious exiters (Ebaugh 1988; Fazzino 2014; Winell 2017) to those who become atheists and secularists (Altemeyer and Hunsberger 1997; LeDrew 2013; Smith 2011), these studies often rely on qualitative methods including interviews, ethnography, and content analysis. Though relying on the words and actions of research participants themselves as a primary source of data can be problematic (Cragun 2016), there are also significant strengths to this approach (Charmaz 2013; Kvale and Brinkmann 2009; Lofland et al. 2005), and such studies have expanded our understanding of both the lived experience of the nonreligious and the cultural processes that underlie them, and shed much light on the topic of secularity and nonreligion in general.

Several related findings have come out of this research. Studies of those who leave religion and become atheists, for instance, show an intellectual process whereby individuals begin to question the claims of religion, finding them increasingly lacking credibility (Altemeyer and Hunsberger 1997; Bradley et al. 2018; Sherkat 2008; Zuckerman 2011). Most of this research suggests a slow, cumulative process of disbelief in specific religious doctrines and supernatural events. Interview participants in such studies tend to identify religious ideas they found they could simply no longer believe. Accordingly, this research reveals the role of religious skepticism (and, in particular, skepticism of organized religion), which may play a part in the growing proportion of the population who claim no religion. Basic components of the process of religious skepticism include increased education, scientific literacy, and greater exposure to competing claims (including other religious claims) about nature and reality. Many participants cite the incompatibility of what is known about the universe through science and the religious teachings they were raised with as reasons for their leaving religion (Sherkat 2016; Smith 2017a; Williamson and Yancey 2013).

Secularization is here again relevant. The interconnected systems of meaning and behaviors that seem to give credibility to religious and supernatural claims, what Peter Berger called *plausibility structures* (Berger 1967), begin to erode in pluralistic contexts where many groups in society have different interests, values, and even competing versions of reality. For instance, the architecture of a place of worship, the rituals performed inside, and the fact that individuals are engaged in these behaviors collectively, endows any associated religious claims or doctrines with a sense of plausibility. But this plausibility structure may be undermined when any of those same individuals obtains a secular education that seems to contradict a religious precept, reads a book critical of religion, or attends a worship service of a different religious group that offers some competing religious doctrine.

Similarly, research finds other elements of secularization at play in causing individuals to disengage with or ignore religion, including "value misalignment" (Cragun 2016). When secular culture and political forces promote values that collide with traditional religious views, it can turn especially young people and the politically active away from religion. As Hout and Fischer (2002) show, the political inclinations of Americans in recent generations have shaped their religious preferences in important ways, and part of the increase of the nones can be attributed to a rejection of the alliance between conservative politics and conservative religion. Again, not all those who are turned off by or disillusioned with religion become atheists. In fact, in the same study by Hout and Fischer, they argue many of those who turn away from religion continue to hold religious beliefs. Thus, religious skepticism alone does not explain the increasing numbers of those with no religion. Cultural, political, and many other forces are at play.

One of those forces that researchers are turning their attention to is secular socialization (Cragun et al. 2013; Merino 2011; Theissen 2016). What happens when young adults with no religious preference begin to have children? Many factors are involved, including generational differences in values and political attitudes between parents and their children (Jones, Cox, and Navarro-Rivera 2014), but when nonreligious parents raise their children it increases the likelihood those children will have no religious preference themselves as adults (Cragun 2016). Interview studies suggest that those who were raised with religion but came to adopt a secular outlook, commit themselves to socializing their children toward autonomy in discovering their own beliefs, be they religious or secular (Manning 2015; Thiessen 2016). Scholars will be keen to follow how the sharp increase in nonreligion in the United States and Canada in the early part of the twenty-first century will affect the (non)religious preferences of subsequent generations.

Finally, a more recent approach to the study of secularity and nonreligion has begun to gain traction, and may offer new theoretical avenues. Lois Lee, in her 2015 book *Recognizing the Nonreligious: Reimagining the Secular* suggests scholars in the area should study neither religion or nonreligion narrowly defined, but *existential cultures*, which she defines as distinct sets of "ideas about the origins of life and human consciousness and about how both are transformed or expire after death—what have been called 'ultimate questions' in the literature" (Lee 2015: 160). The idea here is that religion as a concept in the social sciences has too convoluted a history and may put up artificial parameters on what constitutes its study. Consequently, the risk is that the study of nonreligion would become entangled with the study of religion in ways that might limit understanding of the former. Similarly, Taves et al. (2018) and others suggest that researchers examine behaviors and worldviews that respond to such "ultimate questions" in their own right rather than focusing too narrowly on whether they are religious or nonreligious. It remains to be seen whether the wider research community will adopt this perspective. Despite these issues and the openness of the question regarding what exactly constitutes its object of study, the literature has produced many useful insights that help explain secularity and nonreligion in modern society.

Prejudice Against the Nonreligious

In North America, and in particular the United States, one consistent finding in the research literature is that there exists significant prejudice against those without religion. Atheists receive the bulk of this prejudice, as many studies have shown (Edgell, Gerteis, and Hartmann 2006; Edgell et al. 2016; Gervais 2013; Hammer et al. 2012), but there is also bias against other nonreligious individuals and groups (Cragun 2016; Edgell et al. 2016). One seminal study by Edgell et al. (2006) helps explain this prejudice by showing the symbolic importance of atheism in America. Based on a national survey that asked a variety of questions such as, "This group does not at all agree with my vision of American society" the authors found that atheists are the most stigmatized and distrusted group among a list of other stigmatized minority groups including Muslims, homosexuals, immigrants, Jews, and African Americans. They argued that bias against atheists is rooted in moral and symbolic boundaries. That is, belief in God is seen by the general public as necessary for membership in American culture because it is perceived as a maker and marker of morality. This study was especially notable in light of research showing an overall *increase* of acceptance of diversity over several decades across all other religious and minority groups in America. The authors concluded this increased acceptance does not extend to atheists and that "the boundaries between believers and nonbelievers remains strong" (Edgell et al. 2006: 211). An update to this study ten years later (see Edgell et al. 2016) shows the "spillover" of this prejudice towards other nonreligious individuals including, most notably, the nones and the SBNR.

Many studies since the 2006 "Atheists as Other" have confirmed this prejudice and help offer explanations for it. Several studies by Will Gervais (2013; Gervais and Majle 2017) suggest the major source of this prejudice is distrust. It is thought by many of the religious that lack of belief in a divine supervisory power makes one more susceptible to dishonesty or even criminality (Smith and Cragun 2019), despite no empirical evidence nonbelievers are more likely than believers to engage in immoral behavior (Beit-Hallahmi 2010; Galen 2018). Figure 1.6 illustrates this. When asked how justifiable it is to claim government benefits to which someone is not entitled, there were no differences by belief in God in Mexico, the United States, or Canada. Similar analyses illustrated negligible differences in all of the following situations: avoiding a fare on public transport, cheating on taxes if given the chance, or accepting a bribe as part of someone's duties. In short, religion or belief in God do not make people more or less moral.

The topic of morality and its relationship to religious belief and nonbelief has been the focus of several studies (Stroope and Baker 2018; Sumerau and Cragun 2016). From a historical perspective, other scholars have argued that much of the bias toward atheists today is a consequence of the Cold War. One way Americans (and Western culture generally) could resist the "godless communism" of the Soviet Union was to underscore the necessity of religion and belief in God for a healthy, moral society (Bullivant and Ruse 2013).

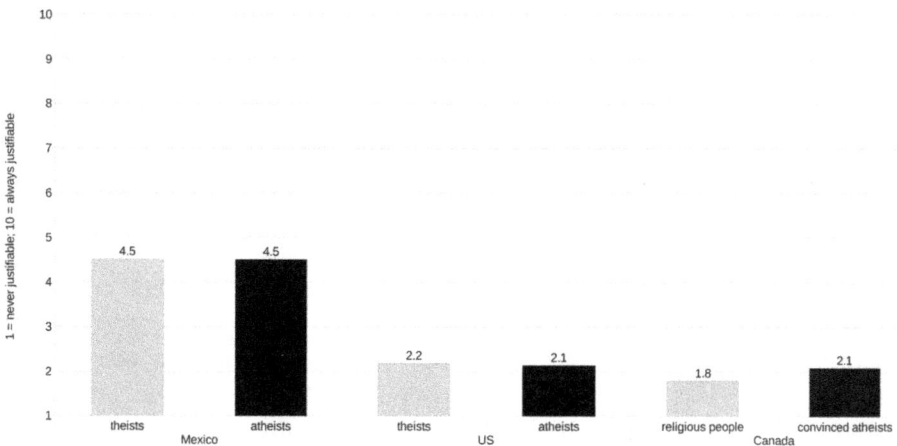

FIGURE 1.6 *How justifiable is it to claim government benefits to which you are not entitled by country and belief in God.* Source: *Created by author from World Values Survey data—for the United States and Mexico 2010–2014; and Canada 2005–2008.*

Whatever its source, prejudice and the perceived threat of discrimination has likely encouraged many nonreligious people not to air their doubts or disbelief publicly. Unlike stigmatized or marginalized groups based on visible traits (e.g., ethnicity, gender, etc.) personal beliefs are invisible and therefore concealable, so atheists' may internalize stigma without actually facing explicit marginalization. As one survey study found (Cragun et al. 2012), 20 percent of nonreligious, and 40 percent of self-identified atheist Americans reported experiencing discrimination in the last five years at places such as work, school, and the military. Other survey and interview studies suggest discrimination ranging from atheist parents being questioned about whether they were fit to raise children, to threats of and actual violence (Hammer et al. 2012; Huang and Kleiner 2001; Smith 2011). Geography plays a role in prejudice as well (see Mann 2015), as Heiner (1992) shows in a study of "evangelical heathens" in the American South. Where religiosity is strongest, greater bias against the nonreligious is expected. In Canada, where there is generally thought to be more widespread secularity, overt prejudice and discrimination against nonbelievers of various stripes appears less prevalent (Cragun, Hammer, and Smith 2013). One—at least symbolic—indication of this comes from a 2007 Gallup poll that found 32 percent of Canadians would not vote for a prime minister who is an atheist, compared to 53 percent of Americans who would vote against a president who was an atheist (Altemeyer 2010). The United States also has a number of organizations devoted to reporting and fighting discrimination against the nonreligious such as the Anti-Discrimination Support Network founded by atheist and secular activist Margaret Downy, which suggests more widespread prejudice than that found in Canadian society. Unfortunately, there is no equivalent research examining the question of prejudice and discrimination against the nonreligious in Mexico, although many scholars have stated the need for such research (Cragun et al. 2013; Keysar and Navarro-Rivera 2014).

Other studies in the United States examine how atheists and other nonreligious individuals negotiate this prejudice with religious family and coworkers through stigma management strategies such as concealing one's identity in these and similar high-cost situations where fear of rejection is high (Hammer et al. 2012; Smith 2011). Zimmerman et al. (2015) studied the consequences of disclosing one's nonbelief by examining the stories of eighty atheists who "came out" to their family members (both religious and nonreligious), finding a considerable amount of rejection and decreased communication, although also occasional sympathy and support. Looking at the role of social networks, Scheitle et al. (2018) found that an individual's connection with friends and family who are more or less open with their nonbelief and lack of religiosity will affect the likelihood of adopting and being open about atheism oneself. Adding to these findings, a study by Abbot and Mullen (2018) found significant relationships between atheists' anticipation of social stigma, whether they decide to disclose their nonbelief, and their overall psychological well-being. Unsurprisingly, individuals will tend to disclose their atheism when the perceived benefits outweigh the costs in any particular private or public situation.

Secular Organizations and Nonreligious Communities

Advocacy of political secularism—defined earlier as the set of beliefs supporting the idea religion should be separate from other aspects of public life—and other forms of secularism in North America reach back to the founding of the United States (Jacoby 2005). The principles of separation of church and state, freedom of religion, and freedom of expression are all enshrined in the First Amendment to the United States Constitution. Canada and Mexico today have similar laws meant to protect the rights of individuals regarding religious preference, though they have very different political and religious histories. As scholars observe, in practice, the actual relationship of political secularism to other public institutions in all three of these democracies (and others around the globe) is much more complicated than the simple church–state division implies (see Fox 2012).

With the exception of historical studies of secularism and atheism (Jacoby 2005; Meagher 2018), most of the contemporary research on secularism has to do with the study of current secular movements and organizations, and the ways in which these facilitate the development of distinct nonreligious communities with particular values, practices, and goals. In the year 2019, there are hundreds of secular organizations in North America and considerable organizational variation in the nonreligious community at large (García and Blankholm 2016; Schutz 2017). Some organizations, such as the American Humanist Association (founded in 1941), Americans United for Separation of

Church and State (founded 1948), and the Humanist Association of Canada (founded 1968) have been actively advocating for political secularism for decades and national organizations of this kind are often part of international secular coalitions that pursue the general interests of the nonreligious (Smith and Cragun 2019). These organizations often have legal teams that see court cases on church–state issues, consider discrimination claims, and advocate for the rights of the nonreligious. Scholars are divided on whether these relatively large national organizations, who aim to represent all secular people in their respective countries, are more or less successful at doing so as they compete for material and other resources (Cimino and Smith 2014; LeDrew 2013). By any measure, compared to their religious counterparts, the secular movement and the organizations it supports enjoy far less funding, lobbying efforts, and representation in congress than do comparable religious organizations (Cragun and Manning 2017).

Hundreds of smaller, local secular groups have arisen in the twenty-first century across the United States and Canada that are more involved with supporting local nonreligious individuals than with political secularism per se. Partly in response to the prejudice discussed earlier, these groups provide social and emotional support to members, conduct volunteer work in local communities, and often seek to destigmatize atheism and other nontheistic worldviews through community engagement (Galen 2018; Smith 2017a). Most of these groups identify themselves by their city/town followed by terms such as humanist, atheist, freethinkers, etc., and offer a space for a variety of social activities for members. These groups build community among the nonreligious, foster solidarity, and fulfill many similar functions to those of religious congregations and nonprofit groups. Researchers have found that in the United States, these kinds of secular groups often fill the role of support group for the formerly religious or for those in the process of leaving religion (Mann 2015; Schutz 2017), something that can be very challenging and emotionally fraught (Winell 2017). Such secular communities provide a social network for individuals who have come to "structure their identities around their nonbelief" (Smith and Cragun 2019). This conclusion is supported by other research that finds, somewhat counterintuitively, that secular groups of this kind tend to thrive in more religiously conservative regions of the United States where nonreligious people feel more embattled and marginalized (Garcia and Blankholm 2016).

The Ethical Culture movement of the late nineteenth century led to the establishment of secular congregations in the United States, and is still headquartered today in New York City. The most notable and recent organization to adopt a religion-like model is the Sunday Assembly, a network of explicitly "secular congregations" based on the motto "Live Better, Help Often, Wonder More" (see Sunday Assembly 2020). Founded in London in 2013, as of April 2020, the Sunday Assembly has forty-five chapters in eight different countries. In 2015, Sunday Assembly reported its total global attendance of 34,604 individuals (Bullock 2018: 60), though those numbers may have gone down since. Though small, the Sunday Assembly signals an interesting development in the secular community where the ritualized services characteristic of religion are embraced rather than avoided. Held usually monthly on Sundays, it follows a similar format to religious gatherings with formal talks and the sharing of personal testimonies, singing and dancing to popular secular songs, recitation of humanist poems, and presentations on scientific, cultural, or other humanism-themed topics. Other organizations, such as the Oasis Network (n.d.), likewise focus on practicing humanist values through communal activities.

This *communal secularity* as it has been identified by Smith (2017a) is an outgrowth of the "new atheist movement" that began in the mid-2000s, and that resulted from the popular writings of the prominent authors noted earlier. Many secularists and nonreligious individuals appeared discontented with, or ready to move on from, the criticism-of-religion aspect of this movement. The Sunday Assembly, though explicitly secular, is promoted as "radically inclusive" and not as focused on atheism or criticism of religion as some other secular groups. Indeed, disagreement on these points created the first split in the group, with some early Sunday Assemblers creating their own group, the Godless Revival, that was more open about its atheism.

The organizational complexity and increasing diversity in the wider secular community has been the subject of several recent studies, a number of which were included in the edited volume *Organized Secularism in the United States* (Cragun, Manning, and Fazzino 2017). For example, Frost (2017) explored the ways in which participants in groups such as the Sunday Assembly negotiated a positive sense of self and moral identity through their interactions with the public and fellow nonreligious. Shook (2017) examined the emerging types and different categories of secularity, arguing there exists a *polysecularity* wherein different individuals and groups assign different meanings to the secular, and express varying secular agendas, some of which are in conflict, while others converge. Furthermore, the ongoing relevance of religion to modern definitions of humanism, secularism, atheism, and other forms of nonreligion was studied by Richter (2017). Finally, although a few studies have focused directly on the politics of the atheist movement (Kettell 2014), in the United States and Canada (Simmons 2017) the political strategies of nonbelievers (Langston, Hammer, and Cragun 2015), and the role of the internet and social media in shaping secular movements and organizations (Addington 2017; Cimino and Smith 2014), scholars agree much more work in this area is needed before any general conclusions can be drawn. However, it is clearly based on the available research that, as with any other social movement or organization, platforms such as Facebook, Reddit, Meetup, and the online world in general has profoundly affected the way members of secular groups connect, communicate, and cooperate; share ideas and values; and construct common goals, many of which become contested within and across groups that are a part of the secular community in North America at large.

Future Research on Secularity and Nonreligion

A great deal has been learned about secularity and nonreligion in North America in the last two decades. In fact, most of the research in the area to date has tended to focus on the United States and Canada (or other Western, developed countries).

Consequently, most scholars agree the greatest need for future research lies in non-Western and developing countries around the globe since very little is known about the nonreligious in these areas, or even whether the Western concept of "nonreligion" makes sense in every cultural context (see Jakobsen and Pellegrini 2008).

One clear need in the North American context, is for much more research to be conducted in Mexico. There is some basic demographic information about the nonreligious in Mexico (see Cragun, Hammer, and Smith 2013), but it is currently an open question to what extent the concepts, models, and observations about the nonreligious in the United States and Canada are applicable to Mexican society. Each cultural setting will have unique characteristics that may curtail the usefulness of the insights gained from the other. For example, although according to the World Values Survey there are at least five million Mexican atheists (people responding "no" to the question, "Do you believe in God?") it is essentially unknown what the actual lived experience of these individuals is like. There are far fewer secular organizations in Mexican society, and basic knowledge about social stigma, discrimination, the process of becoming atheist, and many other issues that have been studied in the United States and Canada remain understudied (or not studied at all) in Mexico.

But as demonstrated throughout this overview, researchers have gathered substantial data on the nonreligious in the United States and Canada; enough to establish important social, demographic, and psychological patterns within the nonreligious community and the many groups it includes. In addition to gathering numerical data on atheists, the nones, and others, a number of theoretical insights have emerged from the literature regarding why people leave religion, how individuals acquire and negotiate secular identities, and many other topics in the field. Though scholarly (and popular) interest in secularity and nonreligion has increased significantly over the last fifteen years, and the research to date indicates multiple lines of research inquiry, no one knows exactly where research in future decades will lead.

There are still many questions and topics left unanswered or underdeveloped that future research can address. For instance, are there inherent personality "types" that make it more or less likely to be nonreligious? How do family dynamics (e.g., closeness, conflict, sibling rivalries, etc.), intimate relationships, and other kinds of interpersonal interactions based on school, work, and leisure shape secular beliefs and identities? What will be the trajectory of secular organizations in North America into the future? Will the proliferation of secular support-type groups continue if the nonreligious population continues to grow, or if being nonreligious loses its social stigma? As researchers respond to questions of this kind, it will likely lead to additional questions that have not yet occurred to anyone.

There is also much more work to be done regarding the relationships between nonreligion and race, gender, sexual orientation, and other sociological variables. Despite clues to these relationships from past and present research, understanding the experience of—for example—atheists who hold other minority statuses is still far too undeveloped. Scholars have generally recognized this deficit (see Smith and Cragun 2019) and some work addressing this has begun to emerge (see Kolysh 2017).

Finally, there is the larger and ongoing question about the changing role of religion in public life as well as its influence on the private lives of individuals. What will be religion's relationship to other social institutions in North America, such as the family, politics, and the economy for the remainder of the twenty-first century? These abstract questions should keep researchers busy studying their more concrete expressions in the decades to come. For instance, if religion in the United States is in fact in decline as a number of the studies outlined in this overview illustrate (also see Voas and Chaves 2018), will this mean a corollary "rise of nonreligion" with more people adopting secular identities, espousing atheism, or adopting a humanist worldview? Or, would the dissolution of religion come to reflect more the character of religious indifference found in Western European societies? Alternatively, perhaps the continued rise of the nones will only mean fewer churchgoers, not more people embracing secularism. Similarly, how will the recent shift in political attitudes regarding marriage equality and new forms of family that depart from traditional and especially conservative religious ideas about it, shape the nonreligious landscape? How will future economic growth or decline affect the appeal of religion and nonreligion to the masses? Will the standing of the United States in the global community play a role in the future growth, decline, or composition of the nonreligious community? What role will environmental threats and the challenges of new technologies play in all this? All of these questions remain open for investigation. Especially because it is still an emerging field, with its "attendant theoretical and methodological implications continuing to take shape" (Smith and Cragun 2019: 328), the study of secularity and nonreligion for students and scholars alike should remain a fruitful area of inquiry for decades to come.

Further Reading and Online Resources

Baggett, J.P. (2019), *The Varieties of Nonreligious Experience: Atheism in American Culture*, New York: New York University Press.

Baker, J.O. and B.G. Smith (2015), *American Secularism: Cultural Contours of Nonreligious Belief Systems*, New York: New York University Press.

Lee, L. (2015), *Recognizing the Nonreligious: Reimaging the Secular*, Oxford: Oxford University Press.

Nonreligion and Secularity Research Network (NSRN) (n.d.), "Home." https://nonreligionandsecularity.wordpress.com/ (accessed September 26, 2020).

Secular Studies (n.d.), "Home." https://brill.com/view/journals/secu/1/1/article-p1_1.xml?language=en (accessed September 26, 2020).

Secularism & Nonreligion (n.d.), "Home." https://secularismandnonreligion.org/ (accessed September 26, 2020).

References

Abbott, D.M. and D. Mollen (2018), "Atheism as a Concealable Stigmatized Identity: Outness, Anticipated Stigma, and Well-Being," *Counseling Psychologist*, 46 (6): 685–707.

Addington, A. (2017), "Building Bridges in the Shadows of Steeples: Atheist Community and Identity Online," in R.T. Cragun, C. Manning, and L.L. Fazzino (eds.), *Organized Secularism in the United States: New Directions in Research*, 135–50, Berlin: De Gruyter.

Altemeyer, B. (2010), "Atheism and Secularity in North America," in P. Zuckerman (ed.), *Atheism and Secularity*, vol. 1, *Issues, Concepts, and Definitions*, 1–22, Santa Barbara, CA: Praeger.

Altemeyer, B. and B. Hunsberger (1997), *Amazing Conversions: Why Some Turn to Faith & Others Abandon Religion*, Amherst, MA: Prometheus Books.

Baker, J.O. and B.G. Smith (2015), *American Secularism: Cultural Contours of Nonreligious Belief Systems*, New York: New York University Press.

Baker, J.O., S. Stroope, and M. Walker (2018), "Secularity, Religiosity, and Health: Physical and Mental Health Differences between Atheists, Agnostics, and Nonaffiliated Theists Compared to Religiously Affiliated Individuals," *Social Science Research*, 75: 44–57. https://doi.org/10.1016/j.ssresearch.2018.07.003.

Beaman, L. and S. Tomlins (2015), *Atheist Identities—Spaces and Social Contexts*, New York: Springer.

Beit-Hallahmi, B. (2010), "Morality and Immorality among the Irreligious," in P. Zuckerman (ed.), *Atheism and Secularity*, vol. 1, *Issues, Concepts, and Definitions*, 113–48, Santa Barbara, CA: Praeger.

Berger, P. (1967), *The Sacred Canopy: Elements of a Sociological Theory of Religion*, New York: Random House.

Bradley, D.F., J.J. Exline, A. Uzdavines, N. Stauner, and J.B. Grubbs (2018), "The Reasons of Atheists and Agnostics for Nonbelief in God's Existence Scale: Development and Initial Validation," *Psychology of Religion and Spirituality*, 10 (3): 263–75. http://dx.doi.org/10.1037/rel0000199.

Brinkerhoff, M.B. and M.M. Mackie (1993), "Casting off the Bonds of Organized Religion: A Religious-Careers Approach to the Study of Apostasy," *Review of Religious Research*, 34: 238–61.

Bromley, D.G., ed. (1998), *The Politics of Religious Apostasy: The Role of Apostates in the Transformation of Religious Movements*, Westport, CT: Praeger.

Bruce, S. (2002), *God Is Dead: Secularization in the West*, London: Blackwell Publishers.

Bruce, S. (2013), *Secularization: In Defence of an Unfashionable Theory*, Oxford: Oxford University Press.

Bullivant, S. and M. Ruse, eds. (2013), *The Oxford Handbook of Atheism*, New York: Oxford University Press.

Bullock, J. (2018), "The Sociology of the Sunday Assembly : 'Belonging without Believing' in a Post-Christian Context," PhD diss., Kingston University, UK.

Campbell, C. (1971), *Toward a Sociology of Irreligion*, London: Macmillan.

Charmaz, K. (2013), *Constructing Grounded Theory*, London: Sage.

Cimino, R. and C. Smith (2014), *Atheist Awakening: Secular Activism and Community in America*, Oxford: Oxford University Press.

Coleman, T.J., R.W. Hood, and H. Streib (2018), "An Introduction to Atheism, Agnosticism, and Nonreligious Worldviews," *Psychology of Religion and Spirituality*, 10 (3): 203–6. http://dx.doi.org/10.1037/rel0000213.

Cragun, D., R.T. Cragun, B. Nathan, J.E. Sumerau, and A.C.H. Nowakowski (2016), "Do Religiosity and Spirituality Really Matter for Social, Mental, and Physical Health?: A Tale of Two Samples," *Sociological Spectrum*, 36 (6): 359–77.

Cragun, R.T. (2016), "Defining That Which Is 'Other to' Religion: Secularism, Humanism, Atheism, Freethought, etc.," in P. Zuckerman (ed.), *Religion: Beyond Religion*, 1–16, New York: Macmillan.

Cragun, R.T. (2019), "Questions You Should Never Ask an Atheist: Towards Better Measures of Nonreligion and Secularity," *Secularism and Nonreligion*, 8: 1–6. https://doi.org/10.5334/snr.122.

Cragun, R.T. and C. Manning (2017), "Introduction," in R.T. Cragun, C.J. Manning, and L. Fazzino (eds.), *Organized Secularism in the United States, Religion and Its Others: Studies in Religion, Nonreligion, and Secularity*, 1–12, Berlin: De Gruyter.

Cragun, R.T. and J.H. Hammer (2011), "'One Person's Apostate Is Another Person's Convert': Reflections on Pro-Religion Hegemony in the Sociology of Religion," *Humanity & Society*, 35 (February/May): 149–75.

Cragun, R.T., B.A. Kosmin, A. Keysar, J.H. Hammer, and M.E. Nielsen (2012), "On the Receiving End: Discrimination toward the Non-Religious," *Journal of Contemporary Religion*, 27 (1): 105–27.

Cragun, R.T., J.H. Hammer, and J.M. Smith (2013), "Atheists in North America," in S. Bullivant and M. Ruse (eds.), *The Oxford Handbook of Atheism*, 601–21, Oxford: Oxford University Press.

Cragun, R.T., V.L. Blyde, J.E. Sumerau, M. Mann, and J.H. Hammer (2016), "Perceived Marginalization, Educational Contexts, and (Non)Religious Educational Experience," *Journal of College and Character*, 17 (4): 241–54.

Cragun, R.T., C. Manning, and L.L. Fazzino, eds. (2017), *Organized Secularism in the United States: New Directions in Research*, Berlin: De Gruyter.

Cragun, R.T., J.H. Hammer, M. Nielsen, and N. Autz (2018), "Religious/Secular Distance: How Far Apart Are Teenagers and Their Parents?," *Psychology of Religion and Spirituality*, 10 (3): 288–95.

Dawkins, R. (2006), *The God Delusion*, New York: Mariner Books.

Demerath, N.J. (1969), "Irreligion, a-Religion, and the Rise of the Religion-Less Church: Two Case Studies in Organizational Convergence," *Sociological Analysis*, 30 (4): 191–203.

Dennett, D.C. (2006), *Breaking the Spell: Religion as a Natural Phenomenon*, New York: Penguin.

Diener, E., L. Tay, and D.G. Myers (2011), "The Religion Paradox: If Religion Makes People Happy, Why Are so Many Dropping Out?," *Journal of Personality and Social Psychology*, 101 (6): 1278–90.

Dobbelaere, K. (2002), *Secularization: An Analysis at Three Levels*, New York: Peter Lang.

Ebaugh, H.R.F. (1988), *Becoming an Ex: The Process of Role Exit*, Chicago: University of Chicago Press.

Edgell, P., J. Gerteis, and D. Hartmann. (2006), "Atheists as "Other": Moral Boundaries and Cultural Membership in American Society," *American Sociological Review*, 71: 211–34.

Edgell, P., D. Hartmann, E. Stewart, and J. Gerteis (2016), "Atheists and Other Cultural Outsiders: Moral Boundaries and the Non-Religious in the United States," *Social Forces*, 95 (2): 607–32.

Fazzino, L.L. (2014), "Leaving the Church Behind: Applying a Deconversion Perspective to Evangelical Exit Narratives," *Journal of Contemporary Religion*, 29 (2): 249–66.

Fox, J. (2012), "The Last Bastion of Secularism? Government Religion Policy in Western Democracies, 1990 to 2008," *Journal of Contemporary European Studies*, 20 (2): 161–80. https://doi.org/10.1080/14782804.2012.685389.

Frost, J. (2017), "Rejecting Rejection Identities: Negotiating Positive Non-Religiosity at the Sunday Assembly," in R.T. Cragun, C. Manning, and L.L. Fazzino (eds.), *Organized Secularism in the United States: New Directions in Research*, 171–90, Berlin: De Gruyter.

Galen, L. (2018), "Focusing on the Nonreligious Reveals Secular Mechanisms Underlying Well-Being and Prosociality," *Psychology of Religion and Spirituality*, 10, 296–306.

García, A. and J. Blankholm (2016), "The Social Context of Organized Nonbelief: County-Level Predictors of Nonbeliever Organizations in the United States," *Journal for the Scientific Study of Religion*, 55 (1): 70–90.

Gervais, W.M. (2013), "In Godlessness We Distrust: Using Social Psychology to Solve the Puzzle of Anti-Atheist Prejudice," *Social and Personality Psychology Compass*, 7 (6): 366–77.

Gervais, W.M. and M.E. Majle (2017), "How Many Atheists Are There?," *Social Psychological and Personality Science*, 9 (1): 3–10.

Hammer, J.H., R.T. Cragun, K. Hwang, and J. Smith (2012), "Forms, Frequency, and Correlates of Perceived Anti-Atheist Discrimination," *Secularism and Nonreligion*, 1: 43–67.

Harris, S. (2004), *The End of Faith: Religion, Terror, and the Future of Reason*, New York: Norton.

Hedström, P. and L. Udehn (2009), "Analytical Sociology and Theories of the Middle Range," in P. Hedström and P. Bearman (eds.), *The Oxford Handbook of Analytical Sociology*, 25–47, Oxford: Oxford University Press.

Heiner, R. (1992), "Evangelical Heathens: The Deviant Status of Freethinkers in Southland," *Deviant Behavior: An Interdisciplinary Journal*, 13: 1–20.

Hitchens, C. (2007), *God Is Not Great: How Religion Poisons Everything*, New York: Hachette.

Hout, M. and C.S. Fischer (2002), "Why More Americans Have No Religious Preference: Politics and Generations," *American Sociological Review*, 67 (2): 165–90.

Huang, C.-C. and B.H. Kleiner (2001), "New Developments Concerning Religious Discrimination in the Workplace," *International Journal of Sociology and Social Policy*, 21 (8–10): 128–36.

Hunsberger, B. and B. Altemeyer (2006), *Atheists: A Groundbreaking Study of America's Nonbelievers*, Amherst, MA: Prometheus Books.

Hwang, K., J.H. Hammer, and R.T. Cragun (2011), "Extending Religion-Health Research to Nontheistic Minorities: Issues and Concerns," *Journal of Religion and Health*, 50 (3): 608–22.

Jacobs, J. (1989), *Divine Disenchantment: Deconversion from New Religious Movements*, Bloomington: Indiana University Press.

Jacoby, S. (2005), *Freethinkers: A History of American Secularism*, New York: Holt Paperbacks.

Jakobsen, J.R. and A. Pellegrini, eds. (2008), *Secularisms*, Durham, NC: Duke University Press Books.

Jones, R.P., D. Cox, and J. Navarro-Rivera (2014), *A Shifting Landscape: A Decade of Change in American Attitudes about Same-Sex Marriage and LGBT Issues*, Washington, DC: Public Religion Research Institute.

Kettell, S. (2014), "Divided We Stand: The Politics of the Atheist Movement in the United States," *Journal of Contemporary Religion*, 29 (3): 377–91.

Keysar, A. and J. Navarro-Rivera (2014), "A World of Atheism: Global Demographics," in S. Bullivant and M. Ruse (eds.), *The Oxford Handbook of Atheism*, 554–86, New York: Oxford University Press.

Kolysh, S. (2017), "Straight Gods, White Devils: Exploring Paths to Non-Religion in the Lives of Black LGBTQ People," *Secularism and Nonreligion*, 6 (2). http://doi.org/10.5334/snr.83.

Kosmin, B.A. and A. Keysar (2006), *Religion in a Free Market: Religious and Non-religious Americans*, Ithaca, NY: Paramount Market Publishing.

Kosmin, B.A., A. Keysar, R.T. Cragun, and J. Navarro-Rivera (2009), *American Nones: The Profile of the No Religion Population*, Hartford, CT: Institute for the Study of Secularism in Society and Culture.

Kvale, S. and S. Brinkmann (2009), *Interviews: Learning the Craft of Qualitative Research Interviewing*, Thousand Oaks, CA: Sage.

Langston, J.A., J.H. Hammer, and R.T. Cragun (2015), "Atheism Looking in: On the Goals and Strategies of Organized Nonbelief," *Science, Religion, and Culture*, 2 (3): 70–85.

LeDrew, S. (2013), "Discovering Atheism: Heterogeneity in Trajectories to Atheist Identity and Activism," *Sociology of Religion*, 74 (4): 431–53.

Lee, L. (2015), *Recognizing the Nonreligious: Reimagining the Secular*, Oxford: Oxford University Press.

Lim, C., C.A. MacGregor, and R.D. Putnam (2010), "Secular and Liminal: Discovering Heterogeneity among Religious Nones," *Journal for the Scientific Study of Religion*, 49 (4): 596–618.

Lofland, J., D. Snow, L. Anderson, and L. Lofland (2005), *Analyzing Social Settings: A Guide to Qualitative Observation and Analysis*, Belmont, CA: Wadsworth.

MacMurray, N.J. and L.L. Fazzino (2017), "Doing Death without Deity: Constructing Nonreligious Tools at the End of Life," in T. Cragun Ryan, C. Manning, and L.L. Fazzino (eds.), *Organized Secularism in the United States*, 279–300, Berlin: De Gruyter.

Mann, M. (2015), "Triangle Atheists: Stigma, Identity, and Community Among Atheists in North Carolina's Triangle Region," *Secularism and Nonreligion*, 4: 1. http://doi.org/10.5334/snr.bd.

Manning, C. (2015), *Losing Our Religion: How Unaffiliated Parents Are Raising Their Children*, New York: New York University Press.

Meagher, R.J. (2018), *Atheists in American Politics: Social Movement Organizing from the Nineteenth to the Twenty-first Centuries*, Lanham, MD: Lexington Books.

Merino, S.M. (2011), "Irreligious Socialization? The Adult Religious Preferences of Individuals Raised with No Religion," *Secularism and Nonreligion*, 1: 1–16. http://doi.org/10.5334/snr.aa.

Oasis Network (n.d.). https://www.oasisnetwork.com/ (accessed September 15, 2020).

Packard, J. and T.W. Ferguson (2018), "Being Done: Why People Leave the Church, but Not Their Faith," *Sociological Perspectives*, 62 (4): 499–517. https://doi.org/10.1177/0731121418800270.

Pasquale, F.L. (2010), "A Portrait of Secular Group Affiliates," in P. Zuckerman (ed.), *Atheism and Secularity*, vol. 1, *Issues, Concepts, and Definitions*, 43–88, Santa Barbara, CA: Praeger.

Pew Research Center (2014), *U.S. Religious Landscape Survey*, Washington, DC.

Price, M.E. and J. Launay (2018), "Increased Wellbeing from Social Interaction in a Secular Congregation," *Secularism and Nonreligion*, 7 (6): 1–9. https://doi.org/10.5334/snr.102.

Quack, J. (2014), "Outline of a Relational Approach to 'Nonreligion'," *Method & Theory in the Study of Religion*, 26 (4–5): 439–69.

Richter, C.L. (2017), "'I Know It When I See It': Humanism, Secularism, and Religious Taxonomy," in R.T. Cragun, C. Manning, and L.L. Fazzino (eds.), *Organized Secularism in the United States: New Directions in Research*, 13–30, Berlin: De Gruyter.

Scheitle, C.P., K.E. Corcoran, and E.B. Hudnall (2018), "Adopting a Stigmatized Label: Social Determinants of Identifying as an Atheist beyond Disbelief," *Social Forces*, 97 (4): 1731–56. https://doi.org/10.1093/sf/soy084.

Schutz, A. (2017), "Organizational Variation in the American Nonreligious Community," in R.T. Cragun, C.J. Manning, and L. Fazzino (eds.), *Organized Secularism in the United States: New Directions in Research, Religion and Its Others: Studies in Religion, Nonreligion, and Secularity*, 113–34, Berlin: De Gruyter.

Schwadel, P. (2010), "Period and Cohort Effects on Religious Nonaffiliation and Religious Disaffiliation: A Research Note," *Journal for the Scientific Study of Religion*, 49 (2): 311–19.

Sherkat, D.E. (2008), "Beyond Belief: Atheism, Agnosticism, and Theistic Certainty in the United States," *Sociological Spectrum*, 28 (5): 438–59.

Sherkat, D.E. (2016), "Religion, Politics, and Americans' Confidence in Science," *Politics and Religion*, 10 (1): 137–60.

Shook, J. (2017), "Recognizing and Categorizing the Secular: Polysecularity and Agendas of Polysecularism," in R.T. Cragun, C. Manning, and L.L. Fazzino (eds.), *Organized Secularism in the United States: New Directions in Research*, 87–112, Berlin: De Gruyter.

Simmons, J. (2017), "Atheism Plus What? Social Justice and Lifestyle Politics among Edmonton Atheists," *Canadian Journal of Sociology*, 42 (4): 425–46.

Smith, G.H. (1980), *Atheism: The Case against God*, 1st paperback edn., Amherst, NY: Prometheus Books.

Smith, J.M. (2011), "Becoming an Atheist in America: Constructing Identity and Meaning from the Rejection of Theism," *Sociology of Religion*, 72 (2): 215–37.

Smith, J.M. (2013), "Creating a Godless Community: The Collective Identity Work of Contemporary American Atheists," *Journal for the Scientific Study of Religion*, 52 (1): 80–99.

Smith, J.M. (2016), "Apostasy," in P. Zuckerman (ed.), *Beyond Religion*, 71–91, Macmillan Interdisciplinary Handbooks: Religion series, Farmington Hills, MI: Macmillan.

Smith, J.M. (2017a), "Can the Secular Be the Object of Belief and Belonging? The Sunday Assembly," *Qualitative Sociology*, 40 (1): 83–109.

Smith, J.M. (2017b), "Secular Living: Many Paths, Many Meanings," in P. Zuckerman and J. Shook (eds.), *The Oxford Handbook of Secularism*, 515–32, Oxford: Oxford University Press.

Smith, J.M. and R.T. Cragun (2019), "Mapping Religion's Other: A Review of the Study of Nonreligion and Secularity," *Journal for the Scientific Study of Religion*, 58 (2): 319–35.

Speed, D. and K. Fowler (2015), "What's God Got to Do with It? How Religiosity Predicts Atheists' Health," *Journal of Religion and Health*, 55 (1): 296–308.

Stark, R. (1999), "Secularization, R.I.P.," *Sociology of Religion*, 60 (3): 249–73.

Stark, R. and R. Finke (2000), *Acts of Faith: Explaining the Human Side of Religion*, Berkeley: University of California Press.

Strawn, K. (2019), "What's Behind All This 'Nones-sense'? Change Over Time in Factors Predicting Religious Non-affiliation in the United States," *Journal for the Scientific Study of Religion*, 58 (3): 707–24. https://doi.org/10.1111/jssr.12609.

Stroope, S. and J.O. Baker (2018), "Whose Moral Community? Religiosity, Secularity, and Self-rated Health across Communal Religious Contexts," *Journal of Health and Social Behavior*, 59 (2): 185–99.

Sumerau, J.E. and R.T. Cragun (2016), "'I Think Some People Need Religion': The Social Construction of Nonreligious Moral Identities," *Sociology of Religion*, 77 (4): 386–407.

Sunday, Assembly (2020) "Welcome to Your London Community." https://www.sundayassembly.com/ (accessed September 15, 2020).

Taves, A., E. Asprem, and E. Ihm (2018), "Psychology, Meaning Making, and the Study of Worldviews: Beyond Religion and Non-Religion," *Psychology of Religion and Spirituality*, 10 (3): 207–17.

Thiessen, J. (2016), "Kids, You Make the Choice: Religious and Secular Socialization among Marginal Affiliates and Nonreligious Individuals," *Secularism and Nonreligion*, 5 (6): 1–16. http://dx.doi.org/10.5334/snr.60.

Tomlins, S. (2018), "Atheism and Religious Nones: An Introduction to the Study of Nonreligion in Canada," in C. Holtmann (ed.), *Exploring Religion and Diversity in Canada*, 237–54, Cham: Springer. https://doi.org/10.1007/978-3-319-78232-4_11.

Vernon, G.M. (1968), "The Religious 'Nones': A Neglected Category," *Journal for the Scientific Study of Religion*, 7 (2): 219–29.

Voas, D. and M. Chaves (2018), "Even Intense Religiosity Is Declining in the United States: Comment," *Sociological Science*, 5: 694–710.

Williamson, D.A. and G. Yancey (2013), *There Is No God: Atheists in America*, Lanham, MD: Rowman & Littlefield.

Winell, M. (2017), "The Challenge of Leaving Religion and Becoming Secular," in P. Zuckerman and J. Shook (eds.), *The Oxford Handbook of Secularism*, 603–20, Oxford: Oxford University Press.

Yamane, D. (1997), "Secularization on Trial: In Defense of a Neosecularization Paradigm," *Journal for the Scientific Study of Religion*, 36 (1): 109–15.

Zimmerman, K., J. Smith, K. Simonson, and B.W. Myers (2015), "Familial Relationship Outcomes of Coming Out as an Atheist," *Secularism and Nonreligion*, 4 (1): 1–13.

Zuckerman, P. (2011), *Faith No More: Why People Reject Religion*, Oxford: Oxford University Press.

Zuckerman, P. (2014), *Living the Secular Life: New Answers to Old Questions*, New York: Penguin Press.

Zuckerman, P. and J.R. Shook (2017), *The Oxford Handbook of Secularism*, Oxford: Oxford University Press.

Glossary Terms

Agnostic A person who claims no knowledge of God or the supernatural.

Apostasy A total departure from, or explicit rejection of, some religious tradition or organization.

Atheist A person who does not believe in the existence of a god(s) or supernatural being.

Humanism A nontheistic, non-supernaturalist interpretation of human existence. It posits that the major domains of human concern such as ethics and morality, human rights, social equality, and the principles by which societies should organize, are best understood and accomplished through science, reason, and other Enlightenment values.

Irreligion To have no religion or in some way work against religion.

Religious exiting The social and psychological process by which an individual exits a former religious identity or ideology.

Religious none A person who does not identify with any religion. Identifying as a religious none does not necessarily mean that one is without any religious or spiritual beliefs or practices. A religious none simply does not identify with any religion.

Secularism The set of beliefs around the idea that religion should be kept separate from the state and its institutions. Coined by the English author George Holyoake (1817–1906), leader of the secularist movement in nineteenth-century Britain, this word has traditionally invoked the political dimension of the secular.

2

Demographics of the Nonreligious in the United States

Ariela Keysar

Introduction

Demographers are concerned with the size, structure, and dynamics of a population (Hauser and Duncan 1959). A demographer asks such questions as: how big is a population, has it grown or declined over time, and why? Populations with a young age structure are usually growing while those dominated by older people tend to be declining (Goldscheider 1971).

To determine the characteristics of a population, demographers rely on statistics. Thus the study of demography is evidence-based. Most demographic data originate from an official census or special survey. A *census* provides a full count of the population. Participation is mandatory and is required by law. The Census Bureau, which is part of the US Department of Commerce, conducts a full census every ten years. Surveys are conducted more frequently, and are based on a subset of the population. They extract a *sample*—a small number of randomly selected people—to represent the entire population (Levy and Lemeshow 1991).

Could we utilize the US Census to determine the size of the nonreligious population in the United States? The simple answer is no. The US Census has not asked questions about religion since the 1950s. The Constitution's separation of religion and state and Public Law 94–521 of 1976 prohibit the Census Bureau from asking any questions about affiliation with a religious group on a mandatory basis (US Census Bureau n.d.).

As a result, the analyses presented here are taken from a host of national samples that collect data on religious indicators as well as demographics of the US adult population, specifically the General Social Survey (GSS), a national survey conducted annually by the National Opinion Research Center (NORC) at the University of Chicago;

the American Religious Identification Survey (ARIS) series 1990–2008; and the Pew Research Center's Religious Landscape Surveys in 2007 and 2014. The sheer size of these surveys (the ARIS series with over 50,000 American adult respondents and the Pew surveys with over 35,000) permits detailed demographic profiles of religious and nonreligious groups in the United States, including small ones (Kosmin and Keysar 2009; Pew Research Center 2012). Moreover, these surveys of American religion are repeated, keeping the same methodological design, which allows scholars who study religion and nonreligion to monitor changes over time and track societal trends.

Definition

Religion is often measured in terms of the 3Bs—belief, belonging, and behavior. Similarly, nonreligion can be defined as lack of belief, lack of identification with a particular religious group, and/or lack of religious behavior, such as attendance at religious services (Keysar and Kosmin 2007).

Nonreligion is a complex concept, the meaning of which varies by individual and by culture (Keysar 2017; Kontala, Keysar and Kheir, forthcoming). Using the strictest interpretation of nonreligion, only 6 percent of Americans were nonreligious by all three of the Bs in 2008 (Keysar 2014). Sherkat (2014) found many people participate in religious rituals without believing in religious dogma; he also found a decline in belief in God among younger cohorts.

Most demographic data that has been collected about the nonreligious is based on just one of the three Bs, namely belonging (or not belonging) to a religious group. Therefore, this chapter will use belonging as its primary metric. When respondents are asked in an open-ended survey question, "What is your religion, if any?" they determine their religious affiliation, or the lack of it, regardless of whether religious institutions consider them to be members. In this regard, the survey captures whether respondents regard themselves as adherents of a religious community. Clearly, there are many options to choose from. These choices are revealing. As I will show, the tendencies to opt for particular choices are changing over time (Chaves 2011; Kosmin and Keysar 2006).

When asked their religion, some people answer atheist, some answer agnostic, and a greater number answer that they profess no religion. All three groups make up what we term the nonreligious, or nones. Some of the people who profess no religion believe in God and even possibly attend religious services. But most of the nones describe themselves as "not religious" (Kosmin and Keysar 2013).

The Pew Religious Landscape Surveys utilized a similar question as ARIS, "What is your present religion, if any? Are you Protestant, Roman Catholic, Mormon, Orthodox such as Greek or Russian Orthodox, Jewish, Muslim, Buddhist, Hindu, atheist, agnostic, something else, or nothing in particular?" However, this is not an open-ended question. Respondents are provided a list of choices of religious/nonreligious groups.

The combined group of atheists, agnostics, and "no religion" are labeled "religiously unaffiliated" by the Pew Research Center's surveys, the "nones" by the ARIS series surveys (Kosmin and Keysar 2009), and "No Religion" in the GSS. There are slight differences in the design of the surveys, question wording, and concepts, but all three surveys capture essentially the same people: the religiously unaffiliated, or nones. The demographic profile of this group is the subject of this chapter.

Often atheism and nonreligious are used as identical categories. They are not identical. The broader nonreligious population encompasses several subgroups of different size: atheists, agnostics, and those who opt for "no religion" when asked their religious identification. As the demographics of the various segments will show, the subgroups are similar but not the same.

For a global perspective one needs to utilize a data source that repeats the same question around the world. The World Values Survey (WVS) asks, "Do you belong to a religious denomination?" The share of people who answer no to this question varies greatly—from 0.6 percent in countries in the Middle East and Africa to over 60 percent in the Netherlands (Keysar 2015).

Size of Nonreligious Population

In 1990, almost 90 percent of adult Americans adhered to a religious group (Kosmin and Lachman 1993) while 8 percent professed no religion. Since the 1990s, the number of people who say that they have no religion has grown rapidly: from 14.3 million adults in 1990, to 29.5 million adults in 2001, to 34.2 million adults in 2008, and to 55.8 million adults in 2014 (ARIS n.d.; Pew Religious Landscape Survey 2014). As a percentage, they are growing as well: the nonreligious adult population rose to about 23 percent in 2014.

Composition of the Nones

The largest group is those who identify as "nothing in particular," comprising about 70 percent of the nones. Atheists and agnostics have increased their share in the US adult population—from only 1 percent at the beginning of the twenty-first century to over 7 percent in 2014 (see Table 2.1). Atheists and agnostics are not a fringe segment anymore.

TABLE 2.1 Percentage of the US Population That Was Atheist, Agnostic, or Nothing in Particular by Time and Data Set.

	2001 (ARIS) (%)	2007 (Pew) (%)	2014 (Pew) (%)
Atheist	0.5	1.6	3.1
Agnostic	0.4	2.4	4.0
Nothing in particular	13.2	12.1	15.8
Total nones	14.1	16.1	22.8

Combined, they now constitute one-third of the nones population. Still, only in a few countries around the world is distancing from a religious group closely synonymous with distancing from God (Keysar 2015). In the United States, atheists are not trusted (Cragun et al. 2012; Edgell, Gerteis, and Hartmann 2006). Openly declaring oneself as an atheist comes with a risk of being ostracized (Zuckerman 2010).

Change Over Time

The American religious landscape is not static (Chaves 2011; Kosmin and Keysar 2006). A society known to be religious for centuries (Finke and Stark 1992; Wuthnow 1999), the United States is transforming and becoming more secular as the nonreligious segment is growing (Altemeyer 2010). The GSS asks several questions on religious belief, behavior, and belonging. The self-identification question is somewhat different from ARIS and Pew referring to "religious preference": "What is your religious preference? Is it Protestant, Catholic, Jewish, some other religion, or no religion?"

Figure 2.1 shows the rise of the nones in the American population from 1972 to 2018. The trend indeed demonstrates the rise of the nones over time from only 5 percent of the adult population in the 1970s to over 20 percent in 2018; the growth is clear and rapid. The ARIS surveys revealed that the first doubling of the nones occurred in the 1990s (Kosmin and Keysar 2009). The GSS time series shows a quadrupling of the nones' share of the population over a span of forty years.

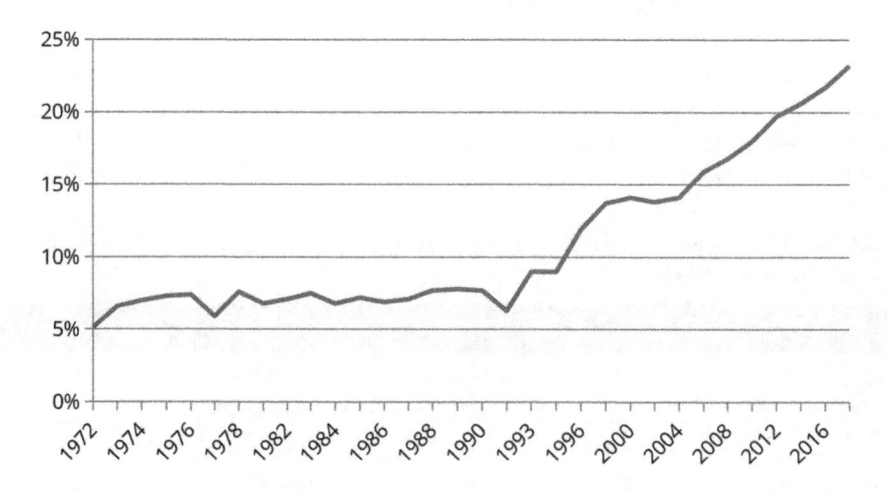

FIGURE 2.1 *Percentage of people identifying with no religion, 1972–2018.* Source: *Created by author from General Social Survey data.*

GSS, ARIS, and Pew surveys corroborate and validate each other. They produce comparable estimates of the size of American nones. All these reputable national surveys also highlight the trajectory of the growth of the nonreligious. While we know the nonreligious are growing, what are the other characteristics of the nones? The following analyses delve into the demographics and geography of American nones.

Demographics

Gender

Women are typically more religious than men in North America (Keysar and Piltzecker 2016; Kosmin and Keysar 2006; Stark 2002). If one were to look around the pews at a religious service on a typical Sunday, one would be more likely to see women than men. Women are more active religiously, more likely to hold religious beliefs, and more likely to report a religious affiliation.

The nonreligious are more likely to be males (see Figure 2.2). Those who self-identify as atheists and agnostics are even more disproportionately male (64 percent) compared with only 47 percent male among the religious. Psychologists of religion have pondered the causes of the religious gender gap. Beit-Hallahmi (2014) asserts that men more

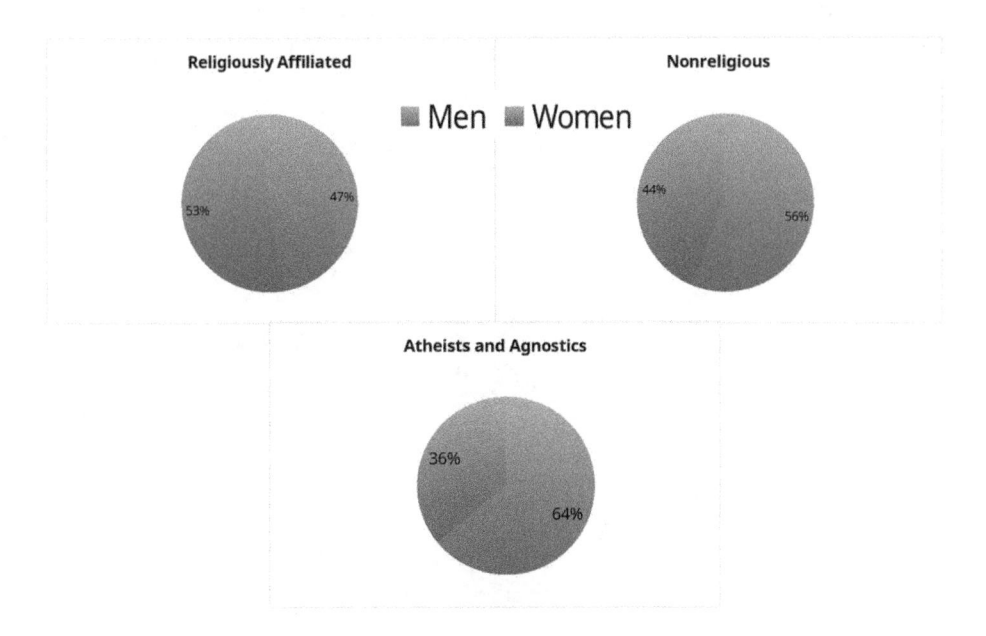

FIGURE 2.2 *Gender composition of the religiously affiliated, nonreligious, and atheists and agnostics.* Source: *Created by author from Pew Research Center (2012) data.*

than women tend to challenge authority, including religious authority, and thus distance themselves from organized religion. Men are also more likely to be independent, take risks, and go against the flow. Persistently across societies males and females are socialized according to their cultural sex-role expectations (Bradshaw and Ellison 2009; Edgell et al. 2017).

Age and generation

Nonreligious Americans are younger than religious Americans (Keysar 2007; Kosmin et al. 2009). Young people are more likely to reject the authority of religious leaders and religious institutions. Many prefer to be independent thinkers. In the words of an American student who professed no religion, "I think for myself. By being a competent learner and analyzing the world for myself everyday, I cut out the middleman and maintain complete control of my beliefs" (Keysar 2016). And who is the middleman? The reference is most likely to organized religion, which the student was clearly distancing from.

As Figure 2.3 illustrates, young adults lead the way in opting not to identify with a religious group. Indeed the most obvious characteristic of the nones is youth. Atheism and agnosticism connote youth as well. Self-identified atheists and agnostics represent a small subgroup of the nones. Atheists/agnostics have an even younger age structure, with 42 percent of them under the age of thirty, according to the Pew Research Center (2012).

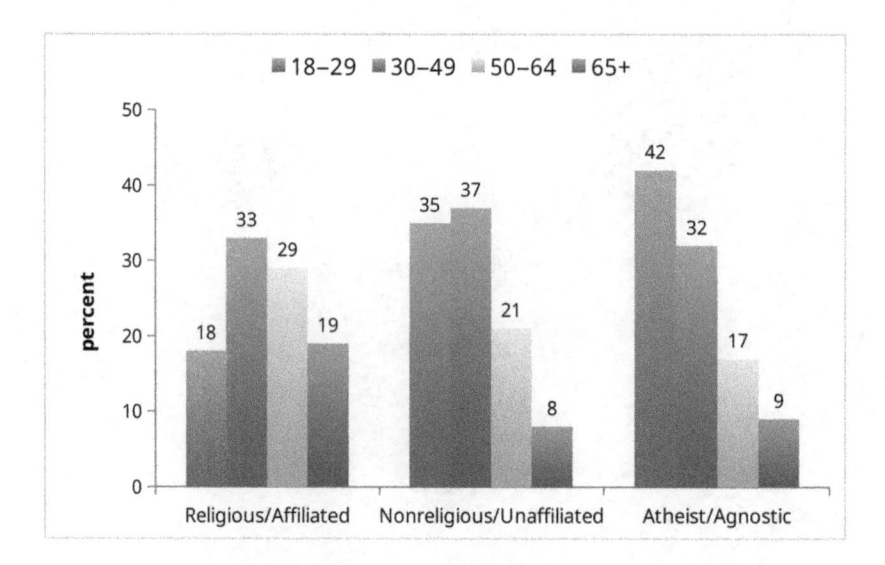

FIGURE 2.3 *Religious and nonreligious by age group.* Source: *Created by author from Pew Research Center (2012) data.*

The millennial generation, born between 1981 and 1996, emerges as the most secular generation: one-third of millennials professed no religion (Pew Research Center 2015). Generation X, born between 1965 and 1980, with about one-quarter nones, preceded them. The most religious generation is the oldest one, the Silent Generation, born between 1928 and 1945 (see Figure 2.4).

One of the most intriguing research puzzles for social scientists is whether young people will become more religious as they age. As people get married, start a family, and raise children, they may reconnect with the religious community of their childhood (Wilson and Sherkat 1994). Will today's nonreligious become religious in the future? It is hard to give a firm answer to this question without embarking on a longitudinal study, which tracks the same cohort over time and monitors attitudinal and behavioral changes.

Still, a secularization trend is documented by the Pew Research Center. The Religious Landscape Survey in 2014 indicated that even older generations have grown somewhat more nonreligious. Comparing older generations, for example, 14 percent of baby boomers were unaffiliated in 2007; by 2014 that number had increased to 17 percent.

Some American students describe drifting away from religion in college. In one student's words, "I'm drifting away from it [my religious upbringing]. You naturally just begin to feel guilty. Because it's more or less of an identity crisis, because you start to realize the way you [were] raised and the way you are, and the way you're thinking forwardly is all conflicting with each other" (Keysar 2016).

Generation	Percent
Silent generation	11
Baby boomers	17
Generation X	23
Millennials	35

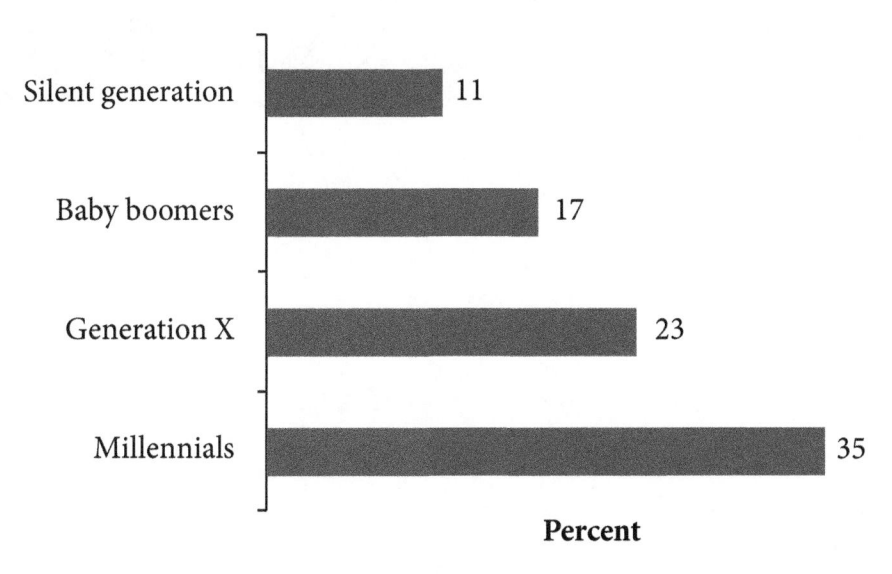

FIGURE 2.4 *Percentage of each generation identifying as having no religious affiliation.*
Source: *Created by author from Pew Religious Landscape Survey 2014 data.*

Race/Ethnicity

The ethnic and racial composition of the United States is changing. So is the racial and ethnic makeup of its religious landscape (Kosmin and Keysar 2009). As minority groups, particularly the Hispanic/Latino population, are gaining in numbers, the white population is losing its plurality (Passel and Cohn 2008). By 2050, the US population is projected to become majority nonwhite, assuming that current demographic processes (such as births, deaths, and immigration) continue. It is projected that the number of American non-Latino whites will decline due to falling birth rates. At the same time, the overall US population is expected to continue to grow. Therefore whites would decline to about 47 percent of the population in 2050—from 67 percent in 2005 (Passel and Cohn 2008; US Census 2018).

Similar patterns are evident among the growing nones population. While a great majority (80 percent) of nones were whites in 1990 (Kosmin and Keysar 2006)—racial homogeneity is gradually lessening. Whites' share of the nonreligious dropped to 68 percent in 2014 (Pew Religious Landscape Survey 2014). Interestingly the racial composition of the religiously unaffiliated is now similar to that of the affiliated (see Table 2.2).

The most striking change among American racial and ethnic groups is among Latinos. In 1990, they made up 6 percent of US adults and 4 percent of adult

TABLE 2.2 Race and Ethnicity of Affiliated and Unaffiliated Americans, 2007–14.

	Year of Survey	Non-Latino				Latino (%)
		White (%)	Black (%)	Asian (%)	Other/Mixed (%)	
Affiliated	2012	68	12	2	4	14
Unaffiliated	2007	73	8	4	4	11
	2014	68	9	5	4	13
Atheist	2007	86	3	4	2	5
	2014	78	3	7	2	10
Agnostic	2007	84	2	4	4	6
	2014	79	3	4	4	9
Nothing in particular	2007	70	10	3	4	12
	2014	64	12	5	5	15

Source: Pew Research Center (2012) and Pew Religious Landscape Survey (2014).

nones. In 2008, Latinos doubled their share of the total adult population and tripled their proportion among nones to 12 percent (Kosmin et al. 2009). This trend of the rise of the nones among Latinos has continued (Pew Research Center 2015). Americanization affects Latinos' religious identification. Language use is an indicator of assimilation. The ARIS 2008 compared four groups of Latinos: those who speak mostly English, those who consider themselves bilingual, those who speak mostly Spanish, and those who speak other languages. We found that the share of nones among English speakers (22 percent) is double the share of nones among Spanish speakers (10 percent). Americanization, measured by English language proficiency, leads to secularization, namely distancing from organized religion (Navarro-Rivera, Kosmin, and Keysar 2010).

Marital status

Patterns of marital status differ greatly between the affiliated and the unaffiliated, emerging especially in recent years (2012–14). Most noticeably, Americans who are engaged in religious activities are more likely to be married while the unaffiliated are more likely to have never been married. The trend data presented in Table 2.3 show the increase in the share of the never married among the "nothing in particular" group

TABLE 2.3 Marital Status of Religiously Affiliated and Unaffiliated Americans, 2007–14.

	Year of Survey	Married (%)	Living with a Partner (%)	Divorced/ Separated (%)	Widowed (%)	Never Married (%)
Affiliated	2012	54	6	20	-	20
Unaffiliated	2007	46	10	12	4	28
	2014	37	11	11	3	37
Atheist	2007	39	11	10	3	37
	2014	36	13	9	2	40
Agnostic	2007	41	10	10	3	36
	2014	35	11	11	2	41
Nothing in particular	2007	48	10	12	4	26
	2014	38	11	12	3	35

Source: Pew Research Center (2012 and 2015).

from 26 percent in 2007 to 35 percent in 2014. The larger nothing in particular group is becoming more similar to atheists and agnostics who are far more likely not to marry—40 percent in 2014. These comparisons reveal distinct differences in the family compositions between Americans who profess a religion and the nones.

One possible explanation for the differences is an age effect. However, a deeper look at the young age group, eighteen to twenty-nine years old, reveals that this difference is not merely an artifact of the higher concentration of young people among the unaffiliated. Even among those aged eighteen to twenty-nine, there are fewer married people among the religiously unaffiliated (12 percent) than among those with the religious nones (23 percent) (Pew Research Centre 2012). The nones seem to be less traditional both in their demographic behavior and in their religious habits.

Education

Overall the levels of educational attainment of religious and nonreligious Americans are similar, as shown in Figure 2.5, within each group a plurality (about 40 percent) are high school graduates or less and about 30 percent have college degrees. These similarities signify the normalization of the nones as they are found in diverse parts of society. Atheists and agnostics, however, exhibit higher educational levels. A plurality, 44 percent, have at least a college degree, and 19 percent of them have postgraduate degrees.

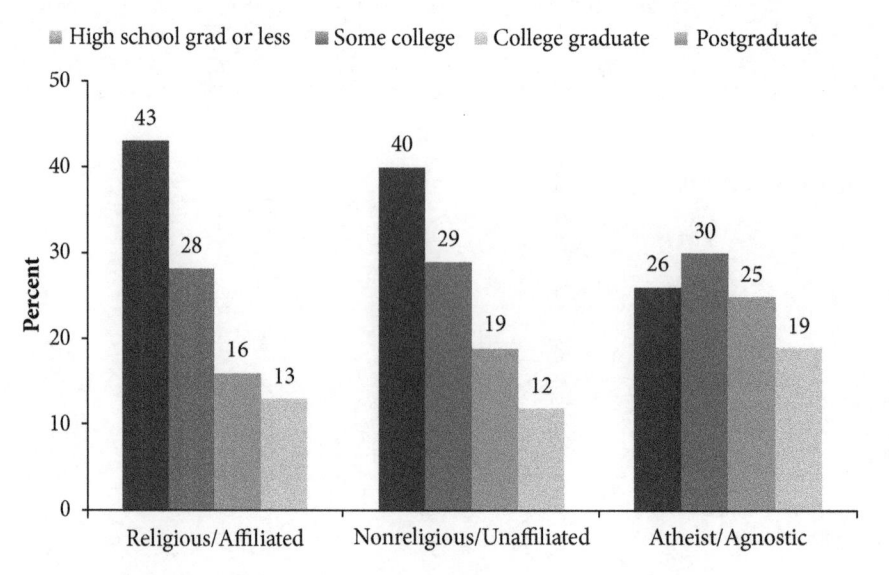

FIGURE 2.5 *Religious and nonreligious by educational attainment.* Source: *Created by author from Pew Research Center 2012 data.*

Geography

Region and religion in the United States are highly linked (Silk and Walsh 2008) with religious areas and nonreligious pockets. According to the Pew Research Center (2012), religiously unaffiliated Americans are more concentrated in the Western region. Almost one-third (30 percent) live in the Western states versus 23 percent of the general population in those states. The nones are less concentrated in the South (28 percent compared with 37 percent of the general population there). In the map of the forty-eight contiguous states (Figure 2.6), the darker colors vividly indicate higher percentages of nones in 2008.

Historically nones have been concentrated in the Western region of the United States, in particular in Oregon and Washington. In 2008, nones accounted for one-quarter of the adult population in the Northwest (Kosmin and Keysar 2009). Regional patterns have begun to change. The Northeast has emerged as a stronghold of the religiously unaffiliated. Vermont had the highest percentage of nones in 2008 with 34 percent, followed by New Hampshire with 29 percent and Maine with 25 percent. As Figure 2.6 illustrates, the nones have also surged in the mountain states. Their share rose in Wyoming from 14 percent in 1990 to 28 percent in 2008, in Idaho from 13 percent in 1990 to 23 percent in 2008, in Nevada from 14 percent in 1990 to 24 percent in 2008, and in Colorado from 13 percent in 1990 to 21 percent in 2008 (Kosmin and Keysar 2009).

Summary

Nones have become the second largest group in the American religious landscape—counting over 55 million adults in 2014—trailing only evangelical Protestants (62 million) and surpassing Catholics (51 million) (Pew Research Center 2015). The traditional

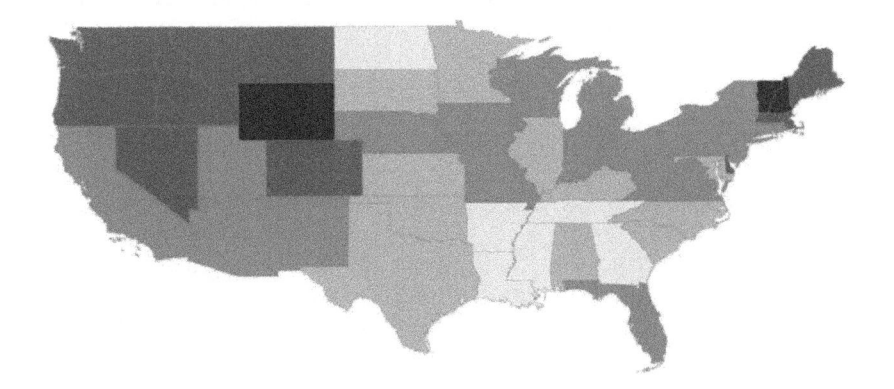

FIGURE 2.6 *Percentage of nonreligious by state, 2008.* Source: *Created by author from ARIS 2008 data.*

stereotype of a none is a young, never-married male living in the Northeast or Pacific Northwest. But as the nones grow in size and as a percentage of the US population, they more resemble the general American population, in part because they make up more of the American population. Most noticeably is their diverse and multiethnic/multiracial composition—nones have become less homogeneously white. Many are Latino/Hispanic, and about 9 percent are black. Their patterns of education also bear a resemblance to the educational levels of religious Americans.

The shift away from organized religion has occurred in every geographical region in the United States. Moreover, every state has experienced a rise of the nones—the most secular one, Vermont (13 percent in 1990 and 34 percent in 2008), as well as the most religious one, Mississippi (3 percent in 1990 and 5 percent in 2008). No religious group has seen such growth in every state (Kosmin and Keysar 2009). The ongoing migration from the Northeast to the Sunbelt most likely involves waves of nonreligious Americans moving to historically religious areas. The rise of the nones will likely have a significant impact on American religious geography over time.

Demography assists us as we ponder whether the nones will continue to rise. The prevalence and the growth of nones among American Latinos could be a revealing prelude. Latinos are a growing segment of the US population and Latinos' transformations are important societal indicators. As they integrate, Latinos adopt American values, attitudes, and conduct. Hence despite their distinctive religious upbringing, Latinos who assimilate into US society adopt American patterns by shifting from religious affiliation toward secularization and contributing to the rise of the nones. Societal transformations might encourage decreased levels of female religiosity. As more American women enter more male-dominant domains, in the workplace and on college campuses, they may come to resemble men in their religious affiliation or non-affiliation.

The sheer number of nones, their wide geographic spread, and their demographic diversity has increased public acceptance of and interest in the no-religion phenomenon. Some people who identify with a religion may feel freer to join the ranks of the nones. The replacement of older religious generations with young nonreligious ones is likely to solidify the place of nones in the American landscape.

Further Reading and Online Resources

Keysar, A. (2014), "Shifts along the American Religious-Secular Spectrum," *Secularism and Nonreligion*, 3: 1–16.

Sherkat, D.E. (2014), *Changing Faith: The Dynamics and Consequences of Americans' Shifting Religious Identities*, New York: New York University Press.

References

Altemeyer, B. (2010), "Atheism and Secularity in North America," in P. Zuckerman (ed.), *Atheism and Secularity*, vol. 2, *Global Expressions*, 1–21, Santa Barbara, CA: Praeger.

ARIS (n.d.), "Series 1990–2008." https://commons.trincoll.edu/aris/about-aris/ (accessed October 21, 2020).

Beit-Hallahmi, B. (2014), *Psychological Perspectives on Religion and Religiosity*, London: Routledge.

Bradshaw, M. and C.G. Ellison (2009), "The Nature-Nurture Debate Is Over, and Both Sides Lost! Implications for Understanding Gender Differences in Religiosity," *Journal for the Scientific Study of Religion*, 48: 241–51.

Chaves, M. (2011), *American Religion: Contemporary Trends*, Princeton, NJ: Princeton University Press.

Cragun, R.T., B. Kosmin, A. Keysar, J.H. Hammer, and M. Nielsen (2012), "On the Receiving End: Discrimination toward the Non-Religious in the United States," *Journal of Contemporary Religion*, 27 (1): 105–27.

Edgell, P., J. Frost, and E. Stewart (2017), "From Existential to Social Understandings of Risk: Examining Gender Differences in Nonreligion," *Social Currents*, 4 (6): 556–74. https://doi.org/10.1177/2329496516686619.

Edgell, P., J. Gerteis, and D. Hartmann (2006), "Atheists as 'Other': Moral Boundaries and Cultural Membership in American Society," *American Sociological Review*, 71: 211–34.

Finke, R. and R. Stark (1992), *The Churching of America—1776–1990: Winners and Losers in Our Religious Economy*, New Brunswick, NJ: Rutgers University Press.

Goldscheider, C. (1971), *Population, Modernization and Social Structure*, Boston: Little Brown.

Hausner, P.M. and O.D. Duncan (1959), *The Study of Population*, Chicago: University of Chicago Press.

Keysar, A. (2007), "Who Are America's Atheists and Agnostics?," in B.A. Kosmin and A. Keysar (eds.), *Secularism & Secularity: Contemporary International Perspectives*, 33–9, Hartford, CT: Institute for the Study of Secularism in Society and Culture, Trinity College.

Keysar, A. (2014), "Shifts along the American Religious-Secular Spectrum," *Secularism and Nonreligion*, 3: 1–16.

Keysar, A. (2015), "The International Demography of Atheists," in B.J. Grim, T.M. Johnson, V. Skirbekk, and G.A. Zurlo (eds.), *Yearbook of International Religious Demography*, 136–53, Leiden: Brill.

Keysar, A. (2016), "'I Think for Myself': American Millennials' Religious and Spiritual Life," presented at *Society for the Scientific Study of Religion Annual Meeting*, Atlanta, Georgia, October 28–30.

Keysar, A. (2017), "Religious/Nonreligious Demography and Religion versus Science: A Global Perspective," in P. Zuckerman and J.R. Shook (eds.), *The Oxford Handbook of Secularism*, Oxford: Oxford University Press.

Keysar, A. and B.A. Kosmin (2007), "The Freethinkers in a Free Market of Religion," in B.A. Kosmin and A. Keysar (eds.), *Secularism & Secularity: Contemporary International Perspectives*, 17–26, Hartford, CT: Institute for the Study of Secularism in Society and Culture, Trinity College.

Keysar, A. and J. Navarro-Rivera (2013), "A World of Atheism: Global Demographics," in S. Bullivant and M. Ruse (eds.), *The Oxford Handbook of Atheism*, 553–86, Oxford: Oxford University Press.

Keysar, A. and T. Piltzecker (2016), "Freedom of Choice: Religion and Gender in a Global Perspective, Young Adults and Religion in a Global Perspective (YARG)," presented at the *Society for the Scientific Study of Religion Annual Meeting*, Atlanta, Georgia, October 28–30.

Kontala, J., A. Keysar, and S. Kheir (forthcoming), "Secular Identities in Context: Emerging Prototypes among Non-Religious Millennials," in P. Nynäs, R. Illman, R. Hernandez, and N. Novis (eds.), *Between Universalism and Particularism in the Study of Religion: Sensitizing "Religious" Variety in a Study of Young Adults in a Global Perspective*, London: Equinox Publications.

Kosmin, B.A. (2007), "Contemporary Secularity and Secularism," in B.A. Kosmin and A. Keysar (eds.), *Secularism & Secularity: Contemporary International Perspectives*, 1–13, Hartford, CT: Institute for the Study of Secularism in Society and Culture, Trinity College.

Kosmin, B.A. and A. Keysar (2006), *Religion in a Free Market, Religious and Non-Religious Americans: Who, What, Why, Where*, Ithaca, NY: Paramount Market Publishing.

Kosmin, B.A. and A. Keysar (2009), *American Religious Identification Survey (ARIS 2008), Summary Report*, Hartford, CT: Institute for the Study of Secularism in Society and Culture, Trinity College.

Kosmin, B.A. and A. Keysar (2013), *Religious, Spiritual and Secular: The Emergence of Three Distinct Worldviews among American College Students, a Report Based on the ARIS 2013 National College Student Survey*, September, Hartford, CT: Trinity College.

Kosmin, B.A. and S.P. Lachman (1993), *One Nation under God: Religion in Contemporary American Society*, New York: Harmony Books.

Kosmin, B.A., A. Keysar, R.T. Cragun, and J. Navarro-Rivera (2009), *American Nones: The Profile of the No Religion Population, A Report Based on the American Religious Identification Survey 2008*, Hartford, CT: Institute for the Study of Secularism in Society and Culture, Trinity College.

Levy, P.S. and S. Lemeshow (1991), *Sampling of Populations: Methods and Applications*, New York: Wiley.

Lipka, M. (2015), "A Closer Look at America's Rapidly Growing Religious 'Nones'," Pew Research Center, May 13. https://www.pewresearch.org/fact-tank/2015/05/13/a-closer-look-at-americas-rapidly-growing-religious-nones/ (accessed September 13, 2020).

Navarro-Rivera, J., B.A. Kosmin, and A. Keysar (2010), *U.S. Latino Religious Identification 1990–2008: Growth, Diversity & Transformation, A Report Based on the American Religious Identification Survey 2008*, March, Hartford, CT: Institute for the Study of Secularism in Society and Culture, Trinity College.

Passel, J.S. and D. Cohn (2008), "U.S. Population Projections 2005–2050," Pew Research Center, February 11. https://www.pewresearch.org/hispanic/2008/02/11/us-population-projections-2005-2050/ (accessed September 13, 2020).

Pew Religious Landscape Survey (2014), https://www.pewforum.org/religious-landscape-study/ (accessed October 21, 2020).

Pew Research Center (2012), "Nones on the Rise," October 9. https://www.pewforum.org/2012/10/09/nones-on-the-rise-demographics/ (accessed September 13, 2020).

Pew Research Center (2015), "Americas Changing Religious Landscape," May 12. https://www.pewforum.org/2015/05/12/americas-changing-religious-landscape/ (accessed September 13, 2020).

Public Law. 1976. https://www.govinfo.gov/content/pkg/STATUTE-90/pdf/STATUTE-90-Pg2459.pdf#page=7 (accessed September 13, 2020).

Sherkat, D.E. (2014), *Changing Faith: The Dynamics and Consequences of Americans' Shifting Religious Identities*, New York: New York University Press.

Silk, M. and A. Walsh (2008), *One Nation, Divisible: How Regional Religious Differences Shape American Politics (Religion by Region)*, Lanham, MD: Rowman &Littlefield.

Stark, R. (2002), "Physiology and Faith: Addressing the 'Universal' Gender Difference in Religious Commitment," *Journal for the Scientific Study of Religion*, 41: 495–507.

US Census Bureau (2018), "Older People Projected to Outnumber Children for First Time in U.S. History," March 13. https://www.census.gov/newsroom/press-releases/2018/cb18-41-population-projections.html (accessed September 13, 2020).

US Census Bureau (n.d.), "Does the Census Bureau Have Data for Religion?." https://ask.census.gov/prweb/PRServletCustom/YACFBFye-rFIz_FoGtyvDRUGg1Uzu5Mn*/!STANDARD?pyActivity=pyMobileSnapStart&ArticleID=KCP-5050 (accessed September 13, 2020).

Wilson, J. and D.E. Sherkat (1994), "Returning to the Fold," *Journal for the Scientific Study of Religion*, 33: 148–61.

Wuthnow, R. (1999), *Growing Up Religious: Christians and Jews and Their Journeys of Faith*, Boston: Beacon Press.

Zuckerman, P., ed. (2010), *Atheism and Secularity*, vol. 2, *Global Expressions*. Santa Barbara, CA: Praeger.

Glossary Terms

Census A complete enumeration of a population of interest, meaning every member of that population is included in the data that are collected.

Demography The study of the size, structure, and dynamics of a population.

Sample A subset of a population of interest. Ideally, samples are randomly chosen to get an accurate representation of the population of interest.

3

Being Nonreligious in the United States

Caitlin Halligan

Becoming Nonreligious

In a country where Christianity is the dominant religion, with 70.6 percent of the population identifying as Christian (Pew Research Center 2015a), nonreligious individuals in the United States often face several challenges—the first of which, for many, is *becoming* nonreligious. Constructing one's nonreligious self is a process that is unique to each individual but commonly occurs in four stages: recognizing the pervasiveness of *theism* in the United States, questioning theism, rejecting theism, and "coming out" (Smith 2011).

The first stage in Smith's (2011) study, recognizing the pervasiveness of theism, consists of individuals beginning to recognize the dominance of religion and religious belief in their society. Because belief is so widespread in the United States, most people are socialized to a belief in God. Many are raised with the same beliefs and religious affiliation as their parents, as families are a primary socializing agent of religious beliefs and upbringing.

Such recognition of the pervasiveness of religion in society then leads many individuals to start questioning why this is the case. Smith's (2011) second stage of becoming nonreligious is just this: questioning theism. In this stage, individuals start questioning where their religious beliefs came from, why their classmate or coworker has a differing belief, how scientific and secular explanations interfere with religious ideas (e.g., the afterlife, the Bible), and having doubts about previously held notions that *morality* stems from religion. For many individuals who leave religion, this stage is sparked as they enter college.

Entering the college campus is a big change for many individuals and often results in less religious activity and more exposure to new ideas and people (Bryant, Choi, and Yasuno 2003; Saenz and Barrera 2007). Students are often far from their homes, meaning that they are also far from their parents and the congregation, synagogue, or mosque that they grew up attending. Having new friends who are critically engaged with religion, such as listening to secular podcasts, debating the "*God question*," or belonging to secular student alliances, can influence individuals to engage with these questions. In fact, the Secular Student Alliance is the country's largest secular student organization with over 315 active chapters (Secular Student Alliance n.d.). Alternatively, exposure to religious students and/or speakers on campus can also lead individuals to question their beliefs. One example of this is evangelical Christian Ross Jackson, better known as "Brother Ross" or "Saint Ross." Brother Ross has been roaming south eastern college campuses and taking advantage of campus free speech areas since 2010. Ross shouts testimonies and stories that often provoke many students who walk by, such as calling women whores for wearing yoga pants or shorts, saying that it is wrong to be a "homo lover," and pronouncing that they (college students) are damned to hell (University of Central Arkansas 2016). As students navigate these college campuses, hearing people such as Brother Ross (or Brother Jed; see figure 3.1) leads many to question both the "illogical" and "immoral" aspects of religious beliefs and teachings.

While attending college may play an influential role for some who leave religion, it is important to note that 44 percent of nonreligious individuals have a high school diploma or less education (Smith et al. 2018). Higher education is not required to leave religion. In fact, many nonreligious individuals report that they started questioning and/ or rejecting religion as early as middle school or high school (Hunsberger and Altemeyer 2006; LeDrew 2013; Perez and Vallières 2019). Zuckerman, Galen, and Pasquale (2017) suggest that it is not being more intelligent or having more education that makes someone nonreligious but, rather, having specific types of cognition. The researchers report that "individuals who have become nonreligious engage in greater complexity of thought" (Zuckerman, Galen, and Pasquale 2017), such as examining issues from multiple perspectives or applying a critical lens. Engaging in complex thought and questioning theism is what eventually leads many to reject theism and religion.

The third stage of Smith's (2011) model is rejecting theism. In this stage, individuals go from questioning to actively rejecting their prior beliefs. Individuals distance themselves from what they perceive as religious doctrines and dogmas and begin to construct their nonreligious identity. The nonreligious often construct their identity in relation to religion. This is typically done by contrasting their view with a religious one, or by describing what they are *not*. For example, a nonreligious individual may begin to construct their identity by saying "I do *not* believe there is compelling evidence for a god to exist" or "I do *not* think a heaven or hell exists" or "I do *not* think a person needs god to be good." However, nonreligious identities are not solely about rejecting religion. In fact, about 34 percent of the nonreligious either believe in God or some form of higher power (Smith et al. 2018). Many nonreligious and nontheistic

FIGURE 3.1 *Brother Jed is confronted by students at Indiana University in Bloomington, Indiana, while preaching about religion.* Source: SOPA Images/Getty Images.

individuals also adhere to humanism, a nontheistic philosophy that provides a set of values for navigating life. When compared to the religious, the nonreligious tend to be less ethnocentric, less prejudiced, less nationalistic, and are more likely to support environmentalism, women's reproductive rights, gay rights, gender equality, doctor-assisted suicide, stem cell research, animal rights, and to be more left-leaning or democratic in their political affiliation (Zuckerman, Galen, and Pasquale 2017).

The fourth and final stage of Smith's (2011) model is "coming out." It is in this stage that nonreligious individuals apply a label to themselves and often let others know their nonreligious standpoint. While Smith's (2011) model is certainly useful in explaining the gradual process of rejecting theism, it is important to note that the model is focused on atheists. Some nonreligious people may not reject theism or religion altogether, and others may never decide to "come out." Additionally, LeDrew (2013) has argued against the linear nature of the model, stating that not all people go through a standard, evolutionary process of having religious beliefs, doubting them, and taking on a new identity. LeDrew (2013) found that many individuals move dynamically between belief, nonbelief, and doubt, returning to religion or atheism and back again a number of times.

Though there are a number of ways people can become nonreligious (LeDrew 2013), Zuckerman, Galen, and Pasquale suggest ten factors that could shape nonreligious identities and beliefs: educational attainment; personal misfortune; exposure to other cultures and religions; friends, colleagues, and/or lovers; political disagreements; moral qualms; sex/sexuality; Satan; malfeasance of religious associates; and suffering, cruelty, and injustice (2017: 97). While education was discussed above, personal misfortunes, such as experiencing loss or pain, can cause individuals to question religion's utility (Zuckerman, Galen, and Pasquale 2017). Individuals might begin to ask themselves why a loss or pain is happening to them or why their prayers have gone unanswered. Exposure to other cultures and religions could also play a role. Moving or traveling to other countries opens people up to new ideas, worldviews, religions, and different ways of living that may lead people to be critical of, or question, their own culture and beliefs. Having friends, colleagues, or lovers with a different religious worldview than one's own may influence beliefs, whether it be through conversations or debates about religion, politics, or other values. Political issues such as abortion; lesbian, gay, bisexual, transgender, and queer/questioning (LGBTQ) equality; prayer in schools; and sex education, are closely tied to religion. Since many conservative Christians associate with the Republican Party, holding more progressive political views may influence individuals to question religion. Some individuals may take issue with biblical or other sacred texts, such as God's lack of fairness or other illustrations of immoral behavior, leading them to question their religion. Sex and sexuality may shape one's relationship with religion, as many religions condemn masturbation, premarital sex, and homosexuality. Religions that teach people to be in a constant state of fear for their eternal fate by worrying about the temptings of Satan and the possibility they will go to hell can cause higher levels of neuroticism. By no longer believing, people can assuage these fears. Hypocritical religious people, such as a coworker or pastor who identifies as religious but has questionable morals—sexually abusing members of the congregation, stealing funds, having a gluttonous lifestyle—can lead people to question religion. A final possible path out of religion is theodicy or the question of suffering in the world. People might wonder why a moral or just God would allow natural disasters to kill millions, or why innocent children suffer from cancer and die when they have done nothing wrong and an all powerful God could intervene.

As noted, every individual's path out of religion is different. Just one or many of the above factors could contribute to them leaving religion. Because every individual's experience is different, the nonreligious have a plurality of worldviews, identities, and behaviors.

Being Nonreligious: Choosing a Label

Just as Christians have a variety of different labels they prefer (e.g., Catholic, Methodist, Presbyterian, Lutheran, etc.), nonreligious individuals have a variety of labels they choose as well. In other words, in the same way "Christian" is an umbrella term used for the variety of religious denominations centered around a monotheistic God and the life and teachings of Jesus, "nonbeliever" is an umbrella term for the variety of belief systems that reject this notion and "nonreligious" is an umbrella term for individuals who report no religious affiliation. Some of the labels are centered around an individual's position towards the concept of a god or gods, while others are more focused on general philosophies (Schnell 2015). Some of the more common labels are atheist, agnostic, spiritual but not religious, and humanist. Atheists lack belief in a god(s) or the divine (Bullivant 2013; Schnell 2015). Agnostics, on the other hand, argue that there is no way to prove or disprove the existence of a god(s) or the divine and therefore they do not take a stance on the "God question," claiming that the existence of a god(s) is not an answerable question. Some individuals identify as "spiritual but not religious." While the meaning behind the label varies from person to person, it is often used to identify those who loosely believe in some form of a higher power but are *unchurched*, dissatisfied with organized religion, or those who adhere to a more "psychological spirituality" in which individuals draw from various belief systems to create their own customized worldview (Chaves 2011; Fuller 2001; Pew Research Center 2018). Spiritual but not religious has seen a recent increase in use; it is the most popular label among the "nonreligious" and is often used by those under forty years old (Chaves 2011). Atheism, agnosticism, and "spiritual but not religious" focus on what people are not. There are other labels nonreligious individuals can and do choose that focus on affirmative philosophies, such as humanism, freethought, skepticism, and naturalism, all of which are discussed in other articles in Bloomsbury Religion in North America.

Often, nonreligious individuals choose more than one nonreligious label to identify themselves. Lee (2014) refers to this as the "atheist plus" identity in which nonreligious individuals respond creatively to a demand for more diverse nonreligious representations. Though Lee's study was primarily focused on atheists, this is common among nonreligious individuals. For example, someone might identify as an atheist because they do not believe god exists but may also identify strongly with humanism because they believe morality should be constructed by human understanding and needs. Another example would be an individual who identifies as an agnostic because they are uncertain as to whether a god exists, but also identifies as a skeptic because they are skeptical of supernatural claims. It is common for nonreligious individuals to choose multiple labels. This is particularly common for atheists due to the *social stigma* associated with the word "atheist" (Galen 2009; Lee 2014; Schietle, Corcoran, and Hudnall 2018). Because of this stigma, atheists often feel the need to explain what they are not and offer a less threatening label. Lee (2014) provides a compelling illustration of this behavior. One of her interviewees, when asked why they use different labels in different circumstances, responded, "Cause if I was talking to someone who was really religious, it might somehow seem a bit, um, *aggressive* to say I was an 'atheist' or something, so I'd probably say 'I'm not religious'" (Lee 2014, emphasis in original). Choosing a nonreligious label is a careful and sometimes context-specific act for many nonreligious individuals.

Choosing an identity or label can provide nonreligious individuals with a sense of independence and empowerment (Smith 2011). For many, this results in individuals "coming out" in a fashion similar to that of the LGBTQ community. They finally feel free to claim their nonreligious identity and let the world know. Similar to the experience of LGBTQ individuals who come out, nonreligious individuals also experience difficulty navigating their new identity with family, friends, and coworkers. Individuals can "come out" in both virtual and personal ways (Smith 2011). Virtually, individuals may opt to change their religious preference on social media to their new label, may write a post

FIGURE 3.2 *An individual holds up a sign telling his mother that he's an atheist.* Source: Elvert Barnes.

on social media about their identity, or may email friends and family to inform them. Nonreligious individuals have even adopted a coming out day, similar to that of the LGBTQ National Coming Out Day, to publicly claim their nonreligious identity (as the individual in figure 3.4 is doing). The National Day of Reason, the first Thursday in May, is held to celebrate reason over religion (American Humanist Association n.d.). The day also coincides with the National Day of Prayer, which many nonreligious individuals believe is an unconstitutional violation of the separation of church and state enshrined in the First Amendment of the Constitution. Nonreligious individuals have used the National Day of Reason as an opportunity to come out to their loved ones.

Individuals also come out in more personal ways, such as direct interactions with family and/or friends. The result of coming out to family members tends to be a more positive experience when the individual has healthy communication with their family, such as being honest and upfront about their nonbelief instead of hinting at the subject or lying. In Zimmerman et al.'s (2015) study on atheists' experiences coming out to their family, individuals reported a positive experience coming out when family members adapted and were respectful. The most common positive responses from family members were acceptance or seeing the change as a nonissue, unconditional love, or gradual acceptance of the change over time (Zimmerman et al. 2015). Parents who responded with acceptance or treating it as a nonissue did so by either focusing on their love and respect for their child (e.g., "We're just glad you're happy") or by expressing ambivalence (e.g., "Okay. Whatever."). Parents who responded to the news with unconditional love often did so by telling their child that they loved and supported them no matter what. Some parents did not immediately respond with acceptance but eventually came around over time. For many parents, their child's atheism may have been shocking, resulting in them needing time to reflect and to figure out how to respectfully handle the situation without upsetting their child.

While many individuals receive positive (or at least neutral) responses to their coming out as nonreligious to their family, others' experiences can be extremely negative and even painful. In one study on atheists in the United States, almost 25 percent reported being "rejected, avoided, isolated, or ignored" by family because of their atheist identity, almost 30 percent said they were asked by family or friends to pretend that they weren't an atheist, and about 38 percent were advised by family or friends to hide their atheist identity (Hammer et al. 2012: 54). These experiences are also reflected in Zimmerman et al.'s (2015) study, along with family members responding by outright anger, despair, lack of connection, denial, dismissiveness, attempts to convert them to religion, and increased religious commitment among family and friends (see Table 3.1).

TABLE 3.1 Negative Familial Responses to Coming Out as an Atheist

Type of Response	Example
Anger	Parent(s) respond with anger, frustration, taking offense, yelling
Rejection	Parent(s) not speaking to their child afterwards, being frowned upon
Despair	Parent(s) crying, feeling as if their child will be damned to hell and cannot be saved
Lack of Connection	Parent(s) feeling like they can no longer relate to their child, especially if religion plays an important role in their life
Denial	Parent(s) refusing to accept (sometimes for years) the individual's nonreligious identity
Dismissiveness	Parent(s) thinking the change is "just a phase" and that the individual will grow out of it
Request of Silence	Parent(s) asking their child not to talk about atheism, not to respond
Conversion Attempt	Parent(s) attempt to convince the individual that they should believe in God, sometimes in direct ways (such as confronting the individual and telling them they need to be saved) or in indirect ways (such as mentioning prayer in passing when discussing a different topic)
Increased Religious Commitment	Parent(s) being more obvious and open about their religious beliefs (such as forwarding the individual religious books, songs, blogs, podcasts, and so forth)
Pressure	Parent(s) pressuring the individual to participate in religious activities (such as prayer at dinner or attending church)

Being Nonreligious: Discrimination

Family is not the only obstacle nonreligious individuals have to overcome once they come out as nonreligious. Many nonreligious individuals have stated that they have lost friends and even been fired from a job due to their identity (Hunsberger and Altemeyer 2006). Issues with family, friends, coworkers, and even strangers is typically a result of the social stigma connected to being nonreligious. Many Americans do not think atheists share the same values and morals as they do. In a national survey, participants were asked which social groups were the least likely to share their vision for American society among Muslims, conservative Christians, Jews, homosexual individuals, immigrants, Hispanics, African Americans, Asian Americans, and atheists (Edgell, Gerteis, and Hartmann 2006). The results showed that out of all the groups, 78.6 percent of Americans believed that atheists did not share their vision of American society, and 47.6 percent would disapprove if their child wanted to marry an atheist (Edgell, Gerteis, and Hartmann 2006). Edgell and colleagues (2016) reexamined Americans' views of atheists again in 2014 and found that anti-atheist sentiment is still strong and persistent in the United States. Additionally, they found that Americans also have a general disdain for the growing number of Americans who claim no religious identification. Americans' disdain for atheists and other nonreligious identities has been shown to be related to morality. Christianity was constructed as part of America's national identity (Jacobs and Theiss-Morse 2013). Additionally, many Christians think that for someone to behave morally they must believe someone or something (i.e., God) must be watching them all the time. Anyone lacking such a belief can, therefore, not be trusted to act morally. As a result, anyone who rejects these long-held cultural values is seen as immoral, an outsider, and as un-American (Edgell et al. 2016). This is also why atheists are seen as being rebellious, immoral, and hedonistic (Harper 2007).

One way to explain the relationship between religious and nonreligious groups in the United States is through advantages (*privilege*) and disadvantages (*oppression*). Groups that are advantaged are seen as superior, have greater social power, and receive unearned benefits, whereas groups that are disadvantaged are seen as inferior, have less social power, and often face *discrimination* (Goodman 2015). This is the case with religious and nonreligious individuals in the United States. Since Christianity is the dominant (majority) religion in the United States with 70.6 percent of the population identifying as Christian (Pew Research Center 2015a), Christians experience privilege, while the nonreligious (minority) often experience disadvantages, such as discrimination. Christian privilege is similar to that of other privileges in the United States. For example, men, white individuals, heterosexual individuals, native-born Americans, the wealthy, and able-bodied people all experience advantages as members of dominant groups in the United States. These privileges can include higher pay for the same job, the ability to walk into a store and not be followed, or the ability to afford a higher education. Similarly, Christians experience privilege in the United States: Christian holidays being recognized as national holidays; discounted child services (e.g., day care, school, summer camp) through their church; Christian prayers at public events; widespread availability of Christian music, movies, and symbols; favor in court systems (Fitzgerald 2017); politicians, teachers, medical, and legal professionals who share their same faith; worship without fear of violence; and the ability to openly discuss beliefs in public without fear of reprisals (Schlosser 2003).

Given that Christian values and practices are woven into American life, it is not surprising that the nonreligious experience discrimination. However, not all nonreligious individuals are discriminated against equally. Studies have found that those who identify as atheist or agnostic are more likely to experience discrimination compared to those whose nonreligious labels are viewed more positively or at least more benignly, such as those who adopt the label "spiritual but not religious" (Cragun et al. 2012; Edgell et al. 2016). Nonreligious individuals report being discriminated against in places of work, at school, and in public spaces.

Workplace Discrimination

Those who identify as atheist or agnostic as well as those who live in the South are more likely to be discriminated against at work than those who identify with other nonreligious labels and live elsewhere in the United States (Cragun et al. 2012; Scheitle and Corcoran 2018). In one study, 36 percent of atheists reported being rejected, avoided, isolated, or ignored by coworkers or classmates. Similarly, 30 percent reported a hostile work or school environment (Hammer et al. 2012). Some examples of discrimination may be helpful. A firefighter in Kentucky experienced continual harassment and retaliation from his coworkers because of his atheism. He stated that one of his colleagues said he would burn down his house because he was an atheist, and in another incident a colleague said atheists "deserve to burn" (Sonka 2016). A manager on a Maine farm was fired for his atheism. The individual was provided with housing on the farm as a part of his employment agreement and lived with his long-term partner to whom he was not married. The owner disapproved of the arrangement and, upon finding out the employee was an atheist, fired him (Boston Globe 2007). Workplace discrimination against the nonreligious can also involve pressuring people to participate in religious practices. A high school German teacher was fired when he spoke out against his religiously devout principal. He lodged complaints against the principal for sending multiple religious emails to the faculty, as well as being forced to pray during school luncheons. The complaints were not ultimately what got the teacher fired, rather, he was fired once he admitted he was an atheist (Wanbaugh 2014).

While many nonreligious individuals experience workplace discrimination, some are even denied jobs for their lack of belief. Hammer et al. (2012) found that almost 10 percent of atheists reported being denied employment, promotion, or educational opportunities because of their beliefs. In support of this finding, Wallace, Bradley, and Wright (2014) sent fake resumes to advertised jobs throughout the South and found that atheists (as well as Muslims and pagans) suffered the highest levels of discriminatory treatment from employers. A clear illustration of this is military discrimination against

FIGURE 3.3 *Military personnel are able to include atheist on their dog tags.* Source: *darwin.wins.*

the nonreligious (though as figures 3.3 and 3.4 show, both military personnel and civilian organizations find creative ways to signal their nonreligious identities). A nonbeliever who had trained to become a humanist chaplain applied to become a chaplain for the Navy and was denied. Navy officials, as well as lawmakers, rejected his application citing no need for an "atheist chaplain" despite a 300 percent increase in service members identifying as nonreligious in the previous ten years (Faram 2018).

Education and Discrimination

Nonreligious individuals also experience discrimination at school. In Hammer's (2012) study, 79 percent of the research participants reported being expected to participate in religious prayers against their will and 59 percent experienced pressure to say "under God" during the US Pledge of Allegiance. While these situations can happen outside of schools, it is not uncommon to see nonreligious individuals being pressured to participate in religious activities in a school environment. For example, a high school student refused to stand during the Pledge of Allegiance because he disagreed with having to say "under God," an action deemed legal by US courts. His teacher threatened to punish him and argued with the student about his atheism, telling him he was not patriotic (Reisman-Brill et al. 2014). Integrating religion into public schools in the United States has resulted in a number of lawsuits. In Cole v. Webster Parish School Board, a Southern public elementary school was accused of unconstitutionally promoting Christianity. The school broadcasted prayers over school speakers, pressured students into saying daily prayers, school sponsored events were accompanied by prayer, and the graduation ceremonies were held in churches (Cole v. Webster Parish School Board 2017). Another instance involved the Carroll County School Board in Maryland. The

FIGURE 3.4 *Nonreligious organizations have posted signs and billboards around the world to help other nonreligious individuals realize they are not alone.* Source: *Sandy Huffaker Getty Images.*

school board consistently opened its meetings with prayers. The American Humanist Association's legal team intervened on behalf of four residents and won in 2019, ending this illegal practice (Henry 2019). Nonreligious students are often harassed and bullied in schools for their lack of belief. A high school student in Oklahoma wanted to take down a Ten Commandment plaque in his biology classroom, only to be bullied by other students who objected to his actions. His mother feared for his safety and his sister suffered consequences as well. His sister was unable to complete a group project because the group members refused to speak to her because of her brother's views (Hamblin 2013).

Discrimination against nonreligious individuals and groups also happens on college campuses. Some college campuses today have nonreligious student organizations, such as the groups of the Secular Student Alliance (n.d.). However, many religiously affiliated universities refuse to recognize nonreligious student organizations as official organizations on campus (Grasgreen 2012). Even when nonreligious student organizations are recognized, they often experience problems with other groups or individuals on campus. One student member of the Secular Student Alliance at a university in Kentucky reported that she received dirty looks when recruiting for the organization, had flyers ripped up in front of her and torn from bulletin boards, and is even hesitant about putting her association with the organization on her resume because employers have scowled at her in the past over being a member (Zuckerman 2017).

Public Discrimination

In addition to work and school, nonreligious discrimination happens in other public spaces as well. In one instance, a nonreligious group put up a legal protest sign near a nativity scene in a public park and it was destroyed multiple times (Ho 2014). A nonreligious group in Texas advertised an upcoming seminar that was going to discuss "In God We Trust" as the national motto. Four of their banners were destroyed (Clarridge 2019). One atheist group adopted a highway, only to have their sign vandalized. Someone had written "pray for" and directional arrows toward the group's name on the sign, and on a different occasion nailed a wooden plaque with the word "pray" to the sign pole (Benziger 2015). Several anti-LGBTQ Christians have sent death threats to well-known TV personality and science advocate Bill Nye (i.e., "Bill Nye the Science Guy"; Stone 2017).

Nonreligious discrimination can also be seen within the US political sphere. A Gallup poll found that 40 percent of Americans say they would not vote for an otherwise qualified atheist candidate for president (McCarthy 2019). As of 2019, only one person in Congress has identified as "unaffiliated," but there has still never been anyone openly atheist in an elected position at the federal level (Pew Research Center 2019). This may be because eight states—Arkansas, Maryland, Mississippi, North Carolina, South Carolina, Tennessee, Texas, and Pennsylvania—still have language in their constitutions that require belief in a god as a prerequisite to hold public office (Moore

2018). While these constitutional requirements are illegal and indefensible in court, the states have not taken them out of their constitutions. This sends a message to those who do not believe in a god that they are not welcome and don't belong within the state government. Additionally, nonreligious individuals face discrimination in the US court system, particularly in cases of child custody and adoption. Because Christianity remains for now the dominant religion in the United States, those who adhere to Christianity are favored over those who do not have a religion when it comes to raising a child. During child custody cases, courts want to establish primary custody with the parent who will act in the "best interest" of the child. In many courts, part of determining the "best interest" of the child involves their spiritual welfare. Given that so many believe it is necessary to believe in a higher power to have morals, some judges argue it is against the child's best interest for a parent to raise a child without religion (Volokh 2006). In one case, a mother was told she could lose custody of her children if she did not pretend to be an ultra-Orthodox Jew around her children, the religion practiced by her ex-husband (Otterman 2018). Volokh (2006) cites over seventy-five other cases with similar stories of nonreligious parents being accused of "neglecting religious training," with many losing custody because of their nonbelief. In these cases, nonreligious individuals were not allowed to openly live their identity to have an ongoing relationship with their own children.

Nonreligious discrimination also happens in US prison systems. Jason Holden, a humanist inmate at the Federal Correctional Institution in Sheridan, Oregon, was denied the right to form a humanist study group and identify as a humanist for official assignment purposes (Miller and Miller 2015). The American Humanist Association's legal team intervened in this case and won in 2015. This case was significant for many humanist individuals in the prison system who were not receiving the same rights, recognition, and treatment as religious individuals.

In addition to the American Humanist Association, the Freedom From Religion Foundation (FFRF) is another nonprofit organization that takes legal action in cases involving the nonreligious and the separation of church and state. The FFRF recently won a lawsuit related to a discriminatory policy in Brevard County, Florida, that favored Christians providing invocations at public meetings (Seering 2020a). Other recent victories include the removal of religious displays in a Texas public school (Seering 2020b) and the removal of a religious organization from providing anti-scientific, religion-based sex education in an Illinois public school (Seering 2019). Nonreligious organizations such as the FFRF continually fight legal battles to combat discrimination and to create a more egalitarian society for the nonreligious.

Everyday Life and Making Meaning

This chapter has illustrated how nonreligious individuals in the United States come to be nonreligious, and how their nonreligious identity is managed across various aspects of American life. Many nonreligious individuals experience discrimination. The final topic this chapter addresses is how the nonreligious find meaning in their lives without religion, belief in a god(s) or divine power.

Many nonreligious individuals carefully choose when and where they will disclose their nonbelief to avoid potential experiences of prejudice and discrimination (Fitzgerald 2003). Like other groups who face prejudice and discrimination (e.g., racial and sexual minorities), nonreligious individuals may turn to supportive others to cope with stigma and/or discrimination, such as family, friends, nonreligious organizations, or therapy. A variety of nonreligious organizations such as the American Humanist Association, American Atheists, Center for Inquiry, and the Secular Student Alliance, offer outlets for nonreligious individuals to express themselves. While many of these organizations have local chapters, many nonreligious individuals join these organizations online to have a space to "come out, speak out, and 'meet up'" (Cimino and Smith 2011: 31).

While nonreligious organizations (either online or face-to-face) may help nonbelievers cope with discrimination, many individuals join these organizations for other purposes. Nonreligious organizations are one venue where individuals make meaning in their lives. There are thousands of nonreligious organizations in the United States devoted to nonreligious values, community, and activism (Garcia and Blankholm 2016). Individuals join these groups to make new friends, learn, volunteer, engage in activism, and/or help others, all of which can help them find meaning in their lives.

Aside from joining nonreligious organizations, nonreligious individuals often have meaning in their lives in similar ways to their religious counterparts, just without a god(s) or higher power. For example, when it comes to morality, nonreligious individuals rely on common sense, philosophy, and science for their basis of morality in contrast to religious teachings or perceived edicts from a higher power (Pew Research Center 2015b). The Center for Inquiry, one of the largest and most well-funded secular and skeptical organization in the United States, argues that moral rules are common to all cultures regardless of religion, and that nonreligious individuals can choose to be kind and compassionate simply because it will make the world a better place (College Foundation Inc. [CFI] 2020). While the religious rely on their religious beliefs during times of hardship, the nonreligious often turn to family and friends for comfort, and if the hardship becomes too much, they may turn to other resources such as therapy or the faith-free support network Grief Beyond Belief (2020). Many nonreligious individuals also enjoy celebrating traditional American holidays and ceremonies. However, instead of celebrating the religious aspect of holidays such as Christmas and Easter, the nonreligious celebrate spending time with their loved ones and being grateful (Mohamed 2013). They also enjoy celebrating ceremonies such as weddings and other life milestones, but instead of the ceremony being religious and having a religious officiant, individuals often prefer a secular or humanist celebrant. Secular and humanist celebrants provide meaningful, distinctively personal ceremonies that honor the uniqueness of those involved (The Humanist Society n.d.).

While nonreligious individuals in the United States face many challenges, the increase in the number of people who are nonreligious has started to improve America's perception of the nonreligious and increased the resources available to them. Much of the research on the nonreligious has focused on atheists, which is somewhat problematic as the nonreligious include many other individuals. Further research on the experiences of all types of nonreligious individuals will provide an even better understanding of what it is like to be nonreligious in the United States today.

Further Reading and Online Resources

Cragun, R.T., B. Kosmin, A. Keysar, J.H. Hammer, and M. Nielsen (2012), "On the Receiving End: Discrimination toward the Non-Religious in the United States," *Journal of Contemporary Religion*, 27 (1): 105–27.

Freedom From Religion Foundation (FFRF) (n.d.), "Home." http://ffrf.org (accessed September 13, 2020).

Pew Research Center (2019), "Religiously Unaffiliated." https://www.pewresearch.org/topics/religiously-unaffiliated/ (accessed September 13, 2020).

Secular Student Alliance (2020), https://secularstudents.org (accessed September 13, 2020).

References

American Humanist Association (n.d.), "National Day of Reason." https://www.nationaldayofreason.org/ (accessed September 13, 2020).

Arnett J.J. and L.A. Jensen (2002), "A Congregation of One: Individualized Religious Beliefs among Emerging Adults," *Journal of Adolescent Research*, 17 (5): 451–67.

Barker, D. and A. Gaylor (2019), "Re: Judge Tammy Kemp, Judge of the Texas 204th Judicial District, Proselytizing in Her Official Capacity," Freedom From Religion Foundation, October 3. https://ffrf.org/images/1JudgeKempletter.pdf (accessed September 13, 2020).

Benziger, J. (2015), "Vandalism of Atheists Sign Opens Up Attack on Those of Faith," *Ceres Courier*, January 21. https://www.cerescourier.com/opinion/editorial/vandalism-of-atheists-sign-opens-up-attack-on-those-of-faith/ (accessed September 13, 2020).

"'Brother Ross' Preaches Controversial Christianity, Causes Stir among Students" (2016), *UCA Echo*, November 29. https://ucaecho.net/news/brother-ross-preaches-evangelical-christianity-angers-students/ (accessed September 13, 2020).

Bryant, A.N., J.Y. Choi, and M. Yasuno (2003), "Understanding the Spiritual and Religious Dimension of Students' Lives in the First Year of College," *Journal of College Student Development*, 44 (6): 723–45.

Bullivant, S. (2013), "Defining 'Atheism'," in S. Bullivant and M. Ruse (eds.), *The Oxford Handbook of Atheism*, 11–21, New York: Oxford University Press.

Chan, M., K.M. Tsai, and A.J. Fuligni (2014), "Changes in Religiosity across the Transition to Young Adulthood," *Journal of Youth and Adolescence*, 44 (8): 1555–66.

Chaves, M. (2011), *American Religion: Contemporary Trends*, Princeton, NJ: Princeton University Press.

Cimino, R. and C. Smith (2011), "The New Atheism and the Formation of the Imagined Secularist Community," *Journal of Media and Religion*, 10: 24–38. doi:10.1080/15348423.2011.549391.

Clarridge, E. (2019), "Atheist Group Says 'In No God We Trust' Banners Vandalized in Downtown Fort Worth," *Fort Worth Star-Telegram*, July 5. https://www.star-telegram.com/news/local/fort-worth/article232354457.html (accessed September 13, 2020).

Cole v. Webster Parish School Board (2017), United States District Court Western District of Louisiana Shreveport Division, Case 5:17-cv-01629. https://www.aclu.org/legal-document/cole-v-webster-parish-school-board-complaint (accessed September 13, 2020).

College Foundation Inc. (CFI) (2020), "Home." http://cfi.org/ (accessed September 13, 2020).

Cragun, R.T., B. Kosmin, A. Keysar, J.H. Hammer, and M. Nielsen (2012), "On the Receiving End: Discrimination toward the Non-Religious in the United States," *Journal of Contemporary Religion*, 27 (1): 105–27.

Edgell, P., J. Gerteis, and D. Hartmann (2006), "Atheists as 'Other': Moral Boundaries and Cultural Membership in American Society," *American Sociological Review*, 71: 211–34.

Edgell, P., D. Hartmann, E. Stewart, and J. Gerteis (2016), "Atheists and Other Cultural Outsiders: Moral Boundaries and the Non-Religious in the United States," *Social Forces*, 95 (2): 607–38.

Edmondson, D. and C. Park (2009), "Shifting Foundations: Religious Belief Change and Adjustment in College Students," *Mental Health, Religion & Culture*, 12 (3): 289–302.

Faram, M.D. (2018), "No 'Atheist' Chaplains, Lawmakers Tell Navy," *Navy Times*, March 26. https://www.navytimes.com/news/your-navy/2018/03/26/no-atheistchaplains-lawmakers-tell-navy/ (accessed September 13, 2020).

"Farm Manager Says Atheism Led to Firing" (2007), *Boston Globe*, May 5. http://archive.boston.com/news/local/articles/2007/05/05/blast_probe_results_to_be_announced/ (accessed September 13, 2020).

Fitzgerald, B. (2003), "Atheists in the United States: The Construction and Negotiation of a Non-normative Identity," PhD diss., State University of New York.

Fitzgerald, J.M. (2017), "An Overview of Religious Considerations in Child Custody Disputes," *The Catholic Lawyer*, 32 (2): 129–38.

Fuller, R.C. (2001), *Spiritual but Not Religious: Understanding Unchurched America*, Oxford: Oxford University Press.

Galen, L.W. (2009), "Profile of the Godless: Results of a Survey of the Nonreligious," *Free Inquiry*, 29: 41–5.

Garcia, A. and J. Blankholm (2016), "The Social Context of Organized Nonbelief: County-level Predictors of Nonbeliever Organizations in the United States," *Journal for the Scientific Study of Religion*, 55: 70–90.

Goodman, D.J. (2015), "Oppression and Privilege: Two Sides of the Same Coin," *Journal of Intercultural Communication*, 18: 1–14.

Grasgreen, A. (2012), "Atheist, Secular Students Becoming Established on Religious Campuses," *Inside Higher Ed*, March 19. https://www.insidehighered.com/news/2012/03/19/atheist-secular-students-becoming-established-religious-campuses (accessed September 13, 2020).

Grief Beyond Belief (2020), "Home." http://griefbeyondbelief.org (accessed September 13, 2020).

Hamblin, J. (2013), "Bullied for Not Believing in God," *The Atlantic*, September 13. https://www.theatlantic.com/health/archive/2013/09/bullied-for-not-believing-in-god/279095/ (accessed September 13, 2020).

Hammer, J.H., R.T. Cragun, K. Hwang, and J.M. Smith (2012), "Forms, Frequency, and Correlates of Perceived Anti-Atheist Discrimination," *Secularism and Nonreligion*, 1: 43–67.

Harper, M. (2007), "The Stereotyping of Nonreligious People by Religious Students: Contents and Subtypes," *Journal for the Scientific Study of Religion*, 46: 539–52.

Henry, S. (2019), "Humanists Score Victory in Longstanding MD Legislative Prayer Case," [Press release] Humanist Legal Center, August 30. https://www.humanistlegalcenter.org/single-post/2019/08/30/Humanists-Score-Victory-in-Longstanding-MD-Legislative-Prayer-Case (accessed September 13, 2020).

Ho, S. (2014), "Atheist Sign near Nativity Scene Damaged in Arlington Heights," *Chicago Tribune*, December 8. https://www.chicagotribune.com/suburbs/arlington-heights/ct-atheist-signs-damaged-arlington-heights-tl-20141208-story.html (accessed September 13, 2020).

The Humanist Society (n.d.). https://www.thehumanistsociety.org/ (accessed September 13, 2020).

Hunsberger, B. and B. Altemeyer (2006), *Atheists: A Groundbreaking Study of America's Nonbelievers*, Buffalo, NY: Prometheus Books.

Jacobs, C.M. and E. Theiss-Morse (2013), "Belonging in a 'Christian Nation': The Explicit and Implicit Associations between Religion and National Group Membership," *Politics and Religion*, 6: 373–401.

Jacoby, S. (2005), *Freethinkers: A History of American Secularism*, New York: Holt Paperbacks.

Law, S. (2013), "Humanism'," in S. Bullivant and M. Ruse (eds.), *The Oxford Handbook of Atheism*, 263–77, New York: Oxford University Press.

LeDrew, S. (2013), "Discovering Atheism: Heterogeneity in Trajectories to Atheist Identity Activism," *Sociology of Religion*, 74 (4): 431–53.

Lee, L. (2014), "Secular or Nonreligious? Investigating and Interpreting Generic 'Not Religious' Categories and Populations," *Religion*, 44 (3): 466–82.

Maroney, E. (2010), "Secular Identity," in R. Jackson and M. Hogg (eds.), *Encyclopedia of Identity*, 663, Thousand Oaks, CA: Sage.

McCarthy, J. (2019), "Less Than Half in U.S. Would Vote for a Socialist for President," *Gallup*, May 9. https://news.gallup.com/poll/254120/less-half-vote-socialist-president.aspx (accessed September 13, 2020).

Miller, M. and M. Miller (2015), "American Humanist Association Secures Equal Rights for Humanist Inmates in Federal Prison," [Press release] American Humanist Association, July 27. https://americanhumanist.org/news/2015-07-american-humanist-association-secures-equal-rights-f/ (accessed September 13, 2020).

Mohamed, B. (2013), "Christmas also Celebrated by Many non-Christians," Pew Research Center, December 23. https://www.pewresearch.org/fact-tank/2013/12/23/christmas-also-celebrated-by-many-non-christians/ (accessed September 13, 2020).

Moore, R.L. (2018), *Godless Citizens in a Godly Republic: Atheists in American Public Life*, New York: W.W. Norton & Company.

Oppy, G. (2013), "Arguments for Atheism," in S. Bullivant and M. Ruse (eds.), *The Oxford Handbook of Atheism*, 53–70, New York: Oxford University Press.

Otterman, S. (2018), "When Living Your Truth Can Mean Losing Your Children," *The New York Times*, May 25. https://www.nytimes.com/2018/05/25/nyregion/orthodox-jewish-divorce-custody-ny.html (accessed September 13, 2020).

Perez, S. and F. Vallières (2019), "How Do Religious People Become Atheists? Applying a Grounded Theory Approach to Propose a Model of Deconversion," *Secularism and Nonreligion*, 8: 3.

Pew Research Center (2015a), "America's Changing Religious Landscape," May 12. http://www.pewforum.org/2015/05/12/americas-changing-religious-landscape/ (accessed September 13, 2020).

Pew Research Center (2015b), "Chapter 1: Importance of Religion and Religious Beliefs," November 3. https://www.pewforum.org/2015/11/03/chapter-1-importance-of-religion-and-religious-beliefs/ (accessed September 13, 2020).

Pew Research Center (2018), "'Spiritual but Not Religious' Label Most Common among 'Nones' Who Say They Believe in a God or Higher Power," May 23. https://www.pewforum.org/2018/05/29/attitudes-toward-spirituality-and-religion/pf_05-29-18_religion-western-europe-05-03/ (accessed September 13, 2020).

Pew Research Center (2019), "Faith on the Hill: The Religious Composition of the 116th Congress," January 3. https://www.pewforum.org/2019/01/03/faith-on-the-hill-116/ (accessed September 13, 2020).

Pigliucci, M. (2013), "New Atheism and the Scientific Turn in the Atheism Movement," *Midwest Studies in Philosophy*, 37 (1): 142–53.

Reisman-Brill, J., J. Bardi, E. Newman, and R. Deitch (2014), "Atheist Student Sits Out the Pledge of Allegiance, Threatened with Punishment," [Press release] American Humanist Association, September 25. https://americanhumanist.org/news/2014-09-atheist-student-sits-out-the-pledge-of-allegiance-th/ (accessed September 13, 2020).

Saenz, V.B. and D.S. Barrera (2007), *Findings from the 2005 College Student Survey (CSS): National Aggregates*, Los Angeles: Higher Education Research Institute.

Scheitle, C. and K. Corcoran (2018), "Religious Tradition and Workplace Religious Discrimination: The Effects of Regional Context," *Social Currents*, 5 (3): 283–300.

Scheitle, C., K. Corcoran, and E. Hudnall (2018), "Adopting a Stigmatized Label: Social Determinants of Identifying as an Atheist beyond Disbelief," *Social Forces*, 97 (4): 1731–56.

Schlosser, L.Z. (2003), "Christian Privilege: Breaking a Sacred Taboo," *Journal of Multicultural Counseling and Development*, 31 (1): 44–51.

Schnell, T. (2015), "Dimensions of Secularity (DoS): An Open Inventory to Measure Facets of Secular Identities," *International Journal for the Psychology of Religion*, 25: 272–92.

Secular Student Alliance (n.d.). https://secularstudents.org (accessed September 13, 2020).

Seering, L. (2019), "Two Victories for State-Church Separation in Illinois," Freedom From Religion Foundation, December 17. https://ffrf.org/legal/other-legal-successes/item/36765-two-victories-for-state-church-separation-in-illinois (accessed September 13, 2020).

Seering, L. (2020a), "Florida County Must Pay $490K in Legal Fees," Freedom From Religion Foundation, February 11. https://ffrf.org/legal/other-legal-successes/item/37118-florida-county-must-pay-490k-in-legal-fees (accessed September 13, 2020).

Seering, L. (2020b), "Religious Display in Texas Public High School Removed," Freedom From Religion Foundation, January 6. https://ffrf.org/legal/other-legal-successes/item/37114-religious-display-in-texas-public-high-school-removed (accessed September 13, 2020).

Simmons, J. (2018), "Not That Kind of Atheist: Scepticism as a Lifestyle Movement," *Social Movement Studies*, 17 (4): 437–50.

Smith, J.M. (2011), "Becoming an Atheist in America: Constructing Identity and Meaning from the Rejection of Theism," *Sociology of Religion*, 72 (2): 215–37.

Smith, T.W., M. Davern, J. Freese, and S. Morgan (2018), "General Social Surveys, 1972–2018," Chicago: NORC at University of Chicago.

Sonka, J. (2016), "Louisville Firm Representing Former Bowling Green Firefighter Who Alleges Harassment from Co-workers for Being Atheist," Louisville Future, August 12. https://louisvillefuture.com/archived-news/former-bowling-green-firefighter-sues-city-over-alleged-harassment-and-retaliation-from-co-workers-based-on-religion/. (accessed December 12, 2020).

Stone, M. (2017), "Bill Nye Receives Death Threats after Mocking Christian Morality." *Patheos*, April 28. https://www.patheos.com/blogs/progressivesecularhumanist/2017/04/bill-nye-receives-death-threats-mocking-christian-morality/?fbclid=IwAR1SDA4ZR6GvTrChnkuFOONhm5wmJP0Bzf4FUsyboZiUOZxjuGQnTcYmOGo (accessed November 25, 2020).

Volokh, E. (2006), "Parent-Child Speech and Child Custody Speech Restrictions," *New York University Law Review*, 81 (2): 631–733.

Wallace, M., R.E. Bradley, and A.H. Wright (2014), "Religious Affiliation and Hiring Discrimination in the American South: A Field Experiment," *Social Currents*, 1 (2): 189–207.

Wanbaugh, M. (2014), "Fired German Teacher Files EEOC Complaint against Middlebury Community Schools," *The Goshen News*, June 15. https://www.goshennews.com/news/local_news/fired-german-teacher-files-eeoc-complaint-against-middlebury-community-schools/article_20e188f5-a16e-5b2d-b060-f0b129c57037.html (accessed August 1, 2019).

Zimmerman, K.J., J.M. Smith, K. Simonson, and W.B. Myers (2015), "Familial Relationship Outcomes of Coming Out as an Atheist," *Secularism and Nonreligion*, 4 (1). http://doi.org/10.5334/snr.aw.

Zuckerman, P. (2017), "Atheist in Appalachia," *Psychology Today*, June 14. https://www.psychologytoday.com/us/blog/the-secular-life/201706/atheist-in-appalachia (accessed September 13, 2020).

Zuckerman, P., L.W. Galen, and F. Pasquale (2016), "The Nonreligious: Understanding Secular People and Societies," *International Journal for the Psychology of Religion*, 27 (3): 154–5.

Glossary Terms

Discrimination The action of treating different groups unfairly, typically on the basis of race, gender, age, sexual orientation, religion, or ability.

God question The philosophical and theological debate about whether or not a god exists.

Morality A distinction between what is good (moral) and what is bad (immoral) in a particular society.

Oppression When a group is subjected to unjust treatment.

Prejudice An intolerant or biased attitude towards a group of individuals, typically on the basis of race, gender, age, sexual orientation, religion, or ability.

Privilege Special rights or power assumed by dominant (majority) groups in society but not granted to other (minority) groups.

Social stigma Having negative characteristics that make a group stand out from others.

Theism Belief in God.

Unchurched Individuals who hold religious views or beliefs but are not connected with a church.

4

Nice, Tolerant, Indifferent Canadians: Religious Nones North of the 49th

Joel Thiessen and
Sarah Wilkins-Laflamme

Introduction

Roman (pseudonym; interviewee from a qualitative study of thirty religious nones—see Thiessen 2016) is an *atheist* who lives in Alberta, Canada. He grew up attending a Presbyterian church weekly with his mom and brother. Roman stopped attending church during his teenage years when his mom no longer wanted to "force the kids to attend." He adds, "Both my father and then my brother identified as atheists. And I don't know if I just did it because I wanted to be like them, or if I actually truly believed it to start with ... For the initial switch ... I was influenced by family. Like if my brother and father weren't, who knows?" Roman was clear though that his father and brother did not try to actively convert him to atheism. Now in his late thirties, working in the information technology sector, a father to two children himself and married to a devout *Evangelical*, Roman shared his views and experiences relative to atheism and religion. We will hear more from Roman in this chapter, but a recurring refrain in Roman's experience, and other Canadians who say they have no religion, is the absence of overt attempts to push one's atheism or religion on to others.

If one were to reflect, like Roman, on their upbringing and current perspectives on religion, what would come to mind? If someone were asked what religion, if any, they identify with, what would they say? Unlike their grandparents or even their parents, chances are that a sizeable proportion would respond by saying "no religion." When someone hears the words "*religious none*," what might come to mind? Atheist? Agnostic? Spiritual but not religious?

Our purpose in this chapter is to draw on the tools of sociology to help us better understand one of the fastest growing "religious" groups in Canada: religious nones. Who are the people who say they have no religion, and how and why are religious nones in Canada different from religious nones in other nations, such as the United States? We argue here that one's social environment—from family to friends to local and national political, educational, and media settings—figures into the perceptions, behaviors, and experiences of religious nones. Moreover, like other modern Western nations, Canadians have become less religious from one generation to the next, a process that started earlier and more rapidly in many parts of Canada than elsewhere in North America.

Snapshot of Religious Nones in Canada

Recent data reveal that 18 percent of Canadian older adults (thirty-five years and older) and 35 percent of Canadian teen and young adult millennials (fifteen to thirty-four years old) say they have no religion (estimates based on our analyses of the 2016 Canadian General Social Survey [GSS]; Statistics Canada 2018). As with the United States, these figures have increased over the last few decades, though the timing and rate of change vary between these two countries. Religious nones grew sooner and faster in Canada, especially in Central Canada (Ontario), the Western Provinces (the Prairies and British Columbia), and the Northern Territories (see figure 4.1 for rates across six different census regions). Most observers point to the early 1970s as the beginning of this increase in these regions (even earlier in the case of British Columbia), compared with the 1990s further to the east in Quebec and Atlantic Canada as well as in the United States. This earlier increase in many parts of Canada is in part due to the country's distinct social and historical environment that opened the door for religious nones to be embraced within mainstream Canadian culture much earlier. More recently though, US rates of no religion have caught up to those in Canada (just under a quarter of the general adult population overall in 2016).

Even in Canada, however, Canadians have not always been as open to religious nones. Canada's roots are largely Christian (Grant 1998; Noll 1992). Schools, hospitals, and other social service agencies were started and run by Christian denominations between the seventeenth and early twentieth century, notably the Anglican and Catholic churches along with the groups that would become the United Church of Canada in 1925. To this day, many Canadian laws, holidays, and practices are informed by Christianity. Two-thirds of Canadians continue to identify with some form of Christian identity, indicative of Christianity's prominent place in Canadian history. Stephen Tomlins (2018) writes of those who were prosecuted through the 1930s for publicly critiquing Christianity. Even in 1965, Dutch immigrants were refused Canadian citizenship because they were atheists and thus perceived as not "of good character, and they could not honestly comply with the oath of allegiance" (Tomlin 2018: 239).

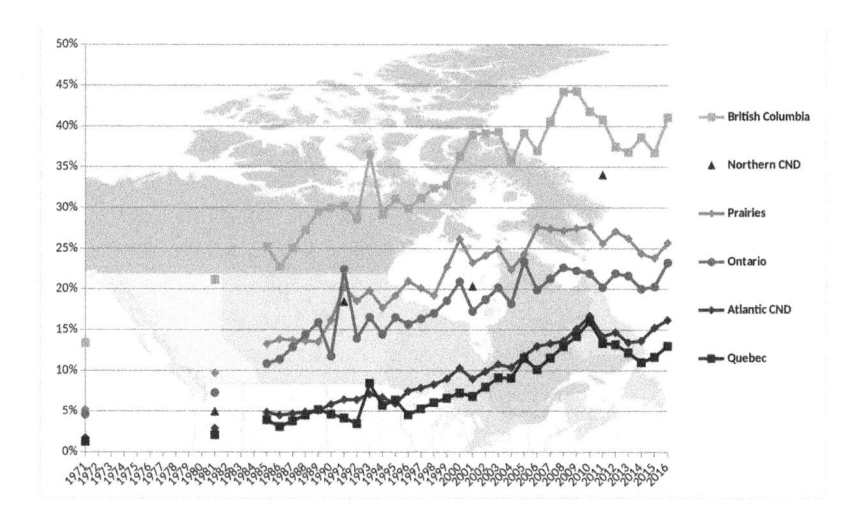

FIGURE 4.1 *Rates of religious nones, six Canadian census regions, 1971–2016.* Source of data: 1971 Census, 1981 Census, 1985–2016 (cycles 1–30) General Social Surveys, Statistics Canada (N British Columbia = 35,497; N Prairies = 78,242; N Ontario = 99,591; N Quebec = 83,299; N Atlantic Canada = 83,093). Missing data for 1987–1988, 1997, 2002 and 2007 replaced by averages from preceding and posterior years. Northern Canada: 1991 Census, 2001 Census and 2011 NHS. All estimates weighted to be representative of general populations.

Still, since the 1960s the magnitude and pervasiveness of a Christian subculture, memory, or self-narrative in Canada has declined, especially in comparison to the strong place of Evangelicalism in the United States that remains to this day (i.e., the United States is still considered by many as a "Christian nation"; Smith 1998). As one example in Canada, the 1965 Dutch immigrant citizenship case resulted in letters of support for atheist immigrants, including vocal support from New Democratic Party leader, founding father of Canada's universal healthcare system and Baptist minister, Tommy Douglas. More recent research shows that Canadians are less likely to believe that an atheist is unfit for political office compared with those in the United States (Bibby 2011).

The support shown for atheist immigrants in 1965 coalesced with other social changes in the immediate decades following the Second World War that progressively weakened Christianity's place in Canada, and strengthened the standing of religious nones. These changes include the waning ethnic-religious ties between English-Protestantism and French-Catholicism, *secularization* at several levels of society (e.g., declining church attendance, withdrawal of religion from public social institutions), and growing support for *multiculturalism* along with increased religious and ethnic diversity. One consequence of these social changes was reduced social stigma associated with saying one had no religion, which opened the door to more people doing so. A defining trait of nones in Canada is that most do not face much social pressure to say they identify with a religion. In fact, there is some research that suggests the social stigma is in the other direction: found more toward those who are actively involved in a religion (Thiessen 2015).

Since the baby boomers, who were born in the postwar period and raised in the 1950s, 1960s, and 1970s, the proportion of those who say they have no religion has increased with each new generation born in most modern Western nations, including Canada (Brown 2013; Crockett and Voas 2006; Wilkins-Laflamme 2015). The *stages of decline* thesis asserts that each generation is less religious than the previous one for a range of social and historical reasons associated with secularization, which include a privileged emphasis on reason and science, strengthened material circumstances, greater pluralism and diversity in a global age, heightened individualism, difficulties in transmitting nominally held religious worldviews across generations, and diminished religious authority throughout the public sphere.

To this point in Canadian history where secularization processes and realities have emerged over time, as in other nations such as the United States, the main pathway leading to no religion is disaffiliation. That is, people like Roman are raised in a religious tradition and then decide for various reasons to leave it behind. Yet, there is also a growing group of religious nones in Canada now who were not raised in any religious tradition, a product of what sociologists call *nonreligious socialization*. Building on the stages of decline thesis (and reflective of widespread secularization in many aspects of social life), as those in one generation leave their religion behind, if or when they have children of their own, they are more likely to raise their children without any religion, and those children are likely to do the same with their own children in future generations. Unlike religious nones raised within a religious tradition, this latter group of "cradle nones" (Bullivant 2017) have little to no familiarity with religion. Given the centrality of family to help socialize people to embrace religious language, attitudes, and practices, one should not necessarily expect such individuals to turn to religious groups for religious holidays or rites of passage, the supernatural in a time of need, or long for the afterlife after a loved one dies (see Thiessen and Wilkins-Laflamme 2017).

Although the proportion of religious nones in Canada has followed a different trajectory than in the United States, when one looks at the demographic characteristics of religious nones, fairly similar qualities arise. When comparing the religiously unaffiliated with the religiously affiliated, religious nones tend to be on average younger, male, not married or having children, and born in the country (see Figure 4.2, and also Clarke and Macdonald 2017; Gee and Veevers 1989; Kosmin and Keysar 2008; Lewis, Currie, and Oman-Reagan 2016; Putnam and Campbell 2010; though see Strawn 2019). This does not mean that, if someone has one or more of these characteristics, they will necessarily be without a religion. It just means that for those who do say they have no religion, they are more likely to have one or more of these demographic traits.

Although they do not differ all that much in terms of demographics, there are nevertheless three other key ways in which Canadian religious nones stand out from their counterparts, notably in the United States. First, Canadian religious nones are

Among all adults

- visible minority (2014 only): Affiliated 17%, No religion 15%
- foreign born: Affiliated 24%, No religion 18%
- male: Affiliated 47%, No religion 57%
- under 35 years old: Affiliated 28%, No religion 49%

■ Affiliated   ■ No religion

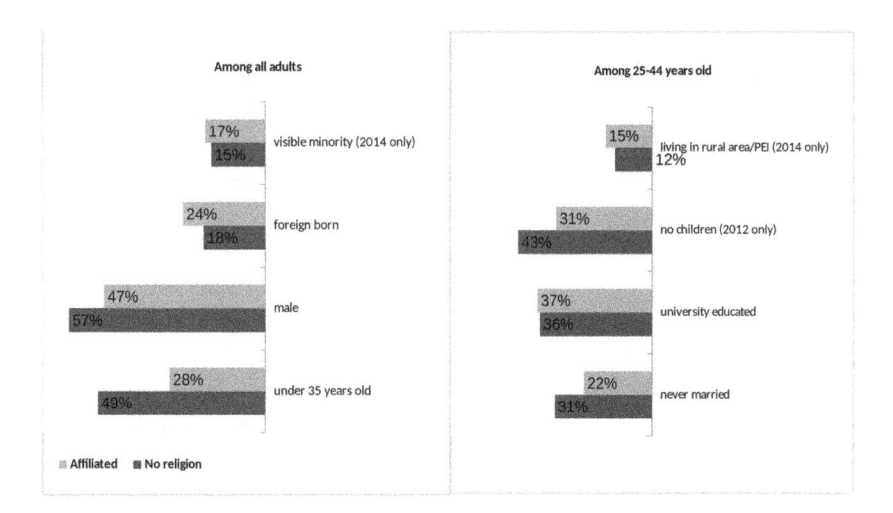

Among 25-44 years old

- living in rural area/PEI (2014 only): Affiliated 15%, No religion 12%
- no children (2012 only): Affiliated 31%, No religion 43%
- university educated: Affiliated 37%, No religion 36%
- never married: Affiliated 22%, No religion 31%

FIGURE 4.2 *Demographic composition of those who are religiously affiliated and those with no religion, Canada, 2010–14, averages.* Source of data: 2010–2014 (cycles 24–28) General Social Surveys, Statistics Canada. Estimates weighted to be representative of the general populations. N 15 years and older = 118,763. N 25–44 years old = 31,856.

even more secular in many ways than religious nones elsewhere in North America. Second, religious nones in Canada are usually less antagonistic toward the religiously affiliated and vice versa. Third, religious nones, like most Canadians regardless of their religious (un)affiliation status, are even more left leaning on a range of sociopolitical issues. We unpack these three observations in more detail in the remainder of this chapter, and along the way we offer sociological explanations as to *why* these data arise as they do.

A Secular Lot

Religious nones are diverse. Some believe in a supernatural being or the afterlife. Others pray, meditate, or consider themselves spiritual persons. Still others say they are atheists, not believing in a god or supernatural beings. Some are agnostic, unsure about the existence of a supernatural entity, while others are completely indifferent to any of these issues. Roman offered the following thoughts on meaning and purpose in life, and the afterlife: "Like, what are we here for? ... lead the best life you can ... But dealing with death, when there's no consolation for going to a better place ... When you're dead, you're dead." Roman also said that although he is an atheist, he is open to attending church services in the future if his wife or kids really want him to. Yet he was quick to qualify, "I wouldn't do it for me, but if my wife said she really wanted me to do this thing, I'd do it ... It would not be for me ... It wouldn't be for me to enhance my spirituality. It would be purely for other people."

Not all religious nones view these topics like Roman. Figure 4.3 details five types of religious nones found among young adults in Canada, including the proportion of nones in each group. This data comes from our 2019 Millennial Trends Survey (MTS). The MTS was administered online over the course of four weeks from March 4–27, 2019, in both English and French, by Sarah Wilkins-Laflamme at the University of Waterloo, Ontario. A total of 2,514 respondents (1,508 from Canada and 1,006 from the United States) aged eighteen to thirty-five years completed the 15-minute web survey. Respondents were recruited through Léger's online panel of registered members (Léger 2020) to complete the survey hosted and maintained by the University of Waterloo's Survey Research Centre (University of Waterloo n.d.).

The first type of religious none, *involved seculars,* include nonbelievers who participate (at least once a year) in organizations that function to advance an atheist, humanist, or secularist worldview. The Sunday Assembly is one example of an organization that started in London, England, and has spread into Canada. This organization regularly gathers secular-orientated individuals together, sometimes in empty church buildings, to sing secular songs, hear speakers on science and nature, volunteer in their community, and raise money to sustain their organization and for other charitable causes. Involved seculars are a small minority among young adult religious nones in Canada, only representing an estimated 3 percent of this demographic.

Inactive nonbelievers are similar to involved seculars in that they do not believe in God or a higher power, but they do not gather with other like-minded individuals to share and discuss this worldview in an organized setting. These inactive nonbelievers are the most common type of religious none, making up nearly half of the religiously unaffiliated young adult Canadian population in 2019.

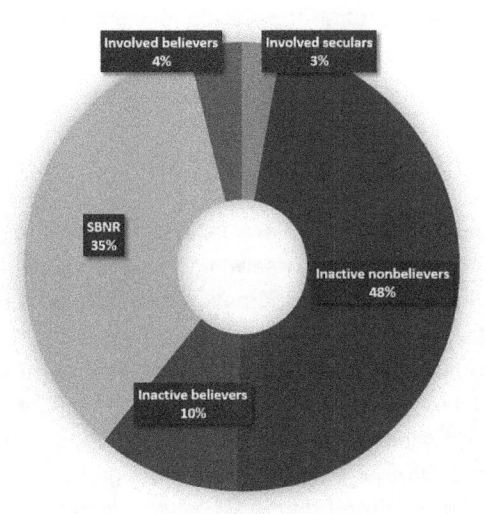

FIGURE 4.3 *Types of religious nones, among unaffiliated respondents eighteen to thirty-five years old, Canada, 2019.* Source of data: Millennial Trends Survey 2019. Estimates weighted to be representative of the young adult population. N = 687.

Inactive believers in turn do believe in God or a higher power, but neither take part in spiritual activities nor attend religious services with any regularity. They represent an estimated 10 percent of young adult religious nones in Canada.

The fourth group, those who are *spiritual but not religious (SBNR)*, also attend religious services less than once a month, but they do say they take part in spiritual activities (activities respondents define as spiritual include meditation, yoga, outdoor nature activities, and so forth). They make up just over a third of the young adult religious none population in Canada.

Finally, the category of *involved believers* include those who believe in God or a higher power and attend religious services at least once a month, despite not affiliating with any single religious group or tradition. As with involved seculars, this category also represents a small minority of young adult religious nones in Canada: an estimated 4 percent.

The Canadian population as a whole is known for scoring lower on most religiosity and belief indicators than in the United States (Bibby 2017; Wilkins-Laflamme 2014). As just one example among many, in 2018 an estimated 11 percent of the US adult population say they do not believe in God or a higher power (based on our analysis of the 2018 GSS; Smith et al. 2018); compared with Canada in 2015 where this estimate reaches 27 percent of the adult population (Angus Reid Institute 2015). This more secular character of the Canadian population compared with the United States also extends to the religious none subpopulations, notably for the indicators of personal religious and spiritual practices. According to data from the 2014 Canadian GSS, only an estimated 12 percent of religious nones said they took part in religious or spiritual practices on their own (including prayer and meditation) at least once a month (Statistics Canada 2018). This compared with the United States where an estimated 36 percent of nones say they meditate at least once a month; and 38 percent say they pray outside of religious services at least a few times a month (based on data from the 2014 Pew Religious Landscape Study). For all intents and purposes then, the largest segment of the religious none population is fairly secular in Canada, more so than nones in the United States.

But why? Here we return to our central thesis of Canada's social environment and the stages of decline framework: there are fewer social cues or pressures north of the 49th parallel to be religious. Sociological research is clear that the family is the single greatest influence over a person's (non)religious development (Bengtson, Putney, and Harris 2013; Clarke and Macdonald 2017; Dillon and Wink 2007; Manning 2015; Merino 2012; Zuckerman 2012). If children are not raised with a religious vocabulary, socialized to believe in a supernatural being or the afterlife, to pray or attend religious services, or turn to religion to find meaning and purpose in life, then it is far less likely that they will do so in their adult years. They are also less likely to pick up religious cues from the surrounding (more secular) Canadian social environment. As we saw in the previous paragraph, the unaffiliated in Canada are further along this stage of decline progression; less likely to believe in God or a higher power, pray, or meditate compared to the United States. Moreover, Canada lacks the strong religious roots or subculture found among Evangelicalism in the United States—including a polarized and public debate between religious and secular groups who are vying for cultural legitimacy in several social institutional spheres (e.g., abortion laws, gay marriage, creationism vs evolution in school curricula)—that adds to the lack of social awareness, knowledge, or pressure to be religious among individuals in Canada.

Less Antagonistic

A key difference between religious nones, particularly nonbelievers, in Canada and the United States is that those north of the 49th parallel are on average less antagonistic toward the religiously affiliated. Roman said the following in response to a question of whether he associates with any particular thinkers or writers on atheism:

> Like somebody sends me a snippet ... of some atheist talking, I always find it a little too militant for my taste. Like I have no beef with religion. Who cares? Okay, so I think it's wrong, but whatever. Who cares? People think wrong things all the time, but who's to say I'm right and they're wrong? Most of the atheist stuff I come across is too militant or too insulting for my taste.

This quotation aligns with Steven Tomlins's (2018) research on the Atheist Community of the University of Ottawa (ACUO). He observed that, while atheists are an internally diverse group, for the most part Canadian atheists are not hostile toward the religiously affiliated. Rather, the atheists he studied sought to live peaceably with those outside the atheist camp; they wanted to dialogue and even partner on shared interests. Tomlins compares Canadian and American atheists this way:

> Unlike findings from American cases, no interviewees from the ACUO mentioned being overly concerned with the status of atheism in their country, nor did they express a desire to develop more positive atheist identities through a club. Members instead stressed the social aspects of the club; most interviewees simply wanted to meet like-minded people in a safe-place where they could engage freely in conversations about controversial issues pertaining to religion and skepticism without causing offense to others. That to me seemed like a quintessentially Canadian answer—that one would want to join an atheist club so as not to cause offense—and it serves as one of the main differences between that Canadian atheist community and American atheist communities. (2018: 247)

As seen earlier, only an estimated 3 percent of young adult religious nones in Canada take part in organized atheist, humanist, or secularist activities at least once a year, compared with an estimated 9 percent in the United States (based on data from the 2019 MTS). The absence of urgency to generate more positive perceptions of atheists or to advance an atheist agenda in society further speak to the more favorable social space that atheists generally inhabit in Canada. In the 2019 MTS, only an estimated 4 percent of young adult nonbelievers say they experience discrimination due to their nonreligious views at least once a month in Canada, compared with 14 percent in the United States. In contrast to the discrimination leveled against atheists earlier in Canadian history, the Canadian government, the law, as well as ordinary Canadians have for the most part progressively embraced nonbelievers as part of the multicultural model in the country (Beaman and Steele 2018). Of course, there are atheists in Canada who are less tolerant toward more religiously devout individuals, as well as atheists in the United States who have positive interactions with more religious folk; there are some in Canada who think negatively about atheists (Evangelicals stand out in this regard) and others in the United States who think positively toward atheists. But in general, it seems there is a striking difference between the atheist experiences in the two nations (This difference is reflected in figure 4.4 below).

The sociological distinction between in-groups and out-groups helps us to understand why these differences exist. In-groups include those groups that one feels an affinity and commitment with, while out-groups are those that one does not feel strong ties to, sometimes to the point of competition. Power matters greatly for these social dynamics between groups. If the in-group is in a position of power, it has the ability to label and define realities and social contexts that can bring harm upon the out-group. Explanations for why atheists in the United States experience higher levels of social stigma than in Canada vary, with some pointing to the historical and current political seat of power that evangelical Christians have enjoyed south of the 49th parallel (see Hout and Fischer 2002), and others linking the Cold War to American perceptions of "godless communists" in the Soviet Union versus Americans who purportedly *should* believe in God (see Cragun 2017). Regardless of the agreed upon explanation, there is no denying that atheists have been labeled an out-group relative to American ideals of a God-believing nation (Cragun et al. 2012; Edgell, Gerteis, and Hartmann 2006; Schmidt 2016; Williamson and Yancey 2013; Zimmerman et al. 2015). To say that one does not identify with a religion, and even worse to not claim belief in God, often comes with a great social cost with one's friends, family, coworkers, or neighbors. Despite the formal separation of church and state in the United States, key social institutions such as education, politics, the law, and health care are battlegrounds for religious versus secular authority and legitimacy. Some atheists in the United States thus appear more emboldened and committed to pursue public credibility and influence because they have more to fight for as a marginalized and ostracized group.

In addition to Roman's earlier reflections on atheists being too militant for his liking, Roman also provided several examples of a quieter and muted expression of atheism in Canada. When asked if his father or brother actively tried to convert him to atheism, Roman quickly replied, "No. Absolutely not." In response to how important identifying as an atheist was to his identity, Roman responded, "Not very. It's not like I go advertising … if people ask me what I am, I mention it." Finally, as Roman talked about being married to a devout Evangelical, he noted, "We just respect each other's boundaries. She doesn't try to convert me and I don't poo poo what she's

Canada

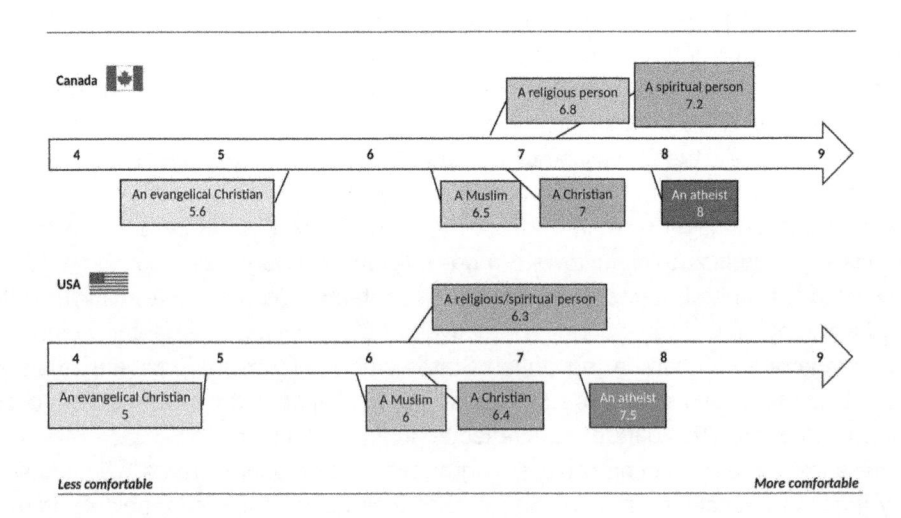

				A religious person 6.8	A spiritual person 7.2	
4	5	6	7		8	9
	An evangelical Christian 5.6		A Muslim 6.5	A Christian 7	An atheist 8	

USA

			A religious/spiritual person 6.3			
4	5	6	7		8	9
	An evangelical Christian 5		A Muslim 6	A Christian 6.4	An atheist 7.5	

Less comfortable — *More comfortable*

FIGURE 4.4 *"On a scale from 0 to 10 (0 indicating very uncomfortable; 10 indicating very comfortable), please indicate what level of comfort you would feel if the following type of person became your relative by marriage (in-law)."* Religiously unaffiliated respondents eighteen to thirty-five years old, Canada and the United States, 2019. Source of the data: Millennial Trends Survey 2019. N Canada = 683; N USA = 420. Estimates weighted to be representative of young adult populations.

doing." As for his kids, Roman commented, "It is not important to me for them to believe what I believe. Whatever works for them is great ... I don't think less of anybody that believes whatever they wanna believe." We do not mean to suggest that all nonbelievers in Canada are nice, tolerant, indifferent Canadians. But the social context and in-group out-group tensions are qualitatively different between Canada and the United States.

Left-Leaning

Research on religious nones in different national contexts shows that they are, in general, more left-leaning on a range of sociopolitical issues compared with the religiously affiliated. This is mainly due to being less exposed to conservative values through organized religion, and more exposed to liberal values in their own family, community, educational and work environments (Ang and Petrocik 2012; Jelen and Wilcox 2003; Leon McDaniel, Nooruddin, and Shortle 2011; Olson, Cadge, and Harrison 2006; Putnam and Campbell 2010; Sherkat et al. 2011; Wilkins-Laflamme 2016). Moreover, it is well known that Canadians are, on many measures, more liberal than are people in the United States. For example, Canadians are more likely to support public health care, immigration, euthanasia, and abortion. When we combine these two findings we discover that not only are religious nones in Canada more liberal than nones in the United States, but on some issues, even the religiously affiliated in Canada are more liberal than religious nones south of the border.

Figure 4.5 (US attitudes among different types of religious nones) and Figure 4.6 (Canadian attitudes among the religiously affiliated and unaffiliated) illustrate some examples of this, notably on issues of abortion, same-sex marriage, women in the workforce, environmental laws and spending, welfare for the disadvantaged, and immigration. It is important to note here that the seemingly lower levels of support for same-sex marriage in Canada than in the United States in Figures 4.5 and 4.6 may be an artifact of how the survey question was asked in the Canadian Election Studies (CES), providing respondents with only three answer options (favor, oppose, or don't know/no opinion) rather than a more detailed Likert scale. The results overall in these two figures are based on logistic regression models run with 2014 Pew Religious Landscape Study and 2011 and 2015 CES data (Fournier et al. 2017). These statistical models measure the likelihood that different types of affiliated and unaffiliated respondents will hold more left-leaning/liberal attitudes while controlling for their other sociodemographic characteristics (including age, gender, marital status, number of children, race [for United States models only], immigrant status, level of education, and region of residence).

Both macro- and micro-level factors in one's social milieu assist us to understand why some of these national differences exist (i.e., why Canadian nones generally show more liberal attitudes). Starting at the macro-level, the combination of Canada's Catholic and mainline Protestant roots and influence (versus Puritan and eventually evangelical roots in the United States), religious decline from the 1960s onward, a

[Bar chart showing predicted probabilities across six categories:]

Abortion should be legal in all or most cases: 88%, 71%, 79%, 47%
Strongly favor or favor same-sex marriage: 92%, 79%, 83%, 53%
Greater participation of women in workforce over the last fifty years a change for the better: 78%, 73%, 74%, 69%
Stricter environmental laws and regulations are worth the cost: 77%, 63%, 72%, 58%
Government aid to the poor does more good than harm, because people can't get out of poverty until their basic needs are met: 66%, 52%, 62%, 50%
A growing population of immigrants over the past fifty years has been a change for the better: 34%, 21%, 32%, 20%

■ Non-believer ■ Inactive believer ■ SBNR ■ Involved believer

Sources: Data from the 2014 Pew Religious Landscape Study. Predicted probabilities generated from logit regression models with robust standard errors, while keeping age, gender, marital status, number of children, race, immigrant status, level of education, and region of residence constant at their mean. Weighted to be representative of the general adult population.

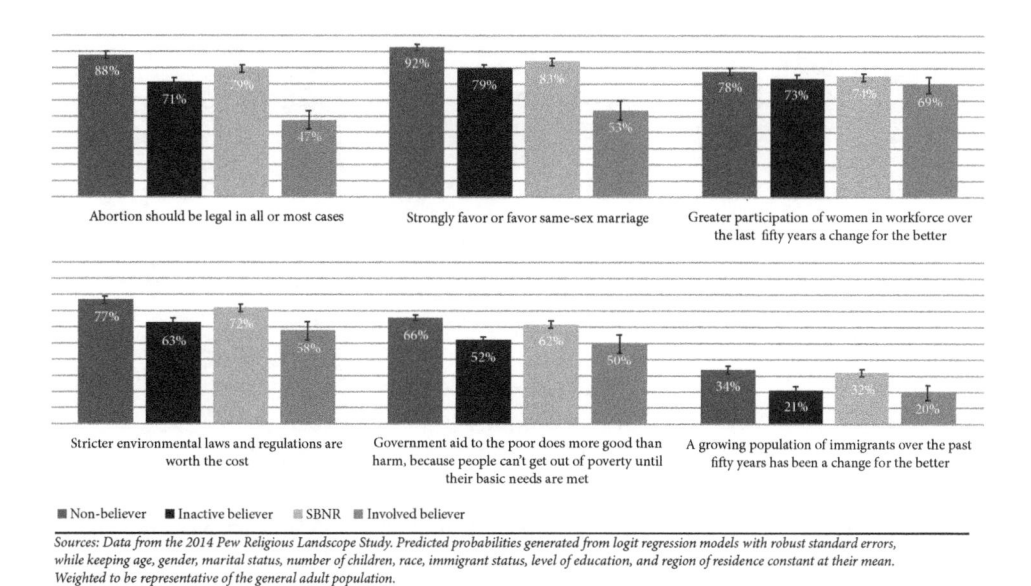

FIGURE 4.5 *Predicted probabilities of left-leaning sociopolitical attitudes among religious none adults, United States, 2014, with CI (95 per cent).* Source: *Created by author.*

gradual and institutionalized shift toward multiculturalism, a lengthier period of broad social acceptance toward religious nones, and deeper and pervasive left-leaning political and legal policies all contribute to the sociopolitical views held among Canada's religious nones. What sets the United States apart is that on top of its strong Puritan Christian origins, the Christian right gained traction in the 1980s in response to the changing sexual morals of the 1960s and 1970s (Hout and Fisher 2002). This generally more conservative environment has impacted many facets of American life. In Canada, not only are there far fewer evangelical Christians, those who do identify as evangelical tend not to be as vocal or public as those south of the border (Reimer 2003). Thus, while religious nones in both nations tend to be more left-leaning than those who affiliate with a religion, religious nones in Canada tend to be even further left of their counterparts south of the 49th parallel.

At the micro-level, the sociological concept of *homophily* is significant. This concept refers to the fact that most individuals are surrounded with people who share values and behavior similar to their own (Lazarsfeld and Merton 1954). The religiously affiliated and unaffiliated tend to associate with others like themselves (Cheadle and Schwadel 2012; McPherson, Smith-Lovin, and Cook 2001; Olson and Perl 2011; Smith, McPherson, and Smith-Lovin 2014), then tend to become more like those around them over time through socialization processes. For example, nonreligious young adults in Canada have an average of three close friends out of five who are not religious at all, compared with only one out of five nonreligious friends among religiously affiliated young adults attending religious services at least once a month (based on data from the 2019 MTS). Consequently, an average religious none is more likely to be

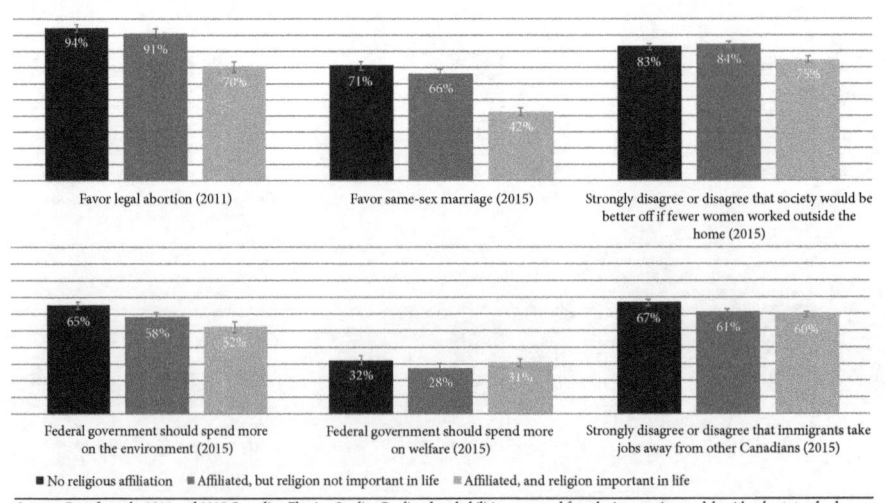

FIGURE 4.6 *Predicted probabilities of left-leaning sociopolitical attitudes among adults, Canada, 2011 and 2015, with CI (95 per cent).* Source: *Created by author.*

surrounded by people who share and support left-leaning values, and there are often few individuals around them to question these views or behaviors. The same goes for actively religious individuals at the opposite end of the spectrum, who on average are surrounded by many who hold a more conservative value orientation.

This homophily process is certainly true for Roman whose closest friends are also religious nones. They rarely talk about their nonreligious worldviews and don't meet to strategize ways to strengthen the public reputation of atheists in Canada, but they do share many of the same views. The combination of Canadians who are embedded in a web of social institutions that often reinforce left-leaning views, and then religious nones who tend to most closely associate with other religious nones, adds credence to our claim that a person's social environment is a major explanation for why religious nones in Canada vary in the ways we have presented from those in the United States. Expressed differently, religious nones in the United States are more likely to be surrounded by social institutions and individuals who do not embrace left-leaning social positions, a reflection of a more conservative undercurrent to many facets of American society.

Conclusion

We return to where we began, with Roman. In some ways he is a bit of an anomaly, an atheist married to an Evangelical. We would argue that this arrangement works for Roman and his wife because Evangelicalism and atheism have different historical and sociopolitical backgrounds, meanings, and implications in Canada than in the United States. Furthermore, the fundamental value in Canada to be nice, tolerant, and relatively indifferent toward many who think and behave differently carries real weight. Roman seems to practice what Lori Beaman (2018) calls "*deep equality*," which is a shared ethos and lived practice to pursue common ground and equality with others in daily life amidst diversity and difference. Canadians like Roman seem to go out of their way to not offend others.

These beliefs and behaviors are a consequence of the social environment that Canadians find themselves in. In case this depiction of Roman and Canada sounds too romanticized, we point back to the notable differences in the quantitative data presented. Religious nones do share many things in common across the 49th parallel, however, religious none perceptions and experiences are different too. Religious nones are diverse in both nations, yet in our estimation they are for the most part more secular, less antagonistic toward the religiously affiliated, and more left-leaning in Canada than their counterparts in the United States.

Why should anyone care about the growth of religious nones in Canada, or anywhere else for that matter? The simple answer is they now comprise a quarter of the population and religious nones often hold distinct social, political, and moral views and behaviors compared with the religiously affiliated. Further, as we show elsewhere (Thiessen and Wilkins-Laflamme 2020) religious nones are generally less socially and civically engaged than the religiously affiliated when measured by volunteering and charitable giving (though, religious nones are more active in these areas than marginal religious affiliates; see Frost and Edgell 2018). This topic matters because Canadian society has changed, is changing, and will continue to change in noticeable ways as the proportion of religious nones grows; political, economic, and moral attitudes and behaviors shift as demographics change in society. Canada may also serve as an exemplar case to other nations on how the religiously affiliated and unaffiliated can peaceably coexist in "deep equality." In this vein, there is some truth to the stereotypes of Canadians. Canadians are generally nice, tolerant, and indifferent—Canadians do not want to offend others, which for religious nones generally means blending into the broader Canadian environment rather than living in a state of conflict with their religiously affiliated fellow Canadians.

Further Reading and Online Resources

Angus Reid Institute (2015), *Religion and Faith in Canada Today: Strong Belief, Ambivalence and Rejection Define Our Views*. http://angusreid.org/wp-content/uploads/2016/01/2015.03.25_Faith.pdf (accessed September 14, 2020).
"Religion in Canada: Are We Godless?" (2015), CBC News. https://www.cbc.ca/news/thenational/religion-in-canada-are-we-godless-1.3073695 (accessed September 14, 2020).
Thiessen, J. and S. Wilkins-Laflamme (2020), *None of the Above: Nonreligious Identity in the U.S. and Canada*, New York: New York University Press.

References

Ang, A. and J.R. Petrocik (2012), "Religion, Religiosity, and the Moral Divide in Canadian Politics," *Politics and Religion*, 5 (1): 103–32.
Beaman, L. (2018), *Deep Equality in an Era of Religious Diversity*, New York: Oxford University Press.
Beaman, L. and C. Steele (2018), "Transcendence/Religion to Immanence/Nonreligion," *International Journal of Human Rights in Healthcare*, 11 (2): 129–43.
Bengtson, V.L., N.M. Putney, and S. Harris (2013), *Families and Faith: How Religion Is Passed Down across Generations*, New York: Oxford University Press.
Bibby, R.W. (2011), *Beyond the Gods and Back: Religion's Demise and Rise and Why It Matters*, Lethbridge: Project Canada Books.
Bibby, R.W. (2017), *Resilient Gods: Being Pro-Religious, Low Religious, or No Religious in Canada*, Vancouver: University of British Columbia Press.
Bibby, R.W., J. Thiessen, and M. Bailey (2019), *The Millennial Mosaic: How Pluralism and Choice Are Shaping Canadian Youth and the Future of Canada*, Toronto: Dundurn.
Brown, C.G. (2013), "The Twentieth Century," in S. Bullivant and M. Ruse (eds.), *The Oxford Handbook of Atheism*, 229–44, New York: Oxford University Press.
Bullivant, S. (2017), "The 'No Religion' Population of Britain," St Mary's University, Catholic Research Forum Reports 3. https://www.stmarys.ac.uk/research/centres/benedict-xvi/docs/2017-may-no-religion-report.pdf (accessed June 21, 2017).

Cheadle, J.E. and P. Schwadel (2012), "The 'Friendship Dynamics of Religion,' or the 'Religious Dynamics of Friendship'? A Social Network Analysis of Adolescents Who Attend Small Schools," *Social Science Research*, 41: 1198–212.
Clarke, B. and S. Macdonald (2017), *Leaving Christianity: Changing Allegiances in Canada since 1945*, Montreal: McGill-Queen's University Press.
Cragun, R. (2017), "The Declining Significance of Religion: Secularization in Ireland," in M.J. Breen (ed.), *Values and Identities in Europe: Evidence from the European Social Survey, Routledge Advances in Sociology*, 17–35, Abingdon: Routledge.
Cragun, R., B. Kosmin, A. Keysar, J. Hammer, and M. Nielsen (2012), "On the Receiving End: Discrimination toward the Non-Religious in the United States," *Journal of Contemporary Religion*, 27 (1): 105–27.
Crockett, A. and D. Voas (2006), "Generations of Decline: Religious Change in 20th Century Britain," *Journal for the Scientific Study of Religion*, 45 (4): 567–84.
Dillon, M. and P. Wink (2007), *In the Course of a Lifetime: Tracing Religious Belief, Practice, and Change*, Berkeley: University of California Press.
Edgell, P., J. Gerteis, and D. Hartmann (2006), "Atheists as 'Other': Moral Boundaries and Cultural Membership in American Society," *American Sociological Review*, 71 (2): 211–34.
Fournier, P., F. Cutler, S. Soroka, and D. Stolle (principal investigators) (2017), "Surveys," 2011–15 Canadian Election Study [Data set]. http://ces-eec.arts.ubc.ca/english-section/surveys/ (accessed March 12, 2017).
Frost, J. and P. Edgell (2018), "Rescuing Nones from the Reference Category: Civic Engagement among the Non-Religious in America," *Nonprofit and Voluntary Sector Quarterly*, 47 (2): 417–38.
Gee, E.M. and J.E. Veevers (1989), "Religiously Unaffiliated Canadians: Sex, Age, and Regional Variations," *Social Indicators Research*, 21 (6): 611–27.
Grant, J.W. (1998), *The Church in the Canadian Era*, 2nd rev. edn., Vancouver: Regent College Publishing.
Hout, M. and C.S. Fischer (2002), "Why More Americans Have No Religious Preference: Politics and Generations," *American Sociological Review*, 67: 165–90.
Jelen, T.G. and C. Wilcox (2003), "Causes and Consequences of Public Attitudes toward Abortion: A Review and Research Agenda," *Political Research Quarterly*, 56 (4): 489–500.
Kosmin, B. and A. Keysar (2008), "American Nones: The Profile of the No Religion Population," Trinity College. http://commons.trincoll.edu/aris/files/2011/08/NONES_08.pdf (accessed February 17, 2010).
Lazarsfeld, P.F. and R.K. Merton (1954), "Friendship as a Social Process: A Substantive and Methodological Analysis," in M. Berger, T. Abel, and C.H. Page (eds.), *Freedom and Control in Modern Society*, 18–66, New York: Octogon Books.
Léger (2020), "Become a LEO Member." https://leger360.com/services/legeropinion-leo/#member (accessed September 14, 2020).
Leon McDaniel, E., I. Nooruddin, and A.F. Shortle (2011), "Divine Boundaries: How Religion Shapes Citizens' Attitudes toward Immigrants," *American Politics Research*, 39 (1): 205–33.
Lewis, J.R., S.E. Currie, and M.P. Oman-Reagan (2016), "The Religion of the Educated Classes Revisited: New Religions, the Nonreligious, and Education Levels," *Journal for the Scientific Study of Religion*, 55 (1): 91–104.
Manning, C. (2015), *Losing Our Religion: How Unaffiliated Parents Are Raising Their Children*, New York: New York University Press.
McPherson, M., L. Smith-Lovin, and J.M. Cook (2001), "Birds of a Feather: Homophily in Social Networks," *Annual Review of Sociology*, 27: 415–44.

Merino, S.M. (2012), "Irreligious Socialization? The Adult Religious Preferences of Individuals Raised with No Religion," *Secularism and Nonreligion*, 1: 1–16.

Noll, M. (1992), *A History of Christianity in the United States and Canada*, Grand Rapids, MI: William B. Eerdmans.

Olson, D.V.A. and P. Perl (2011), "A Friend in Creed: Does the Religious Composition of Geographic Areas Affect the Religious Composition of a Person's Close Friends?," *Journal for the Scientific Study of Religion*, 50 (3): 483–502.

Olson, L.R., W. Cadge, and J.T. Harrison (2006), "Religion and Public Opinion about Same-Sex Marriage," *Social Science Quarterly*, 87 (2): 340–60.

Putnam, R. and D. Campbell (2010), *American Grace: How Religion Divides and Unites Us*, New York: Simon and Schuster.

Reimer, S. (2003), *Evangelicals and the Continental Divide: The Evangelical Subculture in Canada and the United States*, Montreal: McGill-Queen's University Press.

Schmidt, L.E. (2016), *Village Atheists: How America's Unbelievers Made Their Way in a Godly Nation*, Princeton, NJ: Princeton University Press.

Sherkat, D.E., M.P. Williams, G. Maddox, and K.M. Vries (2011), "Religion, Politics, and Support for Same-Sex Marriage in the United States, 1988–2008," *Social Science Research*, 40 (1): 167–80.

Smith, C. (1998), *American Evangelicalism: Embattled and Thriving*, Chicago: University of Chicago Press.

Smith, J.A., M. McPherson, and L. Smith-Lovin (2014), "Social Distance in the United States: Sex, Race, Religion, Age, and Education Homophily among Confidants, 1985 to 2004," *American Sociological Review*, 79 (3): 432–56.

Smith, T.W., M. Davern, J. Freese, and S. Morgan (2018), *General Social Surveys, 2018* [machine-readable data file]/Principal Investigator, Tom W. Smith; Co-Principal Investigators, Michael Davern, Jeremy Freese, and Stephen Morgan; Sponsored by National Science Foundation. –NORC ed.– Chicago: NORC at the University of Chicago [producer and distributor]. Data from the GSS Data Explorer website: https://gssdataexplorer.norc.org/ (accessed July 1, 2019).

Statistics Canada (2018), *Cycles 1–30 (1985–2016), General Social Survey [Canada] Public Use Microdata Files (PUMF): Individual Files* [Data sets].

Strawn, K.D. (2019), "What's Behind the 'Nones-Sense'? Change Over Time in Factors Predicting Likelihood of Religious Nonaffiliation in the United States," *Journal for the Scientific Study of Religion*, 58 (3): 707–24.

Thiessen, J. (2015), *The Meaning of Sunday: The Practice of Belief in a Secular Age*, Montreal: McGill-Queen's University Press.

Thiessen, J. (2016), "Kids, You Make the Choice: Religious and Secular Socialization among Marginal Affiliates and Nonreligious Individuals," *Secularism and Nonreligion*, 5 (1): 1–16.

Thiessen, J. and S. Wilkins-Laflamme (2017), "Becoming a Religious None: Irreligious Socialization and Disaffiliation," *Journal for the Scientific Study of Religion*, 56 (1): 64–82.

Thiessen, J. and S. Wilkins-Laflamme (2020), *None of the Above: Non-Religious Identity in the U.S. and Canada*, New York: New York University Press.

Tomlins, S. (2018), "Atheism and Religious Nones: An Introduction to the Study of Nonreligion in Canada," in C. Holtmann (ed.), *Exploring Religion and Diversity in Canada: People, Practice and Possibility*, 237–54, Cham: Springer.

University of Waterloo (n.d.), "Welcome to the Survey Research Centre." https://uwaterloo.ca/survey-research-centre/ (accessed September 14, 2020).

Wilkins-Laflamme, S. (2014), "Towards Religious Polarization? Time Effects on Religious Commitment in US, UK and Canadian Regions," *Sociology of Religion*, 75 (2): 284–308.

Wilkins-Laflamme, S. (2015), "How Unreligious Are the Religious 'Nones'? Religious Dynamics of the Unaffiliated in Canada," *Canadian Journal of Sociology*, 40 (4): 477–500.

Wilkins-Laflamme, S. (2016), "Secularization and the Wider Gap in Values and Personal Religiosity between the Religious and Non-Religious," *Journal for the Scientific Study of Religion*, 55 (4): 717–36.

Williamson, D.A. and G. Yancey (2013), *There Is No God: Atheists in America*, Lanham, MD: Rowman and Littlefield.

Zimmerman, K.J., J.M. Smith, K. Simonson, and B.W. Myers (2015), "Familial Relationship Outcomes of Coming Out as an Atheist," *Secularism and Nonreligion*, 4 (4): 1–13.

Zuckerman, P. (2012), *Faith No More: Why People Reject Religion*, New York: Oxford University Press.

Glossary Terms

Atheist Someone who does not believe in the existence of a god or supernatural being.

Deep equality A lived process of daily interactions among people who may be different from one another, yet seek areas of common ground, acceptance, respect, and equality with one another. In the context of this chapter, deep equality primarily refers to the ties between the religiously affiliated and unaffiliated.

Evangelical Someone within the Christian tradition who tends to believe that (a) the Bible is the authoritative Word of God, (b) Jesus Christ died on the cross to save humans from their sin and eternal damnation, (c) humans need to convert to Christianity and profess their belief in Jesus Christ, and that Christians have a responsibility to share their faith with others with the expressed intent that others would convert, and (d) one's Christian beliefs should inform human and social behavior in areas such as morality and relationships. How these beliefs are internalized and acted upon varies by social context.

Homophily Individuals who surround themselves with people who are similar to themselves (e.g., race, ethnicity, social class, age, religion), and who over time become more like one another in their social attitudes and values.

Multiculturalism A social framework that discourages any form of social inequality based upon people's differences (e.g., gender, race, religion, sexuality) and encourages individuals and groups to "come as they are" into various social spaces. Multiculturalism is both a practiced and lived reality in society, plus a cultural ideal that many in society aspire toward.

Nonreligious socialization The process, typically within the family setting, where individuals do not receive formal religious instruction of any kind. Nonreligious socialization may involve the complete absence of religious instruction, explicit secular or nonreligious teaching (e.g., atheist worldview), and even anti-religious socialization attitudes and behaviors.

Religious none Someone who says they do not identify with any religion. Identifying as a religious none does not mean that one is without any religious or spiritual beliefs or practices. They simply do not identify as a Christian or Muslim or Jew, for example.

Secularization A series of complex social processes that vary in speed and impact across time and space, which culminate in lower levels of religious belief, behavior, and/or belonging across societal, institutional, and/or personal spheres of social life.

Stages of decline Refers to individuals and/or societies who progressively become less religious over time, from one generation to the next. How exactly religion and religiosity are measured (e.g., belief in God, church attendance, religious identification) and the specific reasons associated with religious decline (e.g., scientific advances, economic prosperity, religious and social pluralism, individualism, diminished religious authority in the public sphere) vary by social and historical context.

5

Nonreligious Organizations in North America

Mathieu Colin

Organizing the Cat Herd: Organized Nonreligion in North America

"In this cat herd, each will decide his own preference" (Cimino and Smith 2014: 139). According to these authors, the cat analogy is used widely in the secular movement to emphasize the high levels of individualism that characterize secular individuals (2014). As Zuckerman, Galen, and Pasquale (2016) have shown, the secular movement is a blurry milieu wherein systems of beliefs are always in motion and evolve according to individual preference, making it difficult to construct analytical frameworks or categories to describe beliefs. There is a diversity of profiles and ideologies reflected in the variety of nonreligious organizations in North America, including atheists, agnostics, humanists, freethinkers, Brights, and many others. Given the diversity—the "cattiness" of secular individuals—how are they able to form a movement? By the end of this chapter, readers will see that even cats sometimes need shelters.

Secular organizations throughout history, and those of the modern secular movement, have not been characterized by their stability. As Fazzino and Cragun remark, "Numerous scholars have argued that American *secularism* is fractured and is better understood as 'disorganized secularism' than 'organized secularism.' There is certainly reason to believe this *was* the case during the twentieth century" (Fazzino and Cragun 2017: 59; emphasis in original). The decentralized nature and heterogeneity of the movement are discussed among scholars either as a sign of its weakness or as an intrinsic characteristic of all social movements, which does not actually undermine their capacity to structure an ideology or to take action in the public sphere (Cimino and Smith 2014;

Fazzino and Cragun 2017; LeDrew 2016). However, all scholars agree on some points. First, there is a lack of research about nonreligious organizations and their history. Second, the secular movement is a relatively recent phenomenon: it has its roots in the twentieth century, but has gained visibility over the past twenty years because of factors including the rise of the "nones" in North America and in the United States especially, the terrorist attacks of 9/11, and the *New Atheism* phenomenon, among other topics. The movement has only garnered sustained academic interest over the last decade. Cimino and Smith (2014) talk about an "Atheist Awakening" to describe the rise and coming out of atheists in the public sphere that has been occurring for the last two decades. Third, the secular movement implies reflection about the nature and process of *secularization* in the West and the polymorphous aspects of religious beliefs in the United States: although religion seems to be waning in the Western world, the United States remains a somewhat religious country despite its modernity and wealth (Zuckerman, Galen, and Pasquale 2016). However, almost 25 percent of the American and Canadian population now describes itself as "nones" (Cragun et al. 2013; Pew Research Center 2013, 2019; Zuckerman, Galen, and Pasquale 2016), and secular organizations such as the Satanic Temple or the Freethought Association of Canada are receiving unprecedented media coverage for their public actions. Consequently, the secular movement should be considered a real and influential force in the political and cultural landscapes of North America.

For this chapter, I analyze and give an overview of the history of the secular movement in the United States and Canada, exemplified by several national secular organizations: American Atheists, and Freedom From Religion Foundation, in the United States; Center for Inquiry Canada, the Humanist Association of Canada, and the Freethought Association of Canada, on the Canadian side (due to the unavailability of information on secular groups in Mexico, we were unfortunately unable to cover this country). Then I will focus on the Satanic Temple as a case study of secular activism in the context of religious pluralism and legal battles in the United States.

Secularism in the United States

The creation of nonreligious structures arose in response to an identity claim and need in a deeply religious country. Nonreligious individuals—especially atheists—felt rejected and unrecognized by official institutions in the United States, and needed structures for political leverage:

> Religion and belief in America receive their legitimacy through the traditional and social institutions in which they are anchored. A theist/religious person in the United States has ready access and recourse to legitimate institutions in which his or her religious identity can find validation and social support. There is a discourse and set of public narratives of belief in America, to which theists may appeal, find meaning, purpose, and social mooring for their religious identities. (Smith 2011: 233)

Because of its prevalence, religion, especially Christianity, has historically been seen as the primary, if not only, source of morality. For most Americans, people who are religious can act in a moral way while nonreligious people have no moral frame. "In a country such as the United States, morality has become synonymous with religious belief, which makes non-religious Americans appear as a moral wildcard to those Americans who believe morality is only derived from religion or God" (Bullivant 2015: 112). People who do not share mainstream religious beliefs and who describe themselves as "nones" are therefore considered an out-group. Nonbelievers, those who deny the existence of a deity, are doubly represented as out-groups and report experiencing twice the discrimination as those who simply identify as nonreligious (Cragun et al. 2013).

In the 1960s, as a result of the Cold War with the Soviet Union, atheism was linked to communism and to socialist "godless enemies," while Christian conservatives reinforced the myth of a "Christian America" facing the threat of decadence presented by liberals, gays, or atheists (Jacoby 2005; Straughn and Feld 2010). Using identity politics to face the growing presence of religion in the public sphere, especially in public schools, Madalyn O'Hair (pictured in figure 5.1) founded American Atheists (AA) in 1963 (LeDrew 2016). Known for opposing compulsory Bible reading in public schools during the Supreme Court case Abington School District v. Schempp in 1963, "the most hated woman in America" intended to transform AA into a group whose mission was to

FIGURE 5.1 *April 18, 1987; Madalyn Murray O'Hair at the atheists convention at the Radisson Hotel.* Source: *Photograph by Dave Buresh/The Denver Post via Getty Images.*

protect atheists as a discriminated minority, while focusing on an active fight for the separation of church and state (Fazzino and Cragun 2017; Jacoby 2005; LeDrew 2016). AA was the most prominent atheist organization at the time, but its importance has waned over the years, especially since the abduction and murder in 1995 of its founder, O'Hair, her son John Murray, and her granddaughter Robin. After O'Hair disappeared, AA lost approximately 60 percent of its membership, as reported by Frank Zindler (Fazzino and Cragun 2017: 68). Its membership is currently estimated at 4,000 members. However, AA was an influential organization, since it was the first to "explicitly advance the interests of atheists and atheism, which had been implicit in earlier organizations defined by secularism, rationalism and humanism" (LeDrew 2016: 106). After a sex scandal resulted in the removal of its long-time Director David Silverman in 2018, Ed Buckner has been serving as the Interim Executive Director of AA.

Another secular movement organization in the United States, the Freedom From Religion Foundation (FFRF), was founded in 1976 to counter the rise of the religious right, and is a good example of the schismatic nature of the secular movement. Initially affiliated with American Atheists, FFRF became a separate entity following an argument between Madalyn O'Hair and FFRF's founder Anne Nicol Gaylor (Fazzino and Cragun 2017: 69). Along with her daughter, Annie Laurie Gaylor and John Sontarck, Gaylor made FFRF an organization dedicated to secular individuals, and whose purpose, according to its website, is "to promote the constitutional principle of separation of state and church, and to educate the public on matters relating to nontheism" (FFRF 2020). Now led by Annie Laurie Gaylor, the daughter of Anne Nicol Gaylor, and her husband, former Christian Evangelist Dan Barker, FFRF is the largest secular organization in the United States with more than 20,000 members (Fazzino and Cragun 2017: 69). The organization focuses on legal battles in favor of the separation of church and state and has won several cases in connection with this issue, such as ending prayer in public schools, removing religious monuments and crosses from public spaces, halting a government chaplaincy that ministered to state workers, and more (Barker in Seidel 2019; FFRF 2020). In 2010, the organization also created the "Out of the Closet" campaign, designed to invite atheists to come out and illustrate to the American people that atheists are an essential part of American society (LeDrew 2016: 131).

One of the oldest humanist organizations in the United States is the American Humanist Association (AHA), formed in 1941. Having its roots in nontheistic religious humanism as promoted by the Unitarian Church in the beginning of the twentieth century and inspired by the work of positivist Frederick James Gould, humanism was a doctrine deemed as religious to emphasize the "profound human experiences and activities while excluding any supernatural beliefs and explanations of reality" (Cimino and Smith 2014: 19; Fazzino and Cragun 2017: 65). The first *Humanist Manifesto* published in 1933 called for the promotion of secular values while integrating religious aspects of life, a reference that was later removed in the *Humanist Manifesto II* published and adopted by the AHA in 1973. In 1991, the AHA joined forces with the Humanist Society of Friends, now the Humanist Society, which trained Humanist Celebrants to conduct ceremonies such as weddings or funerals as a secular equivalent of ceremonies performed by clergy (Fazzino and Cragun 2017: 65).

Paul Kurtz, hired in 1968 to edit the organization's journal, *The Humanist*, split from the organization in 1978 following a conflict over his management of the journal and his disagreement with the religious framework of AHA (Cimino and Smith 2014: 19; Fazzino and Cragun 2017: 70). Subsequently, Kurtz founded the Council for Secular Humanism (CSH) in 1980 and its umbrella organization Center for Inquiry (CFI) in 1991, to promote secular humanism (thus eschewing any religious reference) around the world, since the structure aims at establishing independent Centers for Inquiry, which are self-governing. CFI created the International Blasphemy Rights Day, celebrated since 2009 on September 30 (LeDrew 2016: 129).

The AHA, since its inception, has dedicated its political activism efforts to the dissemination of humanist values through, for example, its support of abortion in the 1960s, its encouragement of the coming out of nonbelievers with several billboard campaigns in 2009, and its effort to remove explicit references to God in public institutions and in the public sphere, focusing for example on the phrase "Under God" in the pledge of allegiance (AHA 2020).

The approach of the New Atheism, an antitheist movement believing in the harmful nature of faith and religion that some may describe as militant, which was popularized by the "Four Horsemen" (Richard Dawkins, Sam Harris, Daniel Dennett, and Christopher Hitchens), polarized the secular movement between two positions: accommodation or confrontation (LeDrew 2016). The accommodationist side considers that secular groups should acknowledge the social role of religion and try to form alliances with liberal and progressive religious groups for political leverage. The confrontationist side opposes compromise with religion, labeling it as its ideological enemy within the public space and constructing the idea of secular identity in strict opposition to religious identity. As we saw with the schism within AHA, there is no consensus about the position that should be adopted toward religion. Should the secular movement reclaim a religious framework to be more accepted in the United States, or should it establish clear boundaries in its opposition to religion? The debate is ongoing, with initiatives such as Camp Quest, where atheists learn how to use a religious framework to frame atheism as a positive system of beliefs, to get rid of the "atheists don't believe in anything" stigma that is still widespread in the United States (Bullivant 2015).

Secularism in Canada

Canadian secularism is deeply linked to American secularism and its secular organizations as well. As is the case for its neighbor, the nonreligious population of Canada has been growing for several decades. Currently about 30 percent of Canadians report having no religion, thus almost one in three is considered a secular individual (Zuckerman, Galen, and Pasquale 2016: 4). Comparatively, in 1951, "Those who said they had no religion had risen slightly, reaching 0.4 percent" (Hanowski 2018: 6). In British Columbia, which is said to be the most secular Canadian province, 35 percent of the population is secular, a 40 percent increase over the past three decades (Zuckerman, Galen, and Pasquale 2016: 4). In Quebec, *La Révolution tranquille* (*the Quiet Revolution*), which began in the 1960s, progressively eliminated Catholic control of education and health, replacing it with secular government control over these institutions (Hanowski 2018). This profound reshaping of Canada and the ways it envisions its religious population and institutions has also spawned several national secular organizations that use the process of secularization to try to influence politics and values by working hand in hand with American or transnational organizations.

The Humanist Association of Canada (HAC), now Humanist Canada, is one of the oldest and largest secular organizations in Canada. Created in 1968 from the fusion

FIGURE 5.2 *Abortion activist Dr. Henry Morgentaler celebrating the Canadian Supreme Court ruling on the Abortion Law, January 28, 1988.* Source: *David Cooper/Toronto Star via Getty Images.*

of the Humanist Fellowship of Montreal (created in 1954) and the Victoria Humanist Fellowship (created in 1956), the HAC was formed to offer a counter force to religious conservatives opposing abortion and to promote secular values (Hanowski 2018: 6). Similar to its American counterpart, Canadian secularism also had strong leaders: the two most important figures were Henry Morgentaler (pictured in figure 5.2 above) and Marian Sherman.

Morgentaler served as president of the Humanist Fellowship of Montreal in 1964 and as president of the HAC between 1968 and 1970. A strong supporter of abortion, before he engaged in illegal abortions in the 1970s, Morgentaler appeared before the Canadian government's House of Commons Health and Welfare Committee in 1967 to urge the Government of Canada to repeal its restrictive abortion laws, stating that they were "barbarous, cruel and unjust" (Weld 2013: 7). The HAC, formed a year later with Morgentaler's help, was also designed to fight for these issues, until the abortion restriction law was finally struck down in 1988. Morgentaler served again on the board of HAC in the 1990s and in the 2000s, and died in 2013.

The other figurehead of Canadian secularism is Marian Sherman. A former interdenominational medical missionary in India and one of the few female fellows of the Royal College of Surgeons, Sherman was an outspoken atheist who helped the secular movement in Canada through her leadership in various organizations (Block 2014). In 1956, she joined the Victoria Humanist Fellowship and from then on worked to develop partnerships between Canadian and American humanist groups, such as the American Humanist Association, to promote secularism and humanist values across North America (Block 2014). She also helped to establish the Humanist Association of Canada in 1968 and became one of its directors (Block 2014: 137). As an influential female atheist, she has been compared to American Atheists' founder Madalyn O'Hair, although she was less controversial. As Block remarks: "The historian Bryan Le Beau notes that O'Hair, who was 'as controversial within American atheist circles as she was in the nation, generally', found little acceptance within the American Humanist Association. Sherman, by contrast, garnered praise from fellow atheists, and emerged by the 1960s as a respected leader of Canadian humanism" (2014: 145). Although Sherman vigorously attacked religion and labeled herself an atheist, stating that religious dogmas were "a curse of mankind," she also embraced the humanist label, winning the Humanist of the Year award in 1975 from the AHA (Block 2014). To what extent the efforts of the secular movement are directly responsible for declining levels of belief is unclear, but by the mid-1970s, the number of Canadians believing in God had decreased to 89 percent. Sherman's efforts of disseminating atheism, humanism and secularism were aided by the Canadian context: the stigma associated with the atheist label was less strong there than in the United States, and British Columbia was the most secular province of Canada (Block 2014). The growth of atheism and nonreligion in Canada decades before a similar trend occurred in the United States suggests there may be somewhat different forces at work in the two countries.

The rise of New Atheism from the mid-2000s and increasing secularity in Canada generated new organizations (Hanowski 2018). The Centre for Inquiry Canada (CFIC) was created in 2006 to replace existing structures that wished to form an alliance: the Toronto Humanist Association and the Toronto Secular Alliance; the latter was formed by two undergraduate students of the University of Toronto, Justin Trottier and Jennie Fiddes. Under the umbrella of the Center for Inquiry Transnational and its subsidiary, the Council for Secular Humanism, the organization founded by Paul Kurtz in the United States in 1991 dedicated to the promotion of secular humanism, CFIC takes a more confrontational approach to disseminating its philosophy, which is described in this way on its website: "Centre for Inquiry Canada works with members, volunteers, supporters and partners to create a better world. We do this through the application of critical thinking skills; promotion of good science; adoption of secular decision-making and through building communities of likeminded people" (CFIC 2020). Its cofounder and first director, Justin Trottier, also created the Freethought Association of Canada a few years later and replicated the British Atheist Bus Campaign in Canada in 2009. Figure 5.3 is a photograph of an initiative of Ariane Sherine supported by the British Humanist Association and Richard Dawkins. The aim of the campaign was to counterbalance the presence of Christian messages in the British public sphere by placing advertising on buses with humanist and atheist messages, such as "There's probably no God. Now stop worrying and enjoy your life" (LeDrew 2016: 127).

In 2013, CFIC also released a video to address Minister of Foreign Affairs John Baird's claim that atheists were not as persecuted as other religious minorities were (LeDrew

FIGURE 5.3 *Comedy writer Ariane Sherine (L), Professor Richard Dawkins (C), and Guardian writer Polly Toynbee (R) pose for pictures beside a London bus displaying an advertising campaign with the words: "There's probably no God. Now stop worrying and enjoy your life," London, January 6, 2009.* Source: *Leon Neal/AFP via Getty Images.*

2016: 137). As a result, Justin Trottier, as a spokesperson for CFIC, asked in the video that the newly opened Office of Religious Freedom consider atheists as a "minority religious identity" that needed protection (LeDrew 2016: 137). Although the American and Canadian political context is different in regard to the perception of atheists and the secular movement in general, Canadian secularists often draw on the strategies of their American neighbors to claim their place in the public sphere. CFIC also campaigned for the repeal of Canada's blasphemy law, which was abolished in December 2018.

Case Study: The Satanic Temple's Fight for Secularism in the United States

Founded in 2012 by Malcolm Jarry and Lucien Greaves (shown below in figure 5.4), the Satanic Temple (TST) is a nontheistic satanic, religious, and secular group whose purpose is to fight for the separation of church and state in the United States by adopting the same strategies as other mainstream religious groups in the public sphere (Colin 2018; Laycock 2020). An official IRS-recognized church since April 2019, TST is one of the most peculiar groups of the secular movement, bridging the gap between religion and secularism.

Readers may be wondering: how can an organization be both religious and secular? TST, despite claiming to be a satanic organization, emphasizes its rational perspective as an heir of the rationalist branch of contemporary *Satanism* codified by Anton LaVey's Church of Satan from 1966 onward. The rationalist branch of Satanism is described as "atheistic, skeptical, epicurean materialism as formulated by Anton LaVey in *The Satanic Bible* and other writings, and then expounded upon by a host of spokespersons in the following years. […] Science, philosophy and intuition are advocated as authority" (Petersen 2009: 7). Thus, TST does not believe in an actual Satan and negates any supernatural beliefs as being backward and obsolete:

> The idea that religion belongs to supernaturalists is ignorant, backward, and offensive. The metaphorical Satanic construct is no more arbitrary to us than are the deeply held beliefs that we actively advocate. Are we supposed to believe that those who pledge submission to an ethereal supernatural deity hold to their values more deeply than we? Are we supposed to concede that only the superstitious are rightful recipients of religious exemption and privilege? (The Satanic Temple 2020)

Satan is seen as the embodiment of rationality, scientific inquiry, struggle against dogmas and tyranny, freedom and free thought, as constructed by the literary works of the so-called "*Satanic School of Romanticism*" (Byron, Shelley, and Blake), and also based on the romantic reading of Milton's *Paradise Lost* (1667) (Colin 2018; Laycock 2020). From its inception, TST has been used as a weapon against the intrusion of religion in public policies, such as in the case of the Faith-Based Initiatives under George

FIGURE 5.4 *Salem, MA—July 25: Lucien Greaves, spokesman for the Satanic Temple, is photographed outside a Salem courthouse, a group of political activists who identify themselves as a religious sect, are seeking to establish After-School Satan clubs as a counterpart to fundamentalist Christian Good News Clubs, which they see as the religious right trying to infiltrate public education and erode the separation of church and state.* Source: *Photograph by Josh Reynolds for* The Washington Post *via Getty Images.*

W. Bush's administration, whereby religious organizations could be granted public funds for their operation. As one of the founders of TST suggested, "I thought, 'There should be some kind of counter.' He had the idea of starting a faith-based organization that met all the Bush administration's criteria for receiving funds, but was repugnant to them. 'Imagine if a Satanic organization applied for funds,' he remembered thinking. 'It would sink the whole program'" (Jarry quoted in Oppenheimer 2015). Besides claiming to be a sincere religious group, TST also takes a provocative and humorous activist approach, using the symbol of Satan as a tool to make statements in the public sphere of a widely Christian country where almost 73 percent of Christians believe with more or less certainty that the devil is real (Newport 2016). Moreover, some moral panics such as the so-called "Satanic Ritual Abuse" panic of the 1980s have shaped the collective unconscious regarding the social meaning of Satan in American society (Dyrendal, Lewis, and Petersen 2016; Introvigne 1997, 2016; Richardson, Best, and Bromley 1984; Victor 1993), making Satan a powerful figure of protest because of intrinsic repulsive characteristics for Christians.

The mission of TST, as presented on its website, is "to encourage benevolence and empathy among all people, reject tyrannical authority, advocate practical common sense and justice, and be directed by the human conscience to undertake noble pursuits guided by the individual will." Their set of beliefs include seven tenets:

- One should strive to act with compassion and empathy toward all creatures in accordance with reason.
- The struggle for justice is an ongoing and necessary pursuit that should prevail over laws and institutions.
- One's body is inviolable, subject to one's own will alone.
- The freedoms of others should be respected, including the freedom to offend. To willfully and unjustly encroach upon the freedoms of another is to forgo one's own.
- Beliefs should conform to our best scientific understanding of the world. We should take care never to distort scientific facts to fit our beliefs.
- People are fallible. If we make a mistake, we should do our best to rectify it and remediate any harm that may have been caused.
- Every tenet is a guiding principle designed to inspire nobility in action and thought. The spirit of compassion, wisdom, and justice should always prevail over the written or spoken word.

These tenets constitute the core religious beliefs of TST, in the way the group conceptualizes religion. "Satanism provides all that a religion should be without a compulsory attachment to untenable items of faith-based belief. It provides a narrative structure by which we contextualize our lives and works. It also provides a body of symbolism and religious practice—a sense of identity, culture, community, and shared values" (TST 2020). Since they are claiming a religious dimension, what they call their "deeply held beliefs," they are thus protected by the First Amendment of the Constitution, are able to act or protest and still be protected by the various clauses of that amendment, that is to say the *free exercise clause* and the *establishment clause*, and to benefit from them. The goal of TST is therefore to identify issues and situations in the public sphere where religion violates separation between church and state, and is endorsed by the federal or the state government. TST only organizes public actions related to situations they consider unfair when compared to the rights of other religions, and they never act simply to provoke. They describe themselves as a "nontheistic organization" producing an "atheistic religion" rather than describing themselves as simply atheists. According to the group, atheism does not offer a moral system and in itself does not propose inner values. It is just a negative way to self-define, by negating the existence of God (DeVito 2015). Thus, Satanism is a positive way to define an individual because it produces a system of "deeply held beliefs" that enables them to act as a regular religious group in the public and in relation to legal issues.

The Oklahoma Ten Commandments monument case of 2014

In 2009, Mike Ritze, a Republican of the Oklahoma House of Representatives, sponsored a bill that allowed him to erect a Ten Commandments monument that he privately funded and then donated to the city of Oklahoma City. The monument was placed just outside the Oklahoma State Capitol in 2012. This monument drew the attention of two secularist groups, first the American Atheists and then the American Civil Liberties Union (ACLU). The Ten Commandments monument was regarded as unconstitutional by the two organizations, because it seemed to be an official endorsement of Christianity by a state government in the public sphere. AA filed a lawsuit in 2014, arguing that the monument violated the establishment clause of the First Amendment, claiming for instance that the fourth commandment that compels people to respect the Sabbath Day was a clear establishment of religion, but the complaint was dismissed (Mehta 2015). The ACLU had also filed a lawsuit in August 2013, claiming the unconstitutionality of the monument on public and government property. They added that if the monument was not to be removed, to respect religious pluralism other religions would also have the right to propose statues representing their faith on public property. Thus, in December 2013, TST applied to erect its own statue next to the Ten Commandments monument. The monument, shown in figure

FIGURE 5.5 *The Baphomet statue is seen in the conversion room at the Satanic Temple where a "Hell House" is being held in Salem, Massachusetts, on October 8, 2019. The Hell House was a parody on a Christian Conversion center meant to scare atheists and other Satanic Church members.* Source: *Photograph by Joseph Prezioso/AFP via Getty Images.*

5.5., is an eight-foot tall an eight-foot-tall Baphomet statue with an estimated cost of $100,000 that was crowdfunded (Laycock 2020; Wexler 2019).

The request was serious, and the Oklahoma representatives feared that they would be compelled to accept a satanic statue on public grounds. As a consequence, the Oklahoma Capitol Preservation Commission froze all requests and declared a moratorium until the lawsuit with the ACLU was finished. Republican representatives were quick to react. Don Armes declared that the commission would never approve a satanic statue in the Bible Belt. Another official, Earl Sears, declared that the statue was "offensive" and refused to consider Satanism as a religion (Morrison 2014). Even ACLU's director, Brady Henderson, said the organization had mixed feelings about the TST's action, declaring that, on the one hand, there should not be any religious statues on public property, but on the other hand, the Baphomet statue triggered reflection on the government's hypocrisy as far as Christianity was concerned (Resnick 2014).

Lucien Greaves, the spokesperson for TST, then declared that he and his lawyers had decided that the Baphomet statue would be placed next to the Ten Commandments monument even if ACLU lost its lawsuit, since the US Constitution states that no religious discrimination will be tolerated. Thus, if the Baphomet statue was rejected, the Ten Commandments monument would have to be removed to prevent an establishment of religion. At this point, the rhetoric of the political discourse of the Oklahoma officials began to shift. The Oklahoma representatives argued that the Ten Commandments monument was not religious but historical, to avoid facing a potential lawsuit regarding the unconstitutionality of the monument. Representative Paul Wesselhoft argued that since laws are made and voted by the Capitol, the Ten Commandments monument represented the oldest form of laws known to man and the basis for American laws, whereas the Baphomet statue had no historical value or significance (Smith 2014). In response, Lucien Greaves declared that the Baphomet statue embodied the pluralistic aspects of free speech and paid homage to the witch hunt of Salem, so it had both cultural and historical value. One year later, the Oklahoma Supreme Court ruled that the Ten Commandments monument was unconstitutional because it violated the state constitution, and thus must be removed: "The 7–2 verdict determined that the monument—which had been funded privately by state Republicans—violated Oklahoma's constitutional ban on using public property to benefit a particular religion. The monument is 'obviously religious in nature' and 'an integral part of the Jewish and Christian faiths', the court ruled" (Vice News 2015). TST canceled the erection of its statue, as there was no longer any reason to insist upon it after the removal of the Ten Commandments monument. The organization's goal was not to promote Satanism on government property but was motivated by the secular purpose of preventing any endorsement of religion by the government (Colin 2018; Laycock 2020; Wexler 2019).

Despite the fact that TST did not file a lawsuit (because it was ACLU's complaint that was first examined by the court), this was a victory for TST that attracted intense media coverage of the organization and its secular goals. Since that time, the organization has been involved in several cases. TST sued the state of Missouri on behalf of Mary

Doe, one of its members who claimed she had been forced to wait seventy-two hours and to read pamphlets saying that life begins at conception before exercising her right to have an abortion, while TST's third tenet, that claims the personal sovereignty of one's body, should have exempted her from this process on a religious basis (Laycock 2020; Wexler 2019: 99). In 2017, TST also tried to place a monument (with a pentagram) dedicated to veterans in a free-speech zone of Veterans Memorial Park in Belle Plaine, Minnesota, after a monument there with a Christian cross was condemned by the Freedom From Religion Foundation. After allowing a "limited public forum," which permitted all religious groups to install a statue in the area, Christian protests against TST's monument led the city council to end the limited public forum, removing any religious statues. TST denounced the city for breach of contract and filed a lawsuit in 2019 (Laycock 2020; Wexler 2019).

The involvement of TST with lawsuits and public policies shows that, despite the fact that secular and atheist organizations are part of a minority that is considered an out-group, they do not intend to remain silent. They seek to be the voice of this minority in the public sphere, to claim their identity and their rights.

Further Reading and Online Resources

Arweck, E., S. Bullivant, and L. Lee, eds. (2013), *Secularity and Non-Religion*, New York: Routledge.
Clements, B. (1989), "Defining Religion in the First Amendment: Functional Approach," *Cornell Law Review*, 74 (3): 532–58.
Jelen, T.G. (2010), *To Serve God and Mammon: Church-State Relations in Americans Politics*, 2nd edn., Washington, DC: Georgetown University Press.
Pew Research Center (n.d.), "Religiously Unaffiliated." https://www.pewresearch.org/topics/religiously-unaffiliated/ (accessed January 27, 2020).
Zuckerman, P. and J.R. Shook, eds. (2017), *The Oxford Handbook of Secularism*, New York: Oxford University Press.

References

American Humanist Association (2020), "Our History." https://americanhumanist.org/about/our-history/ (accessed January 21, 2020).
Block, T. (2014), "Ungodly Grandmother: Marian Sherman and the Social Dimensions of Atheism in Postwar Canada," *Journal of Women's History*, 26 (4): 132–54. https://doi.org/10.1353/jowh.2014.0067.
Bullivant, S.C. (2015), "Believing to Belong: Non-Religious Belief as a Path to Inclusion," in L.G. Beaman and S. Tomlins (eds.), *Atheist Identities — Spaces and Social Context*, 101–17, New York: Springer.
Centre for Inquiry Canada (2020), "What Is CFIC." https://centreforinquiry.ca/what-is-cfic/ (accessed January 20, 2020).
Cimino, R. and C. Smith (2014), *Atheist Awakening: Secular Activism and Community in America*, New York: Oxford University Press.

Colin, M. (2018), *Le satanisme rationaliste: de la mort d'Anton LaVey au Temple satanique*, mémoire de recherche de Master 2, Paris: École Pratique des Hautes Études.

Cragun, R.T., B. Kosmin, A. Keysar, J.H. Hammer, and M. Nielsen (2013), "On the Receiving End: Discrimination toward Non-Religious in the United States," in E. Arweck, S. Bullivant, and L. Lois (eds.), *Secularity and Non-Religion*, 87–110, New York: Routledge.

DeVito, L. (2015), "The Satanic Temple to MT: We're Not Atheists." *Metro Times*, July 3. https://www.metrotimes.com/the-scene/archives/2015/07/03/the-satanic-temple-to-mt-were-not-atheists (accessed January 26, 2020).

Dyrendal, A., J.R. Lewis, and J.A. Petersen (2016), *The Invention of Satanism*, Oxford: Oxford University Press.

Fazzino, L.L. and R.T. Cragun (2017), "'Splitters!': Lessons from Monty Python for Secular Organizations in the U.S.," in R.T. Cragun, C. Manning, and L.L. Fazzino (eds.), *Organized Secularism in the United States*, 57–86, Berlin: De Gruyter.

Freedom From Religion Foundation (FFRF) (2020), "Legal Challenges." https://ffrf.org/legal/challenges (accessed January 22, 2020).

Hanowski, E. (2018), "Activist Unbelief in Canadian History," *Secularism and Nonreligion*, 7 (1): 10. http://doi.org/10.5334/snr.95.

Introvigne, M. (1997), *Enquête sur le satanisme: satanistes et antisatanistes du XVIIe siècle à nos jours*, Paris: Dervy, collection Bibliothèque de l'hermétisme.

Introvigne, M. (2016), *Satanism: A Social History*, Leiden: Brill.

Jacoby, S. (2005), *Freethinkers: A History of American Secularism*, New York: Owl Books.

Laycock, J.P. (2020), *Speak of the Devil: How the Satanic Temple Is Changing the Way We Talk about Religion*, New York: Oxford University Press.

LeDrew, S. (2016), *The Evolution of Atheism: The Politics of a Modern Movement*, Oxford: Oxford University Press.

Mehta, H. (2015), "Judge Dismisses American Atheists' Lawsuit against Ten Commandments Monument on Oklahoma Capitol Grounds," *Friendly Atheist*, March 11. https://friendlyatheist.patheos.com/2015/03/11/judge-dismisses-american-atheists-lawsuit-against-ten-commandments-monument-on-oklahoma-capitol-grounds/ (accessed January 24, 2020).

Morrison, S. (2014), "Satanists, Pastafarians, Hindus, Dudes and PETA Are Trolling Oklahoma," *The Atlantic*, January 6. https://www.theatlantic.com/national/archive/2014/01/satanists-pastafarians-hindus-dudes-and-peta-are-trolling-oklahoma/356752/ (accessed January 25, 2020).

Newport, F. (2016), "Most Americans Still Believe in God," Gallup. https://news.gallup.com/poll/193271/americans-believe-god.aspx (accessed January 25, 2020).

Oppenheimer, M. (2015), "A Mischievous Thorn in the Side of Conservative Christianity," *The New York Times*, July 11. https://www.nytimes.com/2015/07/11/us/a-mischievous-thorn-in-the-side-of-conservative-christianity.html (accessed January 25, 2020).

Petersen, J.A., ed. (2009), *Contemporary Religious Satanism: A Critical Anthology*, Farnham: Ashgate.

Pew Research Center (2013), "Canada's Changing Religious Landscape," June 27. https://www.pewforum.org/2013/06/27/canadas-changing-religious-landscape/ (accessed January 23, 2020).

Pew Research Center (2019), "In U.S., Decline of Christianity Continues at Rapid Pace," October 17. https://www.pewforum.org/2019/10/17/in-u-s-decline-of-christianity-continues-at-rapid-pace/ (accessed January 23, 2020).

Resnick, G. (2014), "Who Are the 'Satanists' Designing an Idol for the Oklahoma Capitol?," *The Atlantic*, February 4. https://www.theatlantic.com/politics/archive/2014/02/who-are-the-satanists-designing-an-idol-for-the-oklahoma-capitol/283567/ (accessed January 25, 2020).

Richardson, J.T., J. Best, and D.G Bromley (1984), *The Satanism Scare*, New York: Aldine de Gruyter.

The Satanic Temple (TST) (2020), https://thesatanictemple.com (accessed January 22, 2020).

Seidel, A.L. (2019), *The Founding Myth: Why Christian Nationalism Is Un-American*, New York: Sterling.

Smith, J. (2014), "Here's the First Look at the New Satanic Monument Being Built for Oklahoma's Statehouse," *Vice*, May 1. https://www.vice.com/en_ca/article/xd5gjd/heres-the-first-look-at-the-new-satanic-monument-being-built-for-oklahomas-statehouse (accessed January 26, 2020).

Smith, J.M. (2011), "Becoming an Atheist in America: Constructing Identity and Meaning from the Rejection of Theism," *Sociology of Religion*, 72 (2): 215–37.

Straughn, J.B. and S.L. Feld (2010), "America as a 'Christian Nation'? Understanding Religious Boundaries of National Identity in the United States," *Sociology of Religion*, 71 (3), (Fall): 280–306. https://doi.org/10.1093/socrel/srq045.

Vice News (2015), "'We Won This Round': Satanic Temple Claims Victory after Oklahoma 10 Commandments Ruling," *Vice*, July 1. https://www.vice.com/en_us/article/wja5dx/we-won-this-round-satanic-temple-claims-victory-after-oklahoma-10-commandments-ruling (accessed January 25, 2020).

Victor, J.S. (1993), *Satanic Panic: The Creation of a Contemporary Legend*, Chicago: Open Court Publishing.

Weld, M. (2013), "A Tribute to Henry Morgentaler," *Humanist Perspectives*, (186) (Autumn): 6–8.

Wexler, J. (2019), *Our Non-Christian Nation: How Atheists, Satanists, Pagans, and Others Are Demanding Their Rightful Place in Public Life*, Stanford, CA: Stanford University Press.

Zuckerman, P., L.W. Galen, and F.L. Pasquale (2016), *The Nonreligious: Understanding Secular People and Societies*, New York: Oxford University Press.

Glossary Terms

Establishment clause One of the two clauses of the First Amendment of the US Constitution, the other one being the free exercise clause. Based on the idea that government and religion must be separate (the famous statement by Jefferson regarding the wall of separation between church and state, leaving the power to courts to debate these issues), the establishment clause stems from the phrasing "Congress shall make no law respecting an establishment of religion, or prohibiting the free exercise thereof" of the First Amendment. The two clauses are always in tension and the definitions of "establishment" and of "religion" are at the core of the debates of the Supreme Court during cases, but the establishment clause deals mainly with issues regarding the involvement of the government with religious institutions (the use of public funds to support them, for example, because the government cannot sponsor or discriminate against any religion in the public sphere) or religious activities.

Free exercise clause The second clause of the First Amendment of the US Constitution asserts the freedom of practicing a religion without the government's intervention. This clause often deals with minority religions that have unconventional practices contravening state or federal laws, for example, the use of drugs (*peyote*) used for some Native American rituals in light of the strict antidrug policy in the United States. This clause deals with the limits and possibilities of religious practice and whether the interference of government is needed or not.

La Révolution tranquille (The Quiet Revolution) The revolution that began in Quebec in the 1960s, that was a period marked by sweeping structural, cultural, and political changes to modernize the province, especially under the Lesage administration. The influence of the Catholic Church, which had previously been in charge of the public education system and the health system, was progressively eliminated by the government that took control of the sectors of education and health.

New Atheism First used by the magazine *Wired* in 2006, "New Atheism" is an expression coined to describe the set of ideas of four prominent figures who helped mediatize atheism in the mid-2000s: Sam Harris, Richard Dawkins, Daniel Dennett, and Christopher Hitchens. Some have described their approach as militant, and their harsh criticism of religion and faith as being intrinsically harmful and dangerous for humankind, especially after the terrorist attacks of 9/11, have been popularized by the media success of their books, which have become best sellers. Sometimes referred as the "four horsemen of atheism" in reference to the four horsemen of the Apocalypse, these authors and their ideas have become widely discussed in the secular movement and have also brought considerable media attention to the phenomenon of "nones" in Western societies.

The Satanic School of Romanticism The "Satanic School" is an expression coined by Robert Southey in the preface to his poem *A Vision of Judgment* in 1821, to condemn Romantic authors who identified Satan as a positive figure in their works: Lord Byron, Percy Shelley, and William Blake. Drawing on the figure of Satan portrayed in Milton's *Paradise Lost* (1667), these "Romantic Satanists" described Satan as a symbol of science and Enlightenment in their works, to mock and criticize religious dogmatism. These authors did not believe in an actual Satan; the "Satanic School" was not a structured movement but was rather characterized by a similar use of Satan by these authors in their works.

Satanism What is sometimes called contemporary Satanism, is a religious and philosophical doctrine that was first codified by Anton LaVey in 1969 in *The Satanic Bible*. Before that time, no instance of codified satanic doctrine has been found. As shown in studies by several scholars, especially Introvigne and Petersen, Satanism is a complex and blurry milieu characterized by its antinomian stance, individualism, and doctrines constructed around the figure of Satan as a post-Christian concept, as a symbol of opposition and of the Self. Three broad categories can be found within Satanism: esoteric Satanism, theistically oriented and drawing on diverse esoteric traditions; rationalist Satanism, characterized by its atheist stance and focus on skepticism and materialism; and reactive Satanism, where Satan is the Christian Devil and can also be a temporary figure of identification during transgression and opposition phases of an individual.

Secularism *Stricto sensu*, the doctrine that aims at separating church and state, but the term has progressively become the name given to the set of beliefs and values of nonreligious people, which encompasses several different worldviews such as agnosticism, atheism, humanism, etc. Secularism is a way of living experienced through a nonreligious frame.

Secularization Widely debated in academia during the 1980s and the 1990s, secularization is still a controversial theory on which there has been no consensus. Generally speaking, secularization is a process that progressively differentiates the religious sphere from the secular sphere because of different factors (modernization, relativism, weakening of religious institutions, anticlerical policies, etc.). Scholars disagree on the process and on the outcomes of such a process. Some, for instance Berger and Stark, regard secularization as a false theory that must be abandoned, because they believe the world is actually de-secularizing and becoming more and more religious. Others such as Bruce think that secularization is a nonlinear process that progressively eliminates the influence of religion in the public sphere because of three factors: privatization of beliefs, relativism, and individualism. However, Bruce does not think that the process leads to complete atheism. Rather, religious beliefs are transformed by these factors and lose their influence in the public sphere.

6

The Organizational Dynamics of Local Secular Communities

Amanda Schutz

Introduction

Every week across North America, atheists meet to socialize, attend educational talks, volunteer, protest injustice, or meditate in the company of other nonbelievers. That people congregate based on a *lack* of belief may seem counterintuitive, yet a significant number of nonbelievers participate in groups that cater explicitly to those who do not believe in God. These *secular organizations*—defined as groups that offer recurring events, activities, services, and/or resources to those who identify with secular labels such as atheist, agnostic, humanist, skeptic, or freethinker—provide spaces for nonbelievers to interact with like-minded others.

Since the early 2000s, atheism has become increasingly visible and emerged as a legitimate social identity, thanks in large part to new technology and social media that has helped connect people who would have previously been socially isolated (Cimino and Smith 2012). Both formal and informal secular organizations have harnessed the power of the internet to coordinate action, which has been especially effective at the local level (Richter 2017).

Local Secular Organizations in North America

National organizations such as the American Humanist Association, American Atheists, and the Freedom From Religion Foundation have existed for decades. At various times, these national organizations have established local chapters. A *national secular organization* is one that is large and professionally organized (often as a tax-exempt nonprofit organization), tends to be further removed from their members, and is more

FIGURE 6.1 *National secular organization American Atheists advertises its holiday message in Times Square.* Source: *Richard Levine/Alamy Stock Photo.*

likely to ask members for monetary support rather than their time (Painter and Paxton 2014). Local groups may also have a national presence, such as a local chapter that is affiliated with a national organization, or a successful grassroots organization that has established "franchises" nationally or even internationally. While national organizations do host events, they do not always happen frequently and may not be within reach geographically for most members. National organizations, like the American Atheists, are often responsible for billboards and other public messages, like the one shown in figure 6.1. Unlike national organizations, *local secular organizations* have the flexibility to cater to their unique populations and focus on activism or charity that directly benefits the local community, and they can more easily host recurring events and meetings.

Social scientists have been learning more about local secular organizations in North America, particularly in the United States and Canada. Much of this research—particularly smaller-scale qualitative research—has occurred in the context of local secular organizations, even if the research hasn't investigated the organizational dynamics themselves. These studies have explored how and why individuals become nonreligious (Fazzino 2014; Hunsberger and Altemeyer 2006; Ritchey 2009; Smith 2011; Zuckerman 2012), the development of collective secular identities (Guenther, Mulligan, and Papp 2013; LeDrew 2013; Smith 2013), and how technology and social media have influenced the prevalence and visibility of nonbelievers (Cimino and Smith 2014).

Little research has explored organized nonreligion in Mexico, which remains a predominately Catholic nation, albeit increasingly less so as religious diversity increases (de la Torre, Hernández, and Gutiérrez Zúñiga 2017). Though the proportion of nones in Mexico is smaller than that in Canada or the United States (~7 percent unaffiliated by some estimates as opposed to over 20 percent, respectively), one study in particular identified patterns among the unaffiliated in Mexico that are similar to those found in Canadian and American contexts. For instance, most nones in Mexico were raised religious, with shifts toward a nonreligious identity developing "over time and through experience" (Mora 2018: 3). This is similar to the findings of research on atheist identity development in Canada (LeDrew 2013) and the United States (Zuckerman 2012). Though it is impossible to know for certain without conducting further empirical research, given the similar patterns of religious affiliation and secular experiences across the United States, Canada, and Mexico, there is reason to suspect that some of the organizational dynamics described throughout this chapter may hold true in local contexts across North America.

The Dynamics of a Local Secular Community: A Case Study

This volume will explore the organizational dynamics of a secular community using the city of Houston as a *case study*. A case study is in-depth research conducted on a particular person, group, or place over a period of time. The data discussed in this volume were collected through participant observation in eight local secular organizations in the Greater Houston area, along with in-depth semi-structured interviews with people who participated in them (Schutz 2019).

If a researcher wishes to learn more about how local organizations interact with one another, there are obvious advantages to an in-depth investigation of a single, geographically confined space, for instance a city. Such data tend to be rich and detailed, providing deep insight into people's lived experiences. The drawbacks include issues associated with limited generalizability: just because people behave a certain way in one setting does not guarantee others will behave similarly in other settings. However, even though we can't know for certain whether secular organizations in other cities will interact in ways similar to those in Houston, there are several reasons why Houston is particularly well suited for a sociological study of local secular organizations.

The case of Houston, Texas

Houston is more religious than most metropolitan areas. Compared to the national average, Houston has more Christians and, in particular, more evangelical Christians (Pew Research Center 2014). It is not surprising then that Houston is home to some of the largest megachurches in the United States. One such megachurch is depicted in figure 6.2. Only about 18 percent of Houstonians are religiously unaffiliated (Kinder 2018); in fact, Houston is among the least secular metropolitan areas in the United States (Public Religion Research Institute [PRRI] 2018). Why, then, choose Houston, Texas, as a field site for research on religious unbelief? Why not conduct research in West Coast cities such as San Francisco, Seattle, or Portland, where the secular populations are nearly double that of Houston's (PRRI 2018)? The simple answer to this

FIGURE 6.2 *Greater Houston is home to some of the largest megachurches in the United States, including Woodland Church, Second Baptist Church, and Lakewood Church (pictured here). Attendance at Lakewood Church averages about 43,000 every week.* Source: Timothy Fadek / Getty Images.

question is that there are a lot of active secular organizations in Houston compared to other cities. By conducting qualitative research in a city with more organizations and a greater variety of meetings, the full range of reasons people give for joining local organizations and the types of meetings they are drawn to could become discernible.

But why are there so many local secular organizations in Houston? On the one hand, Houston is a huge city. It is home to a large number of nonbelievers, if only because it has a large number of people. It is also one of the most diverse cities in the United States, racially, ethnically, and culturally. At the same time, Houston is still a part of Texas, firmly located in the Bible Belt and not far removed from the Deep South. Religion is prevalent enough that nonbelievers expect to encounter it in everyday interactions. Nonbelievers in Houston may feel a greater need to organize in response to religion than somewhere more secular, and they may feel safer doing so than in small rural towns that don't have enough active nonbelievers to form a supportive local community. Further research in a range of settings is needed to confirm any concrete patterns of organizational vitality, though García and Blankholm (2016) suggest that secular organizations tend to emerge in US counties with larger populations of evangelical Protestants.

Variation in a local secular community

Types of events

People join secular organizations for different reasons, which are reflected in the types of events that are held (Schutz 2017). Events hosted by local secular organizations can be social, educational, political, charitable, or spiritual in nature. Some examples of events offered to nonbelievers in Houston include social gatherings at bars and cafes, game nights, book clubs, documentary screenings, protests and political marches, volunteer opportunities, and group meditation sessions. Another example is figure 6.3, which deptics a local secular group's participation at a pride parade. The most popular types of events that local secular organizations host are social events—typically characterized by unstructured conversations in a relaxed atmosphere.

When interviewed, respondents said that one of the main reasons for joining a secular organization was to meet and interact with people who were more like themselves. Leigh, for example, had recently moved to Houston and joined the social networking site Meetup.com to meet people with similar interests. She described being pleasantly surprised by the large group that had assembled for her first meeting: "There were so many people, and it had more scientific-minded talks, and I met a lot of people who were kind of like-minded […] a couple months ago I decided to start up again, make some more friends. Most of my local friends that I have now I made through these groups." Allison also described secular organizations as a way of meeting friends:

> I was 65 and I'm *so* liberal, and I really can't stand religion. I would go places and they'd go, "Oh, have a blessed day!" And [I thought], I've got to find my own tribe,

FIGURE 6.3 *A local secular organization participates in their city's LGBTQ Pride Parade.*
Source: *400tmax / Getty Images*

my own group of people! And I found Meetup […] and I was just blown away that a group would call themselves Houston *Atheists, and* have their meeting [at a restaurant] owned by the Second Baptist Church! And I just loved it. I just thought, this is just thumbing your nose at the Baptists!

Both Leigh and Allison discussed seeking out like-minded others who share characteristics beyond lack of belief—namely, appreciation of science and liberal politics. Mutual nonbelief is often perceived as an indication that two people may have other, more significant qualities in common.

Types of identities

Many studies have found that seeking out people who are similar to themselves is one of the main reasons people seek out organizations (Smith and Cragun 2019). An advantage of local secular organizations is that they are often better suited than national organizations to respond to the needs of their own specific community. For example, Houston is one of the most racially and ethnically diverse cities in the United States (Kinder 2018), and the secular organizations in Houston reflect this diversity. Though nonbelievers as a whole are stigmatized (Edgell, Gerteis, and Hartmann 2006), some racial and ethnic minority groups experience it more intensely, describing experiences that are different from those typical of white nonbelievers: "There is a lot of backlash," said Diego, a Hispanic atheist. "[My family is] very Catholic, to the bone. It's part of our identity to an extent. If you're not Catholic, you're not Mexican [...]. It's hard to talk to relatives [...] because they think it's bizarre or wrong." One humanist group in Houston hosted recurring meetings intended for Spanish speakers and other Latinx nonbelievers.

Houston was also home to a secular organization for black nonbelievers. One member, Tim, spoke about the invisibility of atheism in the black community and the feeling that atheism is not "for" them:

> As black atheists we have challenges that no one else in this country has [...]. For white people there's some intellectual circles where it's not only *not* a liability to be an atheist, it's an advantage ... That don't exist for us, there's no such thing ... I think a lot of black people think atheism is something white people do. That's what *they* do.

Tim's observation sheds light on the importance of context when considering atheist experiences. Though white Americans do experience prejudice as atheists, Tim observed that "white culture" is not as innately religious as black culture, and that white people are more likely to occupy spaces (e.g., some regions of the United States, academia, professional occupations) where nonbelief is tolerated or even expected, and religiosity is unusual or stigmatized (Ecklund 2010; Hyers and Hyers 2008; Yancey, 2010; Yancey, Reimer, and O'Connell 2015). Additionally, though atheists as individuals are a diverse group (like any social category, both demographically and in their attitudes, beliefs, and behaviors), data show that those unaffiliated with religion are more likely to also belong to other privileged groups: white, male, educated, and middle or upper-middle class (Zuckerman 2009). Minority group members, then, are likely to experience nonbelief differently than those from majority groups. Local secular organizations provide a space for minority atheists to share these experiences with others who can relate.

Types of organizational forms

Local secular organizations can take many forms and have different leadership structures and levels of formality. They may have hierarchical leadership, with a president and board of directors who administrate all levels of activity, or they may be structured horizontally with responsibilities diffused among many committed members. They can be run as dictatorships or democracies. They can be formalized with 501(c)(3) status, securing the same legal and monetary benefits granted to other nonprofit organizations that provide a public service, or pursue no such ambitions. Meetings may have strict agendas or none at all.

One striking form that secular organizations can take that is particularly relevant to the local context is the "congregational" form. Social scientists often refer to this type of organization as a *godless congregation*: a secular organization (like the one in figure 6.4) whose structure, organization, and activities resemble a typical religious congregation (usually Protestant Christian) but without belief in a supernatural deity. Every Sunday, a

FIGURE 6.4 *Attendees sing along to pop songs at the Sunday Assembly, a godless congregation in London that has established local franchises around the world.* Source: Leon Neal / Getty Images.

group in Houston called the Houston Oasis (n.d.) hosts an event that includes coffee, musical guests, a secular talk, and donation collection. But these organizations are church-like in ways that go beyond the structure and content of a "Sunday service." They embed themselves into local communities, provide volunteer opportunities, establish children and youth programming, and host weddings and memorial services. While some godless congregations have expanded internationally, they are inherently local institutions, much like religious congregations. Religious people typically think of themselves not as belonging to "the Christian Church" or another religion or denomination but rather to a congregation. While someone may identify with a particular religion, the experience they have with religion is mediated by the local congregation they belong to. The congregation is the organizational center for the "belonging" function of religion.

Interactions between organizations: Coordination, competition, and conflict

Coordination

Nonbelievers who were active in Houston's secular community often belonged to several local secular organizations. Organizations not only shared members but also leaders, organizers, and activities. Secular events in Houston were often promoted by several organizations via social media announcements. The tendency for groups to cross-promote and cohost events across the city fostered an overall collaborative environment in Houston's secular community, and members expressed a desire to support the creation and growth of other secular organizations. One example comes from Matt, a former leader of one of Houston's humanist groups. After hearing that several members of his group were forming a separate organization, he said, "I wished [the other organizer] luck and we talked about it, and I felt that the thing they were doing was different enough in format and focus that I didn't feel like it was competition. I really wanted to see a lot of diversity in the community."

Competition

Despite this friendly environment, organizations still need people to attend their meetings to survive, and people have limited time to attend secular meet-ups. Organizations can attract members in numerous ways. For example, Houston's secular organizations include several different secular labels in their names: atheist, humanist, skeptic, or freethinker. Nonbelievers can use different labels to describe themselves, and organizations differentiate themselves and attract certain types of people by including these labels in their names. Groups can also be generalist or specialist organizations (Carroll and Swaminathan 2000; McPherson 1983). A *generalist organization* hosts a variety of events that target a more diverse population, while a *specialist organization* has a narrower focus and may offer one specific type of event. For instance, if a nonbeliever in Houston was interested in attending events that were social, educational, and charitable in nature, they could join a generalist group that offered a wider variety of events. On the other hand, if they were only interested in attending political events, they could join a specialist organization that devoted all of its meetings to secular political causes, such as the separation of church and state.

Conflict

In addition to passive competition for membership, some organizations in Houston have experienced more direct conflict. Like national secular organizations (Cragun, Manning, and Fazzino 2017), local groups also experience conflict that can lead to splitting. In New York City, members of a godless congregation, the Sunday Assembly (affiliated with the original Sunday Assembly that was founded in London in 2013: Sunday Assembly 2020), left to form their own group, the Godless Revival, when the former stopped referring to itself as an "atheist" group in an effort to be more inclusive of other secular identities. Because members disagreed on the significance of the word "atheist" to describe their organization, they split. Conflict can also cause groups who were once friendly toward one another to stop collaborating and coordinating action altogether. In one example, a cofounder and (now-former)

Executive Director of the Houston Oasis was accused of sexual assault by another member of the group. After interviewing both the Executive Director and the victim, who came forward with the allegation several months after it occurred, the Oasis Board of Directors decided to move forward without disciplinary action, and the Executive Director would continue in his role. After this decision, a letter was sent to those involved in the incident (but not to the community at large) justifying the decision. The letter circulated throughout Houston's secular community, and some members of other secular organizations returned to Oasis before a Sunday gathering to protest and distribute annotated copies of the Board's letter, with "victim-blaming language" highlighted. Those handing out letters claimed they were effectively excommunicated from Oasis afterward, and the Executive Director was banned from attending events at several of Houston's other atheist and humanist organizations.

This example illustrates that this conflict not only affected Oasis members but also created a rift in Houston's larger secular community. Becker (1999) describes conflicts experienced by congregations as "identity conflicts": conflicts that force a congregation to confront fundamental identity questions such as "Who are we?" and "How do we do things?" Questions about identity have been shown to drive group conflict in other types of organizations as well (Pratt et al. 2016). Quotes from Tobin and Bert summarize opposing sides of Oasis's identity conflict:

> Some people left and they're not coming back. And I know several of them, and they told me that. [One friend of mine] left, for a while. And then I think he realized that the group is more important than what either did or didn't happen with [the Executive Director]. And there's no evidence—he was never accused in court or anything like that [...]. We've done a pretty good job of picking up the pieces and going on, but yeah, we took a hit. (Tobin)
>
> Listen, I attended Prairie Bible Institute [a conservative Christian college in Canada]. I saw the way Prairie Bible Institute treated people that called out the rapists, sexual molesters. And it was *identical* to the way Oasis reacted [...] and a lot of different churches have this, where there's been sexual molestation, the church has done everything to bury it, anybody that dares call the church out is trying to destroy the church [...]. And the people who tried to point out that there was a molestation issue at Oasis were called out for the exact same things. And then it occurred to me, [*with disgust*] this is nothing but a church. Call it what it is and walk away. (Bert)

These quotes illustrate two opposing responses to the questions "Who are we?" and "How do we do things?" Is Oasis the type of organization that perseveres through controversy and conflict, making certain sacrifices for the survival of the group? Or is Oasis the type of organization that takes progressive stances and empowers survivors of sexual assault, even in the face of resistance from those in power? For Tobin, this controversy had the potential to destroy Oasis, but he (and others, including women) felt that Oasis' mission was too important to abandon. Bert, on the other hand, felt that the conflict exposed Oasis for what it truly was: another corrupt congregation. Underlying Bert's commentary is the idea that although godless congregations look like churches, they should be held to a different, higher standard than churches. When some people thought Oasis fell short of that standard, they left.

Barriers to Local Secular Participation

Although local secular organizations present opportunities for community building that national organizations cannot, there are still barriers to participation, even for those who would like to attend. (Many, if not most, people who identify as nonbelievers do not participate in such organizations, often because their nonreligious identity is not strong enough to prompt them to join such a group.) These barriers include practical reasons (especially lack of time), disagreements with ideological positions held by other group members, the organization feeling too similar to a church, and stigma against atheists.

Practical reasons

Some people simply don't have time to attend secular events. Even though Houston has a very active secular community, with events offered on different days of the week in different parts of the city, Greater Houston covers as much land area as the state of Vermont. At certain times of day, it can take hours to travel from one side of the city to another, and people cannot always find time to participate. Others pointed to a lack of resources preventing them from participating. For example, Lucia said, "I get limited because I don't have a car. There's a lot more I'd be doing—a lot of networking, a lot of things like that I'd be able to do. I'd be able to go visit my friend in Beaumont [TX]. Or if I had money, I could go visit my family." Lucia's reasons for not participating are twofold: she does not have resources, but even if she did, other priorities would have to be met before she would consider participating in secular organizations.

Ideological disagreement

Sometimes a secular organization doesn't fit someone's expectations when they attend a meeting. The majority of nonbelievers tend to be left-leaning (Sherkat 2017). However, this is not always the case in all organizations—especially at the local level—and people may find that having atheism in common with others is not enough to keep them in the group. For example, Charlie described this experience at a skeptic group meet-up:

> I very much like the skeptical views, but nationwide [...]. I went to one of the [local] meetings, and like, one person that I talked to loved Ayn Rand. And I was like, *Ayn Rand*? No, no, no, I can't deal [...]. Another person was arguing that every war is justified because technological progress is made throughout all these wars and that's worth sacrificing human lives, and I'm like, *no*. Nothing is ever worth sacrificing human life. I am sorry, no. I'm done with those people, I don't want to talk to those people [...]. I don't really buy into libertarian stuff.

In Houston, the local skeptics organization tended to attract more libertarian-minded people than the other groups (several prominent skeptics do identify as libertarian, including Skeptics Society founder Michael Shermer and magician Penn Jillette). Thus, Charlie did not find the local skeptics organization appealing. However, several months after giving this interview, I saw Charlie at an event cosponsored by two local secular organizations that aligned themselves with a more humanist, progressive expression of nonbelief. In Houston, the secular community is large enough—and organizations are varied and diverse enough—that if one organization is unappealing, there are several others to choose from.

Too much like a church

The idea of organizing around nonbelief in and of itself is too church-like for some nonbelievers to even consider participating. However, this is especially the case for godless congregations. While some nonbelievers are drawn to these "godless congregations" *because* they emulate churches and some participate *despite* this resemblance, others avoid the congregation model due to its similarities to religious gatherings. For example, one of Oasis' methods of collecting donations by passing hats around the room made some participants uncomfortable. The Executive Director (a former minister-turned-atheist) said they do this because he knows, from his experience as a minister, that it works. Still, an activity that is entirely appropriate and effective in a church setting may not always be an efficient strategy for a godless congregation. One member told me that prior to hats, they used wicker baskets, but they noticed that sometimes someone would get up and leave at this point during the meeting. The baskets acted as a trigger, bringing to mind religious services for some participants—but this had not been a noticeable issue since switching to hats. In other words, while emulating the church model can be perceived as legitimate in some instances, it can also be taken too far. Frost (2017), for example, also found that people disengaged from godless congregations if they were perceived as too "church-like."

FIGURE 6.5 *Nonbelievers, and atheists specifically, are often associated with other groups that are perceived as lacking morality.* Source: *Education Images/Getty.*

Stigma

Because people often associate religion with moral behaviors, the nonreligious (as suggested in figure 6.5 above) are sometimes stereotyped as immoral, elitist, judgmental, cynical, and hedonistic (Edgell, Gerteis, and Hartmann 2006; Gervais 2014 Harper 2007;). In one study, Christians were asked to imagine their lives without religion; they imagined living chaotic, selfish lifestyles devoid of emotion and meaning (McAdams and Albaugh 2008). These perceptions are so engrained in the public consciousness that it is a common assumption even among nonbelievers (Gervais, Shariff, and Norenzayan 2011; Wright and Nichols 2014). Tracy, for example, held negative assumptions about nonbelievers that made her hesitant to attend a local atheist meet-up:

> Tracy: I just typed in "atheist" on Meetup[.com] and I saw that there was a Houston group. So I joined it, but it took me a year to actually go to my first meet-up because I was so nervous. Aside from my ex-husband I had never met anyone who was an atheist, that I know of. I'd never talked about it, and so I didn't know what to expect. I didn't know if the people would be like me, or if they would be something different, you know, so it took—
> Interviewer: What were you afraid that you might encounter?
> Tracy: I don't know! There's such a negative stereotype of atheists, and that's all I'd ever known of atheists. And so, I don't know, in my head I thought, like, it would be a bunch of goth men or something [*laughs*]! I didn't know! And then I showed up and it was just regular people. And then I just started going all the time and I made a lot of friends [and met my current husband].

Tracy's use of the term "goth" makes an association of atheists with another deviant subculture that is stereotyped as violent and fixated on death and the macabre (Haenfler 2010). It is also telling that she expected to encounter few women at an atheist group meeting, which could have left her feeling even further marginalized.

Secular organizations can be a significant source of support and a strategy for managing atheist stigma, and some social scientists have begun to explore this connection. For example, Cragun (2015) analyzed the mission statements and histories of some of the largest national secular organizations and found a common aim among them: "the normalizing of nonreligion and nonbelief in the US." Several authors contributing to the edited volume *Organized Secularism in the United States* (2017) find through analysis of national organizations' mission statements and nationwide surveys that secular organizations can be used to help reduce the stigma associated with atheism (Cragun and Manning 2017; Langston et al. 2017; MacMurray and Fazzino 2017; Smith 2017). However, while normalizing nonbelief may be a goal of national organizations, is the same true of local organizations? And is macro-level cultural acceptance a common reason given by nonbelievers for attending local secular meetings? Though national organizations might aim to reduce the stigma of atheism, or "normalize nonbelief" (Cragun and Manning 2017; Guenther, Mulligan, and Papp 2013), I find that individual members typically do not describe their involvement in local organizations in these terms. However, if they can overcome the barrier of stigma, normalization appears to be an immediate, micro-level effect in the lives of many of my respondents as they meet others who share their experiences, even if normalization at the cultural level is occurring at a slower pace.

Conclusion

Few sociological studies have explored the dynamics of secular organizations at the local level, so it is unclear whether the findings discussed in this chapter would hold true in other cities across North America. Houston is a unique city in a number of ways, and it is home to more secular organizations than most other large North American cities. In Houston, nonbelievers have alternative options; many people who left the Houston Oasis after the allegations of sexual assault did not disengage from the secular community completely but rather chose to spend their time in one of the other secular organizations Houston had to offer. This may not be the case in other cities; if no alternative options exist, members may be more likely to split from the organization and form new groups, or they may disengage from the community completely. Such movement between local secular organizations should be explored in other cities to better understand the benefits members get from different groups, and it is possible that themes discussed here could also appear in other contexts under certain conditions. Only further empirical research can tell us.

Further Reading and Online Resources

Beaman, L. and S. Tomlins (2015), *Atheist Identities—Spaces and Social Contexts*, Cham: Springer.
Cragun, R., C. Manning, and L. Fazzino (2017), *Organized Secularism in the United States: New Directions in Research*, Berlin: DeGruyter Press.
Oasis Network (2019), "Find an Oasis." https://www.oasisnetwork.com/ (accessed September 15, 2020).
Sunday Assembly (2019), "Find an Assembly." https://sundayassembly.online/find-an-assembly/ (accessed September 15, 2020).

References

Becker, P.E. (1999), *Congregations in Conflict: Cultural Models of Local Religious Life*, Cambridge: Cambridge University Press.
Carroll, G. and A. Swaminathan (2000), "Why the Microbrewery Movement? Organizational Dynamics of Resource Partitioning in the U.S. Brewing Industry," *American Journal of Sociology*, 106 (3): 715–62.
Cimino, R. and C. Smith (2012), "Atheisms Unbound: The Role of the New Media in the Formation of a Secular Identity," *Secularism and Nonreligion*, 1: 17–31.
Cimino, R. and C. Smith (2014), *Atheist Awakening: Secular Activism and Community in America*, Oxford: Oxford University Press.
Cragun, R. (2015), "Time to Name a Movement?," [Blog] *Nonreligion and Secularity*, May 1. https://blog.nsrn.net/2015/05/01/time-to-name-a-movement/ (accessed March 21, 2019).

Cragun, R. and C. Manning (2017), "Introduction," in R. Cragun, C. Manning, and L. Fazzino (eds.), *Organized Secularism in the United States: New Directions in Research*, 1st edn., 1–12, Berlin: DeGruyter Press.

Cragun, R., C. Manning, and L. Fazzino (2017), *Organized Secularism in the United States: New Directions in Research*, Berlin: DeGruyter Press.

de la Torre, R., A. Hernández, and C. Gutiérrez Zúñiga (2017), "Religious Diversity and Its Challenges for Secularism in Mexico," *International Journal of Latina American Religion*, 1: 180–99.

Ecklund, E. (2010), *Science vs. Religion: What Scientists Really Think*, Oxford: Oxford University Press.

Edgell, P., J. Gerteis, and D. Hartmann (2006), "Atheists as 'Other': Moral Boundaries and Cultural Menewmbership in American Society," *American Sociological Review*, 71 (2): 211–34.

Fazzino, L. (2014), "Leaving the Church Behind: Applying a Deconversion Perspective to Evangelical Exit Narratives," *Journal of Contemporary Religion*, 29 (2): 249–66.

Fazzino, L. and R. Cragun (2017), "Splitters!: Lessons from Monty Python for Secular Organizations in the US," in R. Cragun, C. Manning, and L. Fazzino (eds.), *Organized Secularism in the United States: New Directions in Research*, 1st edn., 57–85, Berlin: DeGruyter Press.

Frost, J. (2017), "Rejecting Rejection Identities: Negotiating Positive Non-religiosity at the Sunday Assembly," in R. Cragun, C. Manning, and L. Fazzino (eds.), *Organized Secularism in the United States: New Directions in Research*, 1st edn., 171–90, Berlin: DeGruyter Press.

García, A. and J. Blankholm (2016), "The Social Context of Organized Nonbelief: County-Level Predictors of Nonbeliever Organizations in the United States," *Journal for the Scientific Study of Religion*, 55 (1): 70–90.

Gervais, W. (2014), "Everything Is Permitted? People Intuitively Judge Immorality as Representative of Atheists," *PLoS ONE*, 9 (4): e92302.

Gervais, W., A. Shariff, and A. Norenzayan (2011), "Do You Believe in Atheists? Distrust Is Central to Anti-Atheist Prejudice," *Journal of Personality and Social Psychology*, 101 (6): 1189–206.

Guenther, K., K. Mulligan, and C. Papp (2013), "From the Outside In: Crossing Boundaries to Build Collective Identity in the New Atheist Movement," *Social Problems*, 60 (4): 457–75.

Haenfler, R. (2010), *Goths, Gamers, and Grrrls: Deviance and Youth Subcultures*, New York: Oxford University Press.

Harper, M. (2007), "The Stereotyping of Nonreligious People by Religious Students: Contents and Subtypes," *Journal for the Scientific Study of Religion*, 46 (4): 539–52.

Houston Oasis (n.d.), "Home." https://www.houstonoasis.org/ (accessed September 15, 2020).

Hunsberger, B. and B. Altemeyer (2006), *Atheists: A Groundbreaking Study of America's Nonbelievers*, Amherst, NY: Prometheus Books.

Hyers, L. and C. Hyers (2008), "Everyday Discrimination Experienced by Conservative Christians at the Secular University," *Analyses of Social Issues and Public Policy*, 8 (1): 113–37.

Kinder Institute for Urban Research (2018), *The 2018 Kinder Houston Area Survey: Tracking Responses to Income Inequalities, Demographic Transformations, and Threatening Storms*, Houston, TX: Rice University.

Langston, J., J. Hammer, R. Cragun, and M. Sikes (2017), "Inside the Minds and Movement of America's Nonbelievers: Organizational Functions, (Non)Participation, and Attitudes toward Religion," in R. Cragun, C. Manning, and L. Fazzino (eds.), *Organized Secularism in the United States: New Directions in Research*, 1st edn., 191–220, Berlin: DeGruyter Press.

LeDrew, S. (2013), "Discovering Atheism: Heterogeneity in Trajectories to Atheist Identity and Activism," *Sociology of Religion*, 74 (4): 431–53.

MacMurray, N. and L. Fazzino (2017), "Doing Death without Deity: Constructing Nonreligious Tools at the End of Life," in R. Cragun, C. Manning, and L. Fazzino (eds.), *Organized Secularism in the United States: New Directions in Research*, 1st edn., 279–300, Berlin: DeGruyter Press.

McAdams, D. and M. Albaugh (2008), "What If There Were No God? Politically Conservative and Liberal Christians Imagine Their Lives without Faith," *Journal of Research in Personality*, 42 (6): 1668–72.

McPherson, M. (1983), "An Ecology of Affiliation," *American Sociology Review*, 48 (4): 519–32.

Mora, C. (2018), "Agnostics and Atheists in Mexico," in H. Gooren (ed.), *Encyclopedia of Latin American Religions*, 1st edn., 1–6, Basel: Springer.

Painter, M. and P. Paxton (2014), "Checkbooks in the Heartland: Change Over Time in Voluntary Association Membership," *Sociological Forum*, 29 (2): 408–28.

Pew Research Center (2014), "Adults in the Houston Metro Area." https://www.pewforum.org/religious-landscape-study/metro-area/houston-metro-area/ (accessed November 1, 2018).

Pratt, M., M. Schultz, B. Ashforth, and D. Ravasi (2016), "Introduction: Organizational Identity, Mapping Where We Have Been, Where We Are, and Where We Might Go," in M. Pratt, M. Schultz, B. Ashforth, and D. Ravasi (eds.), *The Oxford Handbook of Organizational Identity*, 1st edn., 1–18, Oxford: Oxford University Press.

Public Religion Research Institute (PRRI) (2018), "The American Values Atlas." http://ava.prri.org/#religious/2018/MetroAreas/religion (accessed November 1, 2018).

Richter, C. (2017), "'I Know It When I See It': Humanism, Secularism, and Religious Taxonomy," in R. Cragun, C. Manning, and L. Fazzino (eds.), *Organized Secularism in the United States: New Directions in Research*, 1st edn., 13–29, Berlin: DeGruyter Press.

Ritchey, J. (2009), ""One Nation under God": Identity and Resistance in a Rural Atheist Organization," *Journal of Religion and Popular Culture*, 21 (2). https://doi.org/10.3138/jrpc.21.2.003.

Schutz, A. (2017), "Organizational Variation in the American Nonreligious Community," in R. Cragun, C. Manning, and L. Fazzino (eds.), *Organized Secularism in the United States: New Directions in Research*, 1st edn., 113–34, Berlin: DeGruyter Press.

Schutz, A. (2019), "Congregation among the Least Religious: The Process and Meaning of Organizing Around Nonbelief," PhD diss., University of Arizona.

Sherkat, D. (2017), "Religion, Politics, and Americans' Confidence in Science," *Politics and Religion*, 10 (1): 137–60.

Smith, J. (2011), "Becoming an Atheist in America: Constructing Identity and Meaning from the Rejection of Theism," *Sociology of Religion*, 72 (2): 215–37.

Smith, J. (2013), "Creating a Godless Community: The Collective Identity Work of Contemporary American Atheists," *Journal for the Scientific Study of Religion*, 52 (1): 80–99.

Smith, J. (2017), "Communal Secularity: Congregational Work at the Sunday Assembly," in R. Cragun, C. Manning, and L. Fazzino (eds.), *Organized Secularism in the United States: New Directions in Research*, 1st edn., 151–70, Berlin: DeGruyter Press.

Smith, J. and R. Cragun (2019), "Mapping Religion's Other: A Review of the Study of Nonreligion and Secularity," *Journal for the Scientific Study of Religion*, 58 (2): 319–35.

Sunday Assembly (2020), "Welcome to Your London Community." https://www.sundayassembly.com/ (accessed September 15, 2020).

Wright, J. and R. Nichols (2014), "The Social Cost of Atheism: How Perceived Religiosity Influences Moral Appraisal," *Journal of Cognition and Culture*, 14: 93–115.

Yancey, G. (2010), "Who Has Religious Prejudice? Differing Sources of Anti-Religious Animosity in the United States," *Review of Religious Research*, 52 (2): 159–71.

Yancey, G., S. Reimer, and J. O'Connell (2015), "How Academics View Conservative Protestants," *Sociology of Religion*, 76 (3): 315–36.

Zuckerman, P. (2009), "Atheism, Secularity, and Well-Being: How the Findings of Social Science Counter Negative Stereotypes and Assumptions," *Sociology Compass*, 3 (6): 949–71.

Zuckerman, P. (2012), *Faith No More: Why People Reject Religion*, New York: Oxford University Press.

Glossary Terms

Case study In-depth research conducted on a particular person, group, or place over a period of time. Such in-depth investigations produce data that are rich and detailed and can provide deep insight into people's lived experiences. The drawbacks include issues associated with limited generalizability: just because people behave a certain way in one setting does not guarantee others will behave similarly in other settings.

Generalist organizations An organization that hosts a variety of events, services, or activities that target a diverse population.

Godless congregation A specific type of secular organization whose structure, organization, and activities resemble a typical religious congregation (usually Protestant Christian) but without belief in a supernatural deity. A recurring weekly, biweekly, or monthly event resembling a church service may include coffee and refreshments, musical guests, a secular talk, and donation collection. Like local churches, they embed themselves into their communities and may provide volunteer opportunities, establish children and youth programming, and host weddings and memorial services.

Local secular organizations Organizations that have the flexibility to cater to their unique populations and focus on activism or charity that directly benefits the local community, and they can more easily host recurring events and meetings. Local groups may also have a national presence, such as a local chapter that is affiliated with a national organization or a successful grassroots organization that has established "franchises" nationally or internationally.

National secular organizations Organization that are large and professionally organized (often as a tax-exempt non-profit organization), they tend to be further removed from their members and are more likely to ask members for monetary support rather than their time. While national organizations do host events, they do not always happen frequently and may not be within reach geographically for most members.

Secular organizations In the context of religious and nonreligious studies, secular organizations are groups that provide spaces for nonbelievers to interact with like-minded others. They offer recurring events, activities, services, and/or resources to those who identify with secular labels such as atheist, agnostic, humanist, skeptic, or freethinker.

Specialist organizations An organization that has a narrow focus and caters to a specific population.

7

Minority Nonreligion in North America

Daniel Swann

Introduction and Overview

The aim of this chapter is to offer a concise overview of racial and ethnic minorities and nonreligion in North America and to illustrate the importance of the intersection of these identities. Included are brief histories of minority atheists when applicable, the histories of these groups in North America, an investigation of specific cultural contexts, religious expectations, how religion operates more broadly in the respective nations and with the respective dominant cultures, and an examination of modern-day organization around this intersection.

Race and ethnicity operate quite differently across the United States, Mexico, and Canada (figure 7.1 is a map geographical map of these three countries). Within countries, and even within states and provinces of countries, race and ethnicity can operate and be applied very differently, and with differing degrees of fluidity. While minority integration into larger national cultures does indeed vary by country, Christianity has been the predominant form of religion in the United States, Mexico, and Canada since shortly after European colonization and settlement began (Glenn 2015). Christianity was the predominant religion at the time when each of the three countries became independent nation-states (Glenn 2015). As should be obvious, none of the indigenous people living in what would become the United States, Mexico, or Canada practiced Christianity before the arrival of Europeans, who brought Christianity with them and forced it upon the indigenous populations. Prior to the arrival of Europeans, there many religious practices that varied by region, culture, and tribe (Hackett 1988; Heyrman 2019).

The demographic profile of the religiously unaffiliated in Canada is similar to their profile in the United States. In both countries, younger people, males, single adults, and college graduates are more likely to be nonreligious than older people, females,

FIGURE 7.1 *Map of Canada, the United States, and Mexico.* Source: *bergserg/Getty.*

those who are married, and those with less education. Despite being more common among certain groups, disaffiliation from religion has occurred among all elements of the Canadian population (Pew Research Center 2013). The percentage of the population that identifies as having no religion in both the United States and Canada is also similar, standing at somewhere between 20 percent and 30 percent in each nation (Pew Research

Center 2013). Mexico, on the other hand, has a much smaller percentage of its population that identifies as nonreligious, at about 7 percent, though some studies suggest the percentage could be as high as 25 percent (Pew Research Center 2014a, 2015). There are also data on how important religion is in the everyday lives of people, a proxy for being nonreligious.[1] For example, Gallup data finds that 57 percent of Canadians, 34 percent of Americans, and 25 percent of Mexicans are functionally nonreligious in this way (Cragun, Hammer, and Smith 2013). This distinction between identities and behavioral practices is important when analyzing nonreligious populations. Regardless of the metric, Mexicans appear to be more religious than people who live in the United States and Canada.

Of particular interest to this chapter are nonreligious individuals in the United States, Canada, and Mexico who identify as black, Hispanic or Latinx, or Asian, along with other minorities in Canada and Mexico.

Black Atheists and Black Nonreligion in America

The racial classification "black" has been deployed in America in a fairly rigid and litigious way, which is important for understanding the way religion and nonreligion intersect with this particular racial classification. Table 7.1 compares four racial classifications based on the composition of Christian, non-Christian, and Unaffiliated groups. Blacks have made up a relatively large percentage (typically between 10 percent and 20 percent of the American population) for over three hundred years (United States Census 2019).

TABLE 7.1 Racial/Ethnic Composition of Religious Groups in the United States (%).

Religion	White, Non-Hispanic	Black, Non-Hispanic	Asian, Non-Hispanic	Hispanic
Full Sample	66	12	4	15
Christian	66	13	2	16
Non-Christian Religions	61	6	21	6
Unaffiliated	68	9	5	13
-Atheist	78	3	7	10
-Agnostic	79	3	4	9
-Nothing in Particular	64	12	5	15

Source: Pew Research Center 2014a. *Note:* Other, non-Hispanic category has been omitted. As a result, the percentages do not total 100 percent.

Black religion and religiosity, as well as the traditions of nonreligion, irreligion, skepticism, humanism, and atheism are inextricably linked to the institution and practices of slavery in America (Hutchinson 2013; Pinn 2011; Swann 2019). The racial formation related to slavery and its incorporation into institutions such as slavery, Jim Crow, the criminal justice system, and national and political rhetoric has resulted in black Americans being among the most—if not the most—stigmatized minority groups in America (Omni and Winant 1994). Despite Christianity being used at times to justify racism and inequality, it reduced racial stigma, serving as a buffer from racism (Swann 2019). Despite the centrality of black religion and Christian spirituality to black America, there is a long history of American black atheists (Cameron 2016). This history includes some of the most prominent African Americans, and atheism and nonreligion likely influenced the leadership of black atheists in important black American social movements (Cameron 2016; Pinn 2011; Swann 2019).

A Brief History of Black Atheists in America

For centuries, very few narratives and histories were preserved from the perspective of African Americans. As a result, very few historical records exist of early black atheism and black skepticism. The stigma surrounding atheism, and the religious tenor of many black social movements, may have resulted in the histories of black atheists and black skeptics being among the last to be reclaimed (Nash, Breschel, and Jude 2015). Cameron (2019) offers one of the most comprehensive histories of black atheists and black skeptics stating that "as long as people have proclaimed the existence of God, others have rejected the idea of a deity." Among black Americans, Cameron mentions that the earliest evidence of atheism and agnosticism comes from slave narratives from the 1800s. He points to Peter Randolph's *Sketches of Slave Life* (1855) and Austin Steward's *Twenty-Two Years a Slave* (1857), as works that suggest that the brutality of slavery drove many blacks to become atheists. Additionally, he points to widespread and prevalent pro-slavery narratives in religion at the time pushed many enslaved blacks away from Christianity, specifically, and religion, generally.

Narratives about the Christian God delivering blacks from bondage were associated with decreases rather than increases in black nonreligion during the Reconstruction era. However, the rise of Jim Crow laws, Black Codes, pogroms directed at black communities, and racial violence that quickly followed the Reconstruction period may have contributed to a sharp increase in black atheism at the beginning of the twentieth century (Cameron 2019). The linking of religion and the Christian God in particular with the negative conditions of American blacks is a fairly consistent theme throughout black atheism and black skepticism (Swann 2019).

The rise of black atheism was particularly prevalent in cultural centers, where progressive ideas were prominent. Luminaries of the Harlem Renaissance, such as Langston Hughes, Nella Larsen, Richard Wright, and Zora Neale Hurston (shown in figure 7.2) were all secular (Cameron 2019). Along with their nonreligion and atheism,

FIGURE 7.2 *Zora Neale Hurston was a prominent member of the Harlem Renaissance.* Source: *Carl Van Vechten. Silver geletin print, 1938.*

these thinkers were committed to improving the human condition and valued reason over faith. The Harlem Renaissance and similar movements of the time did not focus on black atheism per se, but they helped bring about the conditions that gave rise to secular ideas, spaces, and communities. For instance, it became routine that rather than attend church on Sunday mornings, a number of early black freethinkers would gather in the Harlem home of A. Philip Randolph to discuss socialism, anti-imperialist ideas, labor politics, and ways to address the condition of black Americans.

Member of the Harlem Renaissance and other early secular black communities differed from contemporary black atheists in their normalization of Christianity; they did not overtly promote atheism as an ideology. Prominent black freethinkers such as Zora Neale Hurston and Langston Hughes did not see atheism as prescriptive; they did not have as a goal disabusing black Christians and other blacks of their religious ideas. While Hurston and Hughes are more representative of black nonreligion at the time, Hubert Harrison was an exception. A black socialist freethinker in Harlem during the 1910s and 1920s, he believed it was his duty to reduce religiosity, and bring secular and atheist ideas to African Americans. Harrison believed that blacks should

FIGURE 7.3 *A. Philip Randolph was a freethinker and leader of the civil rights movement.*
Source: *Science History Images/Alamy Stock Photo.*

in fact relish in discarding Christian ideology because the religion had historical ties to oppressing blacks by propping up the institutions of slavery and then Jim Crow (Cameron 2016).

Black atheists, black freethinkers, black humanists, and black skeptics also played significant roles in both the civil rights movement, and the Black Power movement. Leaders included Bayard Rustin, James Forman, Eldridge Cleaver, and Stokely Carmichael, all of whom rejected Christianity, which they tended to associate with Martin Luther King Jr's strategies of nonviolent resistance (Cameron 2019; Swann 2019). Randolph pictured in figure 7.3 above, for instance, supported appealing to reason over prayer and signed the Humanist Manifesto II of 1973. Carmichael and Cleaver both connected the religious contexts of blacks in the United States with oppression. However, many black atheist and black skeptic figures of the 1960s often saw themselves primarily as political activists first and freethinkers second (Cameron 2019).

It was not until the 1990s that nonreligious blacks began to build their own groups and institutions. For decades, many had participated in a variety of movements such as the Ethical Culture movement, Unitarian Universalism, and other organizations that, while usually tolerant and hospitable to secular ideas, did not centralize or promote them. There was at least one notable nonreligious African American group, the Black Panther Party for Self-Defense. During this time, a number of prominent, national secular organizations formed, for instance the American Atheists and the Freedom From Religion Foundation. It was not until 1989, when Norm Allen Jr. founded African Americans for Humanism, that there was a group that explicitly embraced the intersection of being both black and nonreligious. National groups, for example, Black Atheists of America and Black Nonbelievers Inc., as well as local groups, such as African American Humanists DC and Black Skeptics Los Angeles, have also recently emerged (Cameron 2019). Given that black atheists and black skeptics in America had not explicitly organized around irreligion until the 1990s suggests that the identity of "Black Atheist"[2] is still emerging and developing. The increasing proliferation of these sorts of racialized *intersectional* groups over time suggests that they are becoming meaningful social spaces for black atheists, black freethinkers, black humanists, and black skeptics (Cameron 2019; Swann 2019). As these black nonreligious organizations continue to grow, they have also begun to develop a unique intersectional language, and in the case of black atheist feminists, newly emerging intersectional ideologies (Hutchinson 2011, 2013; Swann 2019).

Black Atheists in the United States

Some scholars have suggested that blackness transmits religiosity in America (Vassenden and Anderrson 2011). An easy way to understand this is to use a simple analogy. For individuals who fall into the category "National Basketball Association player," their inclusion in this category also transmits the suggestion that they will be tall. Similarly, individuals who are classified as black are associated with religiosity, an association that is more likely for blacks than for any other race or ethnicity (Vassenden and Anderrson 2011).

Since the early 2000s, nonreligious blacks have begun to create their own organizations around the intersection of blackness and nonreligion, with a particular emphasis on humanism and atheism. These organizations are gaining members, and many are becoming more visible as organizations and/or increasing their levels of activism (Hutchinson 2013, 2017; Swann 2019). This includes creating their own advertising campaigns, increasing their online presence, and creating and engaging in a "Black Atheist Day of Solidarity" that has become relatively widely celebrated among these groups and sympathetic individuals (Swann 2019). Additionally, an emerging black feminist atheist identity appears to be emerging as an important ideology within the camps of black atheists (Swann 2019).

While very limited, scholarly attention given to black nonreligion is greater than the attention given to other racial minorities in America, including those of Hispanic or Latinx descent or Asian Americans. There is also very little scholarship on nonreligion and racial/ethnic minorities in Mexico or Canada, perhaps owing to the centrality of the study of race in the United States.

Hispanic and Latinx Atheism in America

While in the twenty-first century people of Hispanic or Latinx descent have become the largest minority group in America, it was not until the 2000 census that this group passed the 10 percent mark (Pew Research Center 2014a, 2015). Black Americans, in contrast, have historically been the largest or one of the largest minorities in America. The shifts in the sizes of these populations is notable for historical and cultural reasons, particularly as it relates to the embeddedness of institutions. As with African Americans, the ethnic or racial category of Hispanic or Latinx is associated with religiosity in the minds of Americans (Swann 2019; Vassenden and Anderrson 2011). Contemporary and historical data show that Americans of Hispanic or Latinx descent have consistently been more likely to be nonreligious than have been black Americans. This includes identifying as atheist as well as identifying as nonreligious (Pew Research Center 2013).

Empirical evidence of the proliferation of Hispanic or Latinx atheist and irreligious groups suggests that they are beginning to follow the path of black Americans in becoming more organized around the intersection of their minority identities and nonreligion, irreligion, or atheism (Mora 2017; Swann 2019).

Asian American Atheists

Asian Americans are more likely than black Americans or Hispanic and Latinx Americans to report being nonreligious (Pew Research Center 2012). Additionally, in recent studies they have consistently identified as nonreligious at higher rates than

Americans as a whole. Asian Americans measure significantly lower on essentially every commonly used metric, for instance religious service attendance or daily prayer, than Americans as a whole (Pew Research Center 2012). As of 2012, 16 percent of Asian Americans said that they did not believe in God, about three times the national average (Pew Research Center 2012).

Unlike black Americans and Hispanic or Latinx Americans, the racial category "Asian" does not transmit or connote religiosity to the average American (Vassenden and Anderrson 2011). Because they do not deviate from expectations in the same way that blacks and Hispanic and Latinx Americans are perceived to have done, their experiences as nonreligious people are likely quite different (Swann 2019). There are schools of atheist thought across many Asian countries (Cohen 2019). Asian immigrants to both the United States and Canada are significantly more likely to report having no religion, and in some cases are likely bringing some of these traditions of nonbelief with them (Cohen 2019; Pew Research Center 2012). The diversity of religion and nonreligion among Asian immigrants and the broad manner in which the racial

TABLE 7.2 Religiosity of Asian Americans Compared with the General Public.

	Asian Americans (%)	General Public (%)
Believe in God		
Yes	79	92
No	16	6
Other	5	2
Frequency of Prayer		
Daily	40	56
Weekly/Monthly	24	23
Seldom/Never	35	19
Don't Know	2	2
Attend Worship Services		
Weekly or more	32	36
Monthly/Yearly	35	34
Seldom/Never	33	28
Don't Know	1	1

category of "Asian" is constructed in North America are contextually significant for understanding Asian nonreligion in North America.

There is a lot of room for work to be done at this intersection. Research on minority nonreligious individuals in North America would help assess the impact of expected religiosity, how different cultural histories help explain the acceptance, or lack thereof, of the presence of nonreligion and atheism among racial minorities, and how intracultural expectations play a role in the development of nonreligious traditions. This sort of work might also address how differing levels of racial stigma affect the way in which nonreligion and irreligious practices are perceived.

Atheism and Agnosticism in Mexico

There are three large racial or ethnic groups in Mexico: white, mestizo,[3] and Indigenous (Pew Research Center 2014b, 2015). All other minority groups comprise 1.2 percent or less of the Mexican population, with black being the most common race or ethnicity of the smaller groups of minorities (Pew Research Center 2014a, 2015). Many of the ways in which racial and ethnic data has been and continues to be collected in Mexico involves the assessment and reporting of phenotypic traits. In this way it becomes more difficult to talk about minority nonreligion in Mexico as opposed to the United States or Canada where being a minority has historically meant being nonwhite. Although the definition of white and nonwhite racial classifications were fluid in these countries, the groups that do not meet contemporary understandings of whiteness are usually fairly clearly delineated, though obviously race, racial identities, and racial classifications can be dynamic and complicated. Blacks and other small minority groups in Mexico have yet to be the subject or focus of specific studies. Perhaps this is due in part to their populations being so small, or perhaps because scholars have yet to encounter a meaningful manifestation of this intersection such as a social movement, visible political activism, or the formation and organization of groups and institutions based around the intersection of irreligion and respective smaller minority identities. Or perhaps this intersectional space has not been neatly defined, given the complex constructed nature of racial categories and ethnicities.

There have been very few studies that examine nonreligion in Mexico, but existing literature does suggest that the tradition of atheism in Mexico dates back about two hundred years (Mora 2017). Mora argues, "the 'invention' of atheism in the country is set in a controversial event; in 1837, the young Ignacio Ramírez, called 'The Necromancer,' in his speech at the Academy of San Juan de Letrán, in Mexico City, pronounced the sentence: 'There is no God! Natural beings sustain themselves'" (Monsiváis 2002; Mora 2017).

While blacks in America appear to have created and used their own atheist traditions relative to slavery, racism, and the condition of being black in America as a means to understand, defang, and combat these forms of discrimination, Mexican atheism appears to have developed in the context of a newly independent nation searching

FIGURE 7.4 *Images from the Mexican Revolution.* Source: *Photo 12 /Alamy Stock Photo.*

for national meaning and self-sufficiency after finally having achieved independence from Spanish rule (Mora 2017; Swann 2019). The concept of atheism was refined to fit the context of the Mexican Revolution (see figure 7.4) roughly one hundred years after Mexican independence (Mora 2017). Through Carlos Monsiváis, Mora argues the armed conflict was a source and a driver of secularization, related to the moral relativism brought about by violence across different factions in the ensuing conflict (Monsiváis 2002; Mora 2017). Though levels of religious affiliation remain high, affiliation with the Catholic Church has waned over time, dropping from roughly 99 percent of the population in earlier decades down to about 89 percent in the 1990s (Mora 2017). Although there has been an increase in religious diversity, especially of Protestant churches, evangelical churches, and Jehovah's Witnesses, one of the sharpest increases in the last century has been among the religiously unaffiliated. Combining the emerging sects of Christianity with the 82 percent of Mexican Catholic adherents, over 90 percent of Mexicans identify as Christian (Pew Research Center 2014a, 2015). However, the religiously unaffiliated actually make up the majority of non-Christians in Mexico (Mora 2017).

Minority Nonreligion in Canada

Very little academic work has been done on the Canadian context about the intersection of nonreligion and minority identities. This is surprising given that the percentage of nonreligious Canadian visible minorities as well as foreign born Canadians is significantly

EMPLOYMENT EQUITY-SELF IDENTIFICATION QUESTIONNAIRE FOR NEW FACULTY AND STAFF

FIPPA Statement
This personal information is being collected under the authority of the Brandon University Act and will be used to assist us in removing barriers to employment and advancement as part of our responsibility to the Federal Contractors Program (http://www.hrsdc.gc.ca/eng/labour/equality/fcp/index.shtml) and the University commitment to employment equity. It will not be used or disclosed for other purposes, unless permitted by The Freedom of Information and Protection of Privacy Act (FIPPA). If you have any questions about the collection of your personal information, contact Human Resources (204 727-7416), Room 337 Clark Hall, 270-18th Street, Brandon, Winnipeg, MB, R7A 6A9

It is **MANDATORY** to complete Section A, *sign at the bottom of page 2*, and return the questionnaire to the address provided at the bottom of the last page even if you choose not to fill out any additional information.

You have the right to review and correct information relating to you at any time. You can self-identify in more than one designated group if applicable.

SECTION A: MANDATORY QUESTIONS

1. Employee Name:_____ Faculty/Department_____

2. ☐ I have decided **not** to answer the employment equity census. (If you select this box, you may disregard the following VOLUNTARY QUESTIONS (#3 to 10), and return the form as per instructions on the bottom of page 2.)

SECTION B: VOLUNTARY QUESTIONS

3. **Women**
For the purposes of employment equity under the Federal Contractors Program (FCP), women are a designated group.

   Do you self-identify as a woman?

   Yes ☐   No ☐

4. **Visible Minority**
For the purposes of employment equity under the Federal Contractors Program (FCP), a member of a visible minority group in Canada is someone (other than Aboriginal Person as defined below in question 5) who self-identifies as non-white visibly or non-Caucasian in racial origin, regardless of birthplace or citizenship. Members of ethnic or national groups (such as Portuguese, Italian, Greek, etc.) are not considered to be racially visible unless they also meet the criteria above.

   Do you consider yourself a member of a visible minority group in Canada, based on the definition under the FCP?

   Yes ☐   No ☐

5. **Aboriginal Person**
For the purposes of employment equity under the FCP, an Aboriginal Person is a North American Indian, Métis or Inuit, or a member of a North American First Nation. An Aboriginal Person may be a treaty status or a non-status, registered or non-registered Indian.

   Do you consider yourself an Aboriginal Person, based on the definition under the FCP?

   Yes ☐   No ☐

   If you answered "yes" to question five (5), please check all that apply:
   ☐ Métis
   ☐ Inuit
   ☐ Status Indian
   ☐ Non Status Indian

FIGURE 7.5 *Example of the way in which "visible minority" appears on many forms in Canada.* Source: *Government of Canada.*

higher than those of other analogous minorities in the larger North American countries of the United States and Mexico (Pew Research Center 2013, 2014a, 2015).

In Canada, visible minorities are defined (as figure 7.5 shows) in the Employment Equity Act as "persons, other than Aboriginals, who are non-Caucasian in race or non-white in colour" (Government of Canada 2019). This makes the conception of what constitutes a minority or visible minority very similar to that of the United States,

TABLE 7.3 Racial/Ethnic Minorities in Canada.

Racial/Ethnic Group	%
South Asian	25.1
Chinese	20.5
Black	15.6
Filipino	10.2
Latin American	5.8

Source: Statistics Canada 2019a.

in that minorities are nonwhites/non-Europeans. About 22 percent of the Canadian population identify as "visible minorities of colour" within the context of this definition, a number that is projected to grow (Statistics Canada 2017, 2019a). Table 7.3 lists the largest visible minority groups in Canada, with the percentage given representing that specific minority populations' composition of Canada's total visible minority population.

Minorities in Canada are more educated than the average Canadian, which holds true specifically relative to non-minority Canadians (Statistics Canada 2019b). Numerous studies in America have shown that there is a correlation between level of education and being atheist (Pew Research Center 2013).

Atheists in Canada

Despite having similar numbers of nonreligious people, the political organization of atheists in Canada has been quite different than that of the United States. Larger scale organizations and groups only recently were formed in Canada, decades after many of the American secular and freethought organizations. For instance, the largest atheist organization in Canada, Canadian Atheists, was formed by Randolph Richardson in 2013 (Canadian Atheists 2019). American secular organizations have had a visible presence for significantly longer, since the 1940s with the American Humanist Association and other groups, well-known atheist Madeline Murray O'Hair's organization, American Atheists, being founded in the 1960s (American Atheists 2019).

There is also evidence that nonreligion, nonreligious people, atheists, and atheism are less stigmatized in Canada than they are in either the United States or Mexico (Edgell et al. 2011). This may result in a social context in which nonreligious and atheist identities are less salient than they might otherwise be (Swann 2019).

Minority Atheists in Canada

Up until at least 2001, foreign-born Canadians had a higher degree of nonreligion than did native-born Canadians (Pew Research Center 2013). The following decade would see native-born Canadians surpass the Canadian national average of religious disaffiliation. The level of religious disaffiliation among foreign-born Canadians at 20 percent is about double that of foreign-born residents of the United States, which stands at approximately 10 percent (Pew Research Center 2013). The provinces that tend to have the highest percentage of the population that identifies as nonreligious tend to be among the provinces with the highest levels of visible minorities and First Nations people's (Edmonston 2016). The Yukon, British Columbia, and Alberta are the three Canadian provinces with the highest degree of religious disaffiliation and these three provinces also have among the highest percentages of visible minorities, with British Columbia having the highest percentage of visible minorities of all Canadian provinces (Edmonston 2016). Edmonston notes that a relatively large proportion of more recent arrived East Asian immigrants identify as having "no religion" (Edmonston 2016).

Although it seems likely that there are meaningful intersectional identities among the visible minorities in Canada, there seems to be significantly less inclination among these respective groups to organize themselves around the intersection of their irreligion and visible minority status. It is possible that because visible minorities in Canada have a history of being religiously disaffiliated at fairly high rates, intragroup or communal pressures might be lower for many visible minority groups in Canada relative to blacks or people of Hispanic or Latinx descent in the United States. Perhaps it is in keeping with the trend in Canada of large atheist organizations and groups being fairly recently organized (Canadian Atheists 2019).

Conclusion

Across the United States, Mexico, and Canada there are many individuals who can be considered racial or ethnic minorities, and these identities vary by nation, region, and historical time period. Additionally, they are fluid identities, with constantly changing degrees of religious affiliation as well as constant changes in the social ethos, social fabric, and cultural understandings in which they are contextually embedded.

Mexico has the lowest percentage of religiously unaffiliated individuals (Mora 2017; Pew Research Center 2014a, 2015). In the United States and Canada, the percentage of all residents who identify as nonreligious is between 20 percent and 30 percent (Pew Research Center 2013, 2014a). However, there are two major differences between those two nations, namely that stigma against atheists and nonreligious people is greater in the United States, and the minority share of the nonreligious population of Canada is much larger than in the United States (Pew Research Center 2013, 2014b).

Some of the social factors that affect minority nonreligion in North America are stigma of particular minority identities, the sources of this stigma, specific national and cultural histories, how race and racial categories are perceived as transmitting religiosity or other thoughts about religion in others, and the cultural and subcultural centrality and import of religion (Swann 2019). In this respect, it is notable that even though they have one of the lowest rates of nonreligion across all minority groups in North America, black Americans have relatively high levels of organization around the intersection of irreligion, nonreligion, and atheism with minority status and identity (Swann 2019).

The percentage of nonreligious people is rising in North America (Pew Research Center 2013, 2014b, 2015). The growth of the nonreligious is also occurring among minority populations. Through understanding these unique populations there is potential not only to learn about these minority groups themselves but also how this unique intersection can shed light on a myriad of social issues and social factors such as stigma, racial and ethnic history, societal expectations, contemporary and historical perceptions of minorities, and how intersectional identities operate.

Further Reading and Online Resources

Cragun, R.T., J.H. Hammer, and J.M. Smith (2013), "North America," in S. Bullivant and M. Ruse (eds.), *The Oxford Handbook of Atheism*, 601–21, Oxford: Oxford University Press.

Hutchinson, S. (2011), *Moral Combat: Black Atheists, Gender Politics, and the Values Wars*, Los Angeles: Infidel Books.

Mora, C. (2017), "Agnostics and Atheists in Mexico," in H. Gooren (ed.), *Encyclopedia of Latin American Religions*, 1–6, Mexico City: Springer.

References

American Atheists (n.d.), "History." https://www.atheists.org/about/history/ (accessed September 15, 2020).

Cameron, C. (2019), *Black Freethinkers: A History of African American Secularism*, Evanston, IL: Northwestern University Press.

Canadian Atheists (2013–20), "Profile (About Us)." https://www.canadianatheists.ca/profile/ (accessed September 15, 2020).

Cohen, S. (2019), "Atheism Has Been Part of Many Asian Traditions for Millennia," *The Conversation*, April 1. http://theconversation.com/atheism-has-been-part-of-many-asian-traditions-for-millennia-113535 (accessed September 15, 2020).

Cragun, R.T., J.H. Hammer, and J.M. Smith (2013), "North America," in S. Bullivant and M. Ruse (eds.), *The Oxford Handbook of Atheism*, 601–21, Oxford: Oxford University Press.

Edgell, P., D. Hartmann, D. Winchester, and J. Gerteis (2011), "How Americans Understand Racial and Religious Difference: A Test of Parallel Items from a Recent National Survey," *Sociological Quarterly*, 52 (3): 323–45.

Edmonston, B. (2016), "Canada's Immigration Trends and Patterns," *Canadian Studies in Population*, 43 (1–2) (2016): 78–116.

Glenn, E.N. (2015), "Settler Colonialism as Structure: A Framework for Comparative Studies of U.S. Race and Gender Formation," *Sociology of Race and Ethnicity*, 1 (1): 52–72. https://doi.org/10.1177/2332649214560440.

Government of Canada (2019), "Employment Equity Act." https://laws-lois.justice.gc.ca/eng/acts/e-5.401/ (accessed September 15, 2020).

Hackett, D. (1988), "Sociology of Religion and American Religious History: Retrospect and Prospect," *Journal for the Scientific Study of Religion*, 27 (4): 461–74. https://doi.org/10.2307/1386944.

Heyrman, C.L. (2019), "Native American Religion in Early America," Divining America, TeacherServe®, National Humanities Center. http://nationalhumanitiescenter.org/tserve/eighteen/ekeyinfo/natrel.htm (accessed August 24, 2019).

Hutchinson, S. (2013), *Godless Americana: Race and Religious Rebels*, Los Angeles: Infidel Books.

Hutchinson, S. (2017), "10 Fierce Atheists: Unapologetically Black Women beyond Belief," *Huffington Post*, December 6. http://www.huffingtonpost.com/sikivu-hutchinson/10-fierce-Atheists-unapol_b_9532692.html (accessed September 15, 2020).

Monsiváis, C. (2002), "Notas sobre el destino (afin de cuentasventuroso) del laicismo en México," *Fractal*, 26: 69.

Mora, C. (2017), "Agnostics and Atheists in Mexico," in H. Gooren (ed.), *Encyclopedia of Latin American Religions*, 3, Mexico City: Springer.

Nash, S., E. Breschel, and D. Jude (2015), "Black Religious Skeptics and Non-Theists: A Call to Research," *Contemporary Journal of Anthropology and Sociology*, 5: 36–47.

Omi, M. and H. Winant (1994), *Racial Formation in the United States: From the 1960s to the 1990s*, 2nd edn., New York: Routledge.

Pew Research Center (2012), "Asian Americans: A Mosaic of Faiths," July 19. https://www.pewforum.org/2012/07/19/asian-americans-a-mosaic-of-faiths-overview/ (accessed September 15, 2020).

Pew Research Center (2013), "Canada's Changing Religious Landscape," June 27. https://www.pewforum.org/2013/06/27/canadas-changing-religious-landscape/ (accessed September 15, 2020).

Pew Research Center (2014a), "Religión en América Latina: Cambio Generalizado en una Región Históricamente Católica," November 13. https://www.pewresearch.org/wp-content/uploads/sites/7/2014/11/PEW-RESEARCH-CENTER-Religion-in-Latin-America-Overview-SPANISH-TRANSLATION-for-publication-11-13.pdf (accessed September 15, 2020).

Pew Research Center (2014b), Religious Landscape Survey.

Pew Research Center (2015), "The Future of World Religions: Population Growth Projections: 2010–2050." https://assets.pewresearch.org/wp-content/uploads/sites/11/2015/03/PF_15.04.02_ProjectionsFullReport.pdf (accessed September 15, 2020).

Pinn, A., ed. (2001), *These Hands: A Documentary History of African American Humanism*, New York: New York University Press.

Pinn, A. (2011), *What Is African American Religion?*, Minneapolis, MN: Fortress Press.

Statistics Canada (2017), *Visible Minority and Population Group Reference Guide, Census of Population, 2016*, October 25.

Statistics Canada (2019a), "Diversity of the Black Population in Canada: An Overview," *Ethnicity, Language, and Immigration Thematic Series*, February 27.

Statistics Canada (2019b), "Population by Visible Minority Group and Median Age, Canada, 2011 and 2016," *Focus on Geography Series*, 2016 Census.

Statistics Canada (2019c), "Visible Minority (15), Highest Certificate, Diploma or Degree (15), Generation Status (4), Age (9) and Sex (3) for the Population Aged 15 Years and Over in Private Households of Canada, Provinces and Territories and Census Metropolitan Areas, 2016 Census–25% Sample Data," Data Tables, 2016 Census.

Swann, D. (2019), *A Portrait of Black Atheists: Don't Tell Me You're One of Those!*, Lanham, MD: Rowman Littlefield.

United States Census (2019), "Population Distribution Over Time." https://www.census.gov/history/www/reference/maps/population_distribution_over_time.html (accessed September 15, 2020).

Vassenden, A. and M. Anderrson (2011), "Whiteness, Non-whiteness and 'Faith Information Control': Religion among Young People in Gronland, Ohio," *Ethnic and Racial Studies*, 34 (4): 574–93.

Notes

1. Such data is important given cultural contexts of social desirability around religion in these countries.
2. The term itself is very likely to be contested.
3. Typically counted as unaffiliated, with the majority either citing or assumed to be mestizo.

Glossary Terms

Intersectional A theoretical perspective that suggests the combination of two identities can result in different outcomes than either of the identities individually. For instance, women experience discrimination because of their sex and blacks experience discrimination because of their race. When you intersect sex with race, this raises questions about the experience of black women. Do those with these intersected identities experience more discrimination?

Minority Categories of people who have experienced marginalization or discrimination based on a shared characteristic such as race or biological sex. The term is somewhat confusing because such individuals may not be numerically in the minority (e.g., blacks in South Africa) but are still considered minorities because of a history of oppression or marginalization.

8

Morality, Prosociality, and Nonreligion

Luke Galen

Socrates once asked his pupils, "Is what is morally good commanded by God because it is morally good, or is it morally good because it is commanded by God?" to encourage them to consider whether morality is independent of God's existence. This chapter will examine the hallmarks of the morality of nonreligious individuals and investigate whether or how it differs from the morality of the religious.

This chapter is written primarily from a social sciences perspective, including disciplines such as psychology, sociology, anthropology, economics, and philosophy. Most of our focus will be on the topic of moral psychology: the study of how people form judgments of right or wrong. I will start broadly with an examination of subjective moral attitudes and judgments.

Moral Foundations, Attitudes, and Judgments

What characterizes the moral attitudes and judgments of nonreligious individuals? Virtually everyone has formed judgments on social and political issues regarding what is permissible or impermissible. Social scientists use various methods or theories to categorize these separate issues into a small number of basic moral factors. One example of this is outlined in Figure 8.1, the Moral Foundations Theory (Graham and Haidt 2010), which suggests that moral issues and actions are judged on the bases of five domains: (1) Is the action or concept harmful as opposed to caring? (2) Is it fair? (3) Does it maintain respect for authority? (4) Does it show loyalty to one's group? and (5) Is it impure or deviant as opposed to pure, sanctified, or conventional? Particular issues may differentially activate one or more of the separate moral foundations, and

TABLE 8.1 Moral Foundations Theory.

Foundation Domain	Moral Concerns	Higher Order Cluster
Care/Harm	Cherishing and protecting	Individualizing
Fairness/Cheating	Justice based on shared rules	
Loyalty	Standing by the ingroup	Binding
Respect for authority	Submission to traditional authority	
Purity/Sanctity	Abhorrence for disgusting or non-normative things	

Source: Haidt (2012).

conversely, a given issue can be also addressed by more than one foundation. For example, one's reaction to abortion could be based on concerns about harm such as "abortion is wrong because it harms life." Alternatively, one's sense of fairness may be offended by actions restricting abortion such as "Banning abortion unfairly penalizes women, especially those who are not wealthy."

Nonreligious people tend to disproportionately utilize the domains of care and fairness (referred to as "individualizing" foundations), to the exclusion of the other three domains (Graham and Haidt 2010). This ethical stance prioritizes personal autonomy, such that people can act as they choose as long as others are not harmed and their actions are fair to others. By contrast, those who are more religious emphasize all five domains relatively equally, including the three "group binding" domains: purity, in-group, and authority. Consequently, religious people may view actions that violate group norms as being immoral in a way that nonreligious people do not recognize as valid. As a result, although many moral issues are judged similarly regardless of religiosity (e.g., "Murder is wrong"), there is a separate set of issues that elicits disagreement.

Nonreligious and religious individuals are relatively indistinguishable in terms of their attitudes regarding major forms of social deviance (e.g., lying, cheating, stealing). Rather, religious differences occur most regarding "*ascetic*" issues. *Asceticism* refers to personal restraint, discipline, and self-denial. This could include refraining from gambling, smoking, drinking alcohol, drug use, and nonmarital sex. Nonreligious people show relative moral leniency on these issues (Middleton and Putney 1962). This has led some to suggest that religiously-based morality has a moralizing effect only as it pertains to hedonism or unconventional sexuality, as opposed to issues involving social cooperation or helping others, where the effect of religion is relatively weak (Weeden and Kurzban 2013). As a result, secular individuals tend not to condemn actions that are harmless and are merely objectionable because they are unconventional or hedonistic, in contrast to the values of religious people, which tend to emphasize traditionalism and conformity (Schwartz and Huismans 1995).

Another factor that differentiates the religious from the nonreligious is their relative degree of moral inclusion and the extent to which their concerns are *parochial*, referring to a limited or narrow outlook. This concept refers to the extent to which an individual feels morally obligated to others as a function of shared similarity or in-group membership (i.e., one's family, clan, tribe, community, or culture). One person may feel obligated to help strangers and friends alike, whereas another person showing more parochialism may be kind only to familiars. On average, nonreligious individuals have a broader circle of moral inclusion. For example, nonreligious people report having greater generalized trust in others, including strangers (Gore et al. 2019; Loveland, Capella, and Maisonet 2017), whereas the religious show greater concern for helping fellow in-group rather than out-group individuals, a phenomenon known as "parochial altruism" (Choi and Bowles 2007).

Similar trends can be seen in personality traits. Those who are high on the trait of agreeableness are described as kind, warm, and trusting toward familiar people. Another trait, openness, refers to a preference for new and different experiences, people, and ideas. Personality profiles of nonreligious people reflect lower agreeableness but higher openness compared to religious people (Saroglou 2010). Relatedly, nonreligious people's values prioritize universalism (protecting the welfare of *all* people) more highly than benevolence (enhancing the welfare of *familiar* people), whereas the reverse is true of the religious (Saroglou, Delpierre, and Dernelle 2004). Thus, across a range of such traits, religious people morally prioritize those who are close to them, whereas the nonreligious are less group-oriented and more universal when it comes to moral obligations. This pattern characterizes many specific moral choices (e.g., who should receive assistance). However, some moral concepts pertain broadly to the ultimate foundation or origin of morality.

Metaethics

Metaethics refers to the underlying nature of ethical judgments, such as beliefs about the basis for morality itself, as opposed to attitudes regarding specific issues. One metaethical stance called *deontology* views the morality of judgments or actions as determined by rules or obligations. For example, "Stealing is always wrong because it is illegal," is a deontologically-based view. This contrasts with *consequentialism*, which refers to judgments based on the objective outcome of the action. "Lying is usually wrong, but lying that protects someone from a greater harm is acceptable," reflects a concern with consequences beyond obedience to a fixed rule. In general, nonreligious people use more consequentialist ethics, whereas the religious are more often deontologists (Piazza 2012). For the nonreligious, morality is perceived to be more subjective or situationally dependent, such as the belief that two people with different

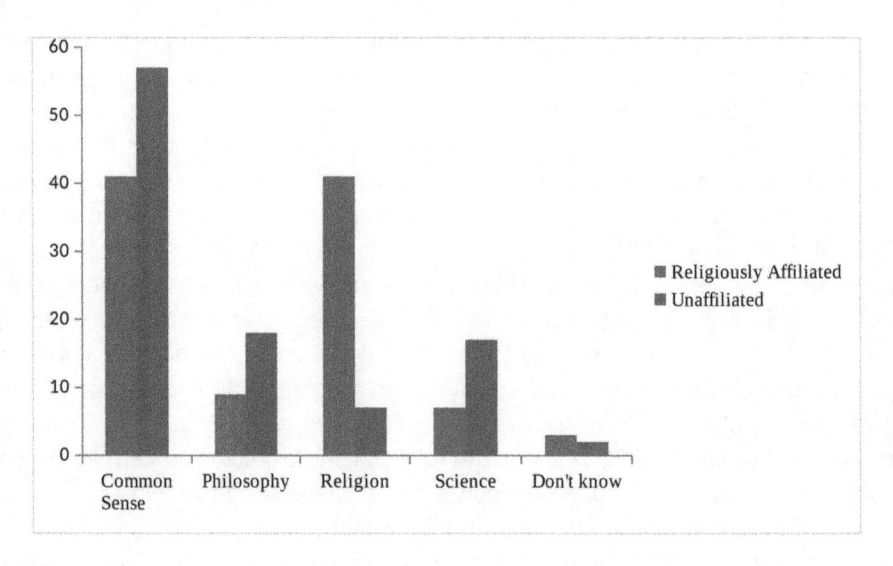

FIGURE 8.1 *Guidance on questions of right and wrong (Pew Research Center 2015). Percentage of Americans who say they "look to ___ for guidance on questions of right and wrong."* Source: *Created by author from Pew 2015 data.*

perspectives could both have equally legitimate claims (Yilmaz and Bahçekapili 2016). This is not surprising if one considers that religious individuals typically refer to God as being the source of moral rules, increasing the likelihood of deontological ethics (e.g., "Stealing is wrong because the Bible says so"). The nonreligious do not endorse moral rules based on perceived divine authority and therefore they must generate reasons or consequentialist arguments for *why* something is moral. As an example of this, in Figure 8.1, the nonreligious are more likely to report relying on common sense, philosophy, and science to determine what is right (Pew Research Center 2015).

Despite these contrasting patterns, there are more similarities than differences as a function of religion in the way people make communal or social moral decisions. Psychologists often study moral choices by using hypothetical dilemmas featuring difficult trade-offs. In the "Trolley Problem," participants are asked to choose between actively sacrificing one person (by shoving them in front of a trolley) to save five others who are standing on the tracks. Similarly, the "Lifeboat" scenario asks participants who they would choose to throw out of a sinking boat to save others. Studies of these (somewhat dramatic) scenarios find few differences as a function of religiosity (Petrinovich et al. 1993). Likewise, the ability to reason or think in complex ways about moral issues does not differ greatly as a function of religiosity (Baumsteiger, Chenneville, and McGuire 2013). Rather, factors such as education or training in ethical reasoning are more predictive of moral choices than is religiosity (Maclean, Walker, and Matsuba 2004). Given that metaethics and moral judgments can be somewhat hypothetical and abstract, social psychologists often prefer to assess morality by examining actual behaviors.

Prosocial Behaviors

Prosociality refers to actions that benefit others, including bystander assistance, charity, or volunteering. Some researchers have suggested that religiosity promotes prosociality in the form of greater helpfulness, cooperation, generosity, and self-control, and that the nonreligious are deficient in these behaviors (McCullough and Willoughby 2009; Putnam and Campbell 2010; Saroglou et al. 2005). However, under closer scrutiny, many of these findings have a different interpretation (Galen 2012). Although it may appear that behaviors varying as a function of religiosity must result from the influence of beliefs themselves, they may be more attributable to other factors correlated with both religion and with prosocialty. This phenomenon is known as a "third variable problem." It can be illustrated in this context using three different examples: demographics, the strength of convictions, and social engagement.

Religious and nonreligious people differ in regards to demographic characteristics such as gender, age, marital status, and education. For example, men are, on average, less religious than women, a trend that is particularly marked among atheists and agnostics (Pew Research Center 2012). There are also gender differences in prosocial motivations and behaviors (Einolf 2011). Therefore, any attempt to isolate the influence of religion on prosociality must separate the effect of gender from that of religion. Likewise, religious people tend to be older and married, whereas nonreligious people tend to be younger and single (Pew Research Center 2012). Older people (who also tend to be wealthier) donate more money to charity and engage in more volunteering than young people (Pew Research Center 2015; Wilcox et al. 2012). Therefore, it is difficult to determine whether religiosity itself has an effect on prosocial behaviors, or whether any effect is actually more attributable to demographics. Similar problems occur with the effects of education, family size, and urban versus rural residence, all of which differ as a function of religiosity and are also correlated with prosocial behaviors.

Another factor that differs as a function of religion is engagement in group-based social activity in the form of membership and attendance at a church, temple, mosque, or other organization. Many of the studies of prosociality mentioned earlier use religious attendance as the measure of religiosity. Not surprisingly, most nonreligious people report that they rarely attend such services. But religious attendance involves aspects other than those specifically related to religion, which themselves are correlated with prosociality (Campbell and Yonish 2003; Merino 2013). Religious services attract people who are "joiners" who want to socialize rather than "loners" who stay at home. Membership in a religious organization involves social networking and recruitment into prosocial activities (e.g., volunteering). These group factors constitute third variables that correlate both with religious belief as well as with prosociality.

Similarly, people with devout religious beliefs can be characterized as having a strong worldview. A *worldview* is a commitment to a particular coherent philosophy of life or conception of the world. Many people who are nonreligious, particularly those who fall into the "none" or "not particularly religious" camp, may not have strong worldviews. However, others, such as those atheists and agnostics who firmly reject supernatural concepts such as gods or a god, can be described as having strong (secular) worldviews. Therefore, as figure 8.2 illustrates one characteristic shared in common by devoutly religious people as well as staunch atheists is a high degree of worldview certainty. Unfortunately, many studies of religion and prosocial behavior have used a "nonreligious" comparison group that actually consists mainly of those who simply lack a religious affiliation ("nones"), or who do not attend religious services. Most of those categorized as unaffiliated actually believe in God (Pew Research Center 2012). Consequently, any comparison of frequent church attenders or devout believers with those who never attend or who are unsure of their beliefs is actually a combination of two separate comparisons: "religious versus nonreligious" and "strong versus weak conviction."

Returning to the original question, one must ask: "If the religious and nonreligious differ in terms of their prosociality, is this attributable to religious belief itself?" When statistical techniques are used to control for such factors, it turns out that the initial, uncontrolled relationships between religion and prosociality are often diminished, nullified, or even reversed. For example, controlling for demographic differences such as gender, marriage, income, and education eliminates much of the relationship between religious belief and engagement in volunteering (Galen and Kloet 2011; Galen, Sharp, and McNulty 2015; Manning 2010). Another study found no difference

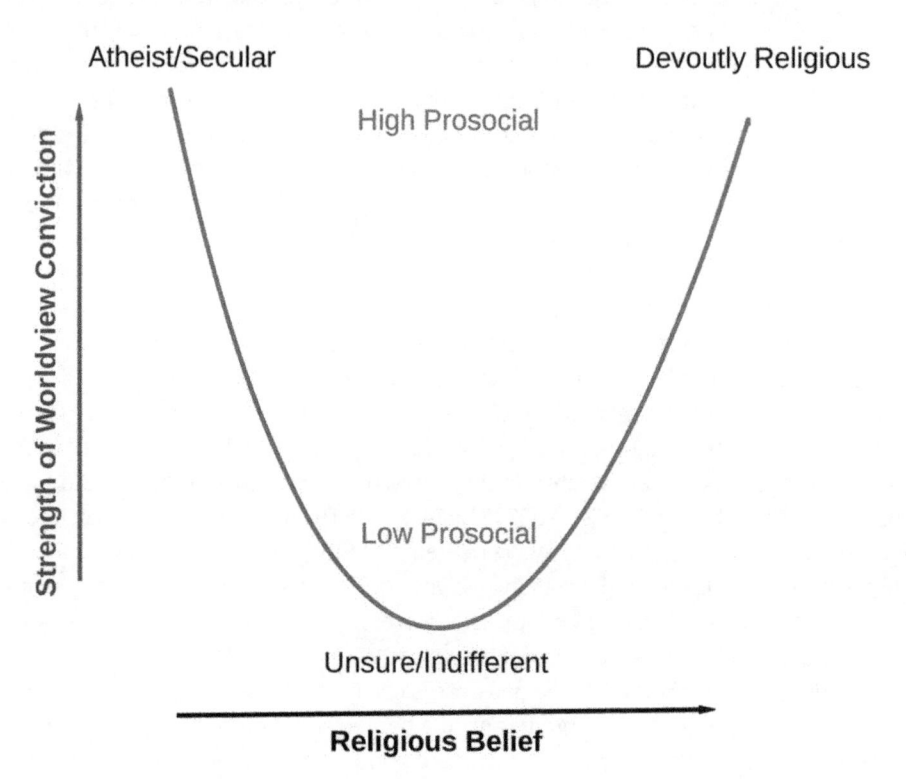

FIGURE 8.2 *Curvilinear model of morality and prosociality by strength of worldview conviction.* Source: *Created by author.*

between religious and nonreligious youth in the likelihood of engaging in deviant acts after controlling for demographic factors (DeCamp and Smith 2019). Likewise, one method to separate the effect of religious belief from worldview conviction is to measure the two variables separately, one regarding belief or nonbelief in God, and one regarding the strength or personal importance of worldview conviction. Another method is to test for curvilinear effects by examining the entire range of beliefs and comparing high religious believers to not only weak religious believers but also complete atheists. This allows the examination of whether any differences are the result of religious beliefs themselves or whether they are attributable to the strength of worldview conviction.

Perhaps the most important third variable effect that must be controlled when studying prosociality is group attendance and social engagement. An examination of how prosocial behaviors correlate with religious membership and service attendance must involve separating belief-specific factors (i.e., worship, prayer) from things such as general motivation, conscientiousness, and engagement in group activities. Religious groups typically engage in activities closely related to prosociality including social networking, volunteering, and the solicitation of donations (Becker and Dhingra 2001; Campbell and Yonish 2003; Merino 2013). Studies have found that the group-related factors associated with religious membership have a stronger impact on prosociality than does any religious content (Brown and Ferris 2007; Gore et al. 2019). In fact, even nonbelievers who happen to attend religious services (e.g., because they have friends and family who are believers) engage in greater prosociality than religious believers who do not attend (Lim and MacGregor 2012; Putnam and Campbell 2010).

Another method of separating the influence of group social activity from belief itself is to compare religious group members with nonbelievers who are members of secular-themed groups with a shared worldview, such as clubs for atheists or humanists. These groups are analogous to religious groups in many ways except they lack religious content. Some secular groups (e.g., Sunday Assembly) specifically adopt many of the features found in religious congregations, including those pertaining to prosocial activities such as volunteering and charity work (J.M. Smith 2017). Studies have found that both religious as well as secular group members who are equally engaged with their groups exhibit equivalent prosociality (Galen, Sharp, and McNulty 2015; Gore et al. 2019). In sum, although many studies claim to find lower levels of behavioral prosociality and morality among the nonreligious, most of the study designs do not properly account for third variables that exert their influence independently of religious belief. Generally, to the extent that studies have controlled for demographic effects, strength of worldview conviction, and social engagement, they typically fail to find any effect of religious belief on prosociality. The best predictors of prosocial behavior, for the nonreligious and religious alike, is engagement with a group of others who share a coherent worldview; one that provides social support and opportunities to engage in productive activities. However, these are not the only third variables that can make it difficult to identify specific nonreligious or religious influences on morality and prosociality.

Politics, Authoritarianism, and In-Group Favoritism

Many moral attitudes and values are related much more strongly to characteristics such as social class, socio-economic status, and political orientation than they are to religion. One example of this includes the political and social attitudes of those who share the Roman Catholic religion but differ in their ethnicity and socio-economic status. White Catholics in the United States are more supportive than Hispanic Catholics of both legal abortion (56 percent vs 43 percent), as well as the death penalty (47 percent vs 30 percent; Public Religion Research Institute [PRRI] 2012). This illustrates that many individuals who report that their religion is the primary motivating factor for their moral views are nonetheless influenced by other factors as well.

The nonreligious are much more likely than the religious to be socially liberal, which also must be considered as a third variable that potentially influences moral attitudes. Similarly, in the United States, the nonreligious are more likely to identify as Democrat or Independent rather than Republican (Pew Research Center 2012). Therefore, we should be cautious about suggesting that the moral attitudes and behavior of the nonreligious are solely due to their lack of belief in God without accounting for the influence of their sociopolitical orientation, which often has a stronger relationship with moral attitudes than does religious affiliation (Koleva et al. 2012).

Another trait that is related closely to both moral attitudes and religiosity is *authoritarianism*. *Authoritarianism* is the tendency to value obedience and conformity to traditional social norms and figures of authority. Authoritarians' most evident characteristics include a strong preference for their in-group (whether racial, ethnic, religious, or national identity) and a dislike of out-groups. Although authoritarianism is not necessarily religious in terms of content (i.e., most measures of authoritarianism do not mention religion), authoritarians tend to be religious. Of the major religious designations, Jews, atheists, and agnostics tend to be the least authoritarian, those who are theologically more fundamentalist, such as evangelical Protestants, are the most authoritarian (Altemeyer 2006). Many of the moral attitudes mentioned earlier, particularly those involving parochial and negative views toward out-group members, are strongly predicted by authoritarian traits. Authoritarians are supportive of the use of punishment (whether legal, corporal, or capital) and are more likely to be aggressive (Altemeyer 2006). For example, those who never attend church services are less supportive of inflicting torture on suspected terrorists than frequent attenders (Pew Research Center 2009). Further, studies with statistical controls have found that authoritarianism, rather than religiosity per se, is chiefly responsible for many sociopolitical and moral attitudes, including in-group favoritism and prejudice (Johnson et al. 2011). In other words, when members of groups such as conservative Protestants display hostility towards out-group members, it is primarily because they also tend to be high in authoritarianism.

The influences of political traits and authoritarianism are relevant to drawing conclusions about the relationship of religion to morality. Recall that nonreligious people tend to be morally individualistic and less parochial. This tendency is also one of the defining features of low authoritarianism. That is, one reason that nonreligious people show lower in-group favoritism is because they are also less authoritarian than the religious. Facets of religiosity actually include a mixture of moral influences that can work at cross-purposes in promoting as well as inhibiting prosocial behavior. Some components of religion (e.g., an emphasis on empathy and the Golden Rule) promote prosociality, but other aspects, such as authoritarianism, erode prosociality (Malka and Soto 2011; Tarrant et al. 2012). By contrast, the nonreligious are less likely to have authoritarian impulses that limit prosociality to only in-group members. This can be observed by examining prosocial behaviors from the standpoint of who they are intended to benefit (i.e., who or what is being helped).

The influence of religious belief or the lack thereof on prosocial behavior, such as community volunteering can be affected by individuals' in-group favoritism. Although some studies find that those who are religious engage in more volunteering than the nonreligious, other studies find that this volunteering advantage is specific only to groups and causes that are associated with religion (e.g., church-sponsored charity; Cragun 2013). Rather, being religiously affiliated is negatively associated with volunteering for groups in which religious individuals are in the minority (Storm 2015). Those who are lower in religiosity tend to give more charitable donations to out-group members (Manesi et al. 2018). Thus, religiosity narrows the scope of prosociality, making it more parochial, a phenomenon known as "minimal prosociality," similar to parochial altruism (Blogowska and Saroglou 2011; Putnam and Campbell 2010).

Sociocultural Influences

Most of the previously discussed material has pertained to nonreligious morality at an individual or group level. What about at a broader cultural level? Are countries or regions with more nonreligious people distinct in terms of moral values or prosocial behaviors? Countries differ markedly in the prevalence of nonreligious people. In North America, the proportion of people saying religion is "very important" to them is, on average, much lower in Canada (27 percent) than in the United States (53 percent) and Mexico (45 percent; Pew Research Center 2018). There is little evidence that countries or states with a higher proportion of religious people have a higher aggregate level of prosociality. To the contrary, research suggests that countries with higher proportions of nonreligious or secular people have lower rates of crime, corruption, and violence (Paul 2009; Zuckerman 2008). In keeping with the third variable problem, however, these countries also differ in other ways, notably with respect to socio-economic development. Affluent countries and regions with higher living standards on average tend to be less religious (Paul 2009). As with analyses on an individual level, this makes it difficult to link secularity with country-level prosociality in a causal manner.

Nonetheless, some researchers have pointed out that prosociality is still associated with individuals' personal level of religiosity within a given region even as the opposite is true at the collective level (i.e., more secular regions are more prosocial as a whole). This problem exemplifies a type of *ecological fallacy*, when an incorrect inference is made about individuals based on information about the group to which they belong. In this case, a "religious engagement paradox" (Myers 2012) exists in that individuals with more frequent religious attendance tend to show greater prosociality on many measures even though at an aggregate level, countries with a greater proportion of religious people tend to have lower overall prosociality.

Other studies have also found that the relationship between religious beliefs (or the lack thereof) and prosociality is dependent upon whether the beliefs are relatively normative compared to the predominant beliefs in the surrounding culture. Religiosity is associated with prosociality in less religious countries or those with no social pressure to follow a religion, but not in more religious countries or those with high social enforcement of religion (Guo, Liu, and Tian 2018; Stavrova and Siegers 2014). These types of interactions are examples of "culture-fit" models. They predict that prosocial traits can be associated with either religiosity or nonreligiosity primarily based on how individuals' own worldviews match those of their surrounding culture. For instance, prosocial personality traits such as being communally oriented are correlated with religiousness only within predominantly religious cultures. By contrast, communal traits are associated with being nonreligious within secular countries such as those in Northern Europe (Gebauer, Paulhus, and Neberich 2013). In sum, there is little evidence that either religion or nonreligion in and of themselves has a consistent prosocial effect in either direction.

TABLE 8.2 Do Americans Believe It Is Necessary to Believe in God to Be Moral? Percentage of US Adults Who Say It Is Not Necessary to Believe in God to Be Moral and Have Good Values.

Black Protestant	26%
White Evangelical Protestant	32%
White Mainline Protestant	63%
Catholic	49%
Unaffiliated	85%

Source: G.A. Smith (2017).

Stereotypes and Situational Prosociality

Many people view the concepts of religiosity and morality as being synonymous. There is a widespread stereotype that being religious promotes morality or that religion is necessary for morality (see Table 8.2; G.A. Smith 2017). Experiments have found that nonreligious individuals, particularly atheists, are viewed as being less moral and trustworthy (Galen, Williams, and Ver Wey 2014; Gervais, Shariff, and Norenzayan 2011). These stereotypes are internalized such that religious people tend to view themselves as being more moral (Sedikides and Gebauer 2010). By contrast, because nonreligious individuals have a lower expectation of being moral, there is less of a tendency to "self-enhance" or boost their moral credentials. In keeping with a lower desire to appear particularly virtuous, the nonreligious are also on average more morally humble and lower in narcissism than those who are religious/spiritual (Gebauer, Sedikides, and Schrade 2017; Hermann and Fuller 2017). Some nonbelievers who are aware that they are viewed as morally suspect may attempt to disprove or counteract that stereotype by behaving virtuously in situations where their atheist identity is conspicuous (Cowgill et al. 2017). As mentioned above, some members of organized secular groups are also motivated to engage in prosocial activities to publicly demonstrate their moral credentials (J.M. Smith 2017).

This is relevant to investigating the relationship between religion and prosociality because most studies rely on self-reports of moral attitudes and behaviors (e.g., asking "Are you a helpful person?"). Therefore, an internalized stereotype about one's own prosociality can lead to biased or enhanced responses. This may explain why the relationship between religion and morality is greater when assessed via self-reports or hypothetical situations as opposed to actual prosocial behaviors (Galen 2012). Although religious individuals self-report that they value honesty to a greater extent than less religious people, there is little or no relationship between religiosity and actual behavioral honesty (Hood et al. 2009). Rather, self-report measures or hypothetical scenarios are colored by how one believes one "ought" to be. Even though this effect represents a type of bias, or distortion, internalized stereotypes can actually help us understand the specific motivations to engage in moral and prosocial behaviors, because a motivation to "look good" differs from a motivation to "do good."

One way to minimize biases inherent to prosocial stereotypes is to focus on behaviors that are spontaneous and unplanned. This can be seen in experiments in which individuals believe they are engaged in one type of task but then are unexpectedly asked to provide assistance to a bystander or "victim." Social psychologist C. Daniel Batson has conducted a series of studies designed to assess not only whether individuals will help but also, by varying the context, to provide information regarding their motives for helping. Batson and colleagues (1989) found that some people may act prosocially out of a sense of personal or egoistic motivation to appear helpful, such as providing help regardless of what the victim or "helpee" wants. Other individuals help because they are motivated by genuine empathy for the victim or "helpee." Results across numerous experiments indicate that those who are less traditionally religious are more likely to

TABLE 8.3 Summary of Moral, Ethical, and Prosocial Differences Between the Nonreligious and Religious.

Dimension	Nonreligious	Religious
Moralized Issues	Restricted to social/cooperative	Social/cooperative as well as ascetic and sexual/reproductive
Moral Foundations	Individualizing: Harm/empathy and fairness	Group binding: Authority, in-group, and purity as well as individualizing
Metaethics	Consequentialist and subjective	Deontological and objective
Radius of Concern	Universal, out-group-inclusive	Greater in-group concern, parochial
Helping	Lower planned, equivalent spontaneous	Greater planned, equivalent spontaneous
Self-enhancement	Low	High
Prosocial Motivation	Empathy-based	Personal/Reward-based

have the latter, more empathy-based helping motivation. By contrast, those who are traditionally religious tend to help more in situations where they can appear (to others, to God, as well as to themselves) as being more helpful, and thus are motivated more by a desire to project a prosocial image. One problem with having a belief that one's morality is motivated by one's religious beliefs is that this may lead some believers to rationalize any negative inclinations, whereas those who do not believe in divine authority for morality are less likely to have a rationalization for engaging in immorality (Jackson and Gray 2019). Some research has also found that less religious individuals are focused to a greater extent on having compassion for victims, whereas the religious may be driven more by doctrine or reputational concerns (Saslow et al. 2013).

Summary

As can be seen in Table 8.3, compared to the religious, the nonreligious moralize a narrower range of issues and rely disproportionately on individualistic moral foundations. Their metaethics are grounded in the consequences of actions and they acknowledge the subjectivity of morality. The nonreligious have a universalist scope of moral obligation and a lesser tendency to base their decisions on in-group concerns. The helping behaviors of the nonreligious are marked by relatively lower levels of planned helping, but there is no overall religious difference in spontaneous assistance. Their helping is based more on empathy rather than reward-based concerns. Finally, many of these apparent effects are intertwined with third-variable differences between the religious and nonreligious including demographic, social, political, and culturally normative characteristics.

Beyond simply cataloging these characteristics, can we make inferences about the underlying motivation for secular morality? Consider two cases that, by any definition, are exemplars of moral action. Leopold Socha was a Polish sewer inspector who, at great personal risk, sheltered and saved many Jews during the Nazi occupation of the city of Lvov by hiding them in underground tunnels. Accounts of the motivation for Socha's heroism often mention his devout Catholicism (Marshall 1991). Perhaps because religions contain moral and ethical codes and guidelines, many people presume that when believers, such as Socha, behave morally it is attributable to these tenets. However, this assumption is an example of the logical fallacy known in Latin as *cum hoc ergo propter hoc* (with this, therefore because of this), or as stated in the social sciences, "correlation does not imply causation."

Consider a second case of someone who also sheltered Jews during the Holocaust at great personal risk. Tina Strobos was a Dutch atheist resistance fighter who said "I never believed in God, but I believed in the sacredness of life" (Langer 2012). Few accounts of Strobos or indeed other heroic atheists presume that they were specifically motivated by their *lack* of religious beliefs. Studies have found that both highly religious and strongly nonreligious people were more likely to have sheltered Jews during the Holocaust than the moderately religious (Oliner and Oliner 1988). In such cases of heroic helping, a high degree of personal moral conviction and a history of positive parental role models are more relevant than religious beliefs to such behaviors (Midlarsky, Jones, and Corley 2005).

As discussed, a general stereotype exists such that religion must provide a motivation for morality, and that without religion, there would be a lack of motivations for good behavior (Zell and Baumeister 2013). However, the evidence outlined in Table 8.3 does not support such a connection. When asked to state a reason for their prosocial actions, many people may refer to the tenets of their worldview (e.g., "my religion teaches kindness"). However, these beliefs may have more to do with relatively specific factors, such as who is helped or in what circumstances, rather than the underlying motivation to act morally. Perhaps more importantly, people with strong worldviews and convictions, regardless of any religious content, are especially likely to act morally and decisively.

Further Reading and Online Resources

Batson, C.D. (1991), *The Altruism Question: Toward a Social-Psychological Answer*, Hillsdale, NJ: Lawrence Erlbaum.
Galen, L.W. (2012), "Does Religious Belief Promote Prosociality?: A Critical Examination," *Psychological Bulletin*, 138: 876–906.

Galen, L.W. (2016), "Secular Morality and Ethics," in P. Zuckerman, L.W. Galen, and F. Pasquale (eds.), *The Non-Religious: Understanding Secular People and Societies*, 146–73, New York: Oxford University Press.

Haidt, J. (2012), *The Righteous Mind: Why Good People Are Divided by Politics and Religion*, New York: Pantheon.

Pew Research Center (2012), "Nones on the Rise," October 9. https://www.pewforum.org/2012/10/09/nones-on-the-rise/ (accessed September 13, 2020).

Shariff, A.F., J. Piazza, and S.R. Kramer (2014), "Morality and the Religious Mind: Why Theists and Nontheists Differ," *Trends in Cognitive Sciences*, 18: 439–41.

References

Altemeyer, B. (2006), *The Authoritarians*, Winnipeg: University of Manitoba.

Batson, C.D., K.C. Oleson, J.L. Weeks, S.P. Healy, P.J. Reeves, P. Jennings, and T. Brown (1989), "Religious Prosocial Motivation: Is It Altruistic or Egoistic?," *Journal of Personality and Social Psychology*, 57: 873–84.

Baumsteiger, R., T. Chenneville, and J.F. McGuire (2013), "The Roles of Religiosity and Spirituality in Moral Reasoning," *Ethics & Behavior*, 23 (4): 266–77.

Becker, P.E. and P.H. Dhingra (2001), "Religious Involvement and Volunteering: Implications for Civil Society," *Sociology of Religion*, 62: 315–35.

Blogowska, J. and V. Saroglou (2011), "Religious Fundamentalism and Limited Prosociality as a Function of the Target," *Journal for the Scientific Study of Religion*, 50: 44–60.

Brown, E. and J. Ferris (2007), "Social Capital and Philanthropy: An Analysis of the Impact of Social Capital on Individual Giving and Volunteering," *Nonprofit and Voluntary Sector Quarterly*, 36: 85–99.

Campbell, D.E. and S.J. Yonish (2003), "Religion and Volunteering in America," in C. Smidt (ed.), *Religion as Social Capital: Producing the Common Good*, 87–106, Waco, TX: Baylor University Press.

Choi, J.K. and S. Bowles (2007), "The Coevolution of Parochial Altruism and War," *Science*, 318 (5850): 636–40.

Cowgill, C.M., K. Rios, and A. Simpson (2017), "Generous Heathens? Reputational Concerns and Atheists' Behavior toward Christians in Economic Games," *Journal of Experimental Social Psychology*, 73: 169–79.

Cragun, R. (2013), *What You Don't Know about Religion (But Should)*, Durham, NC: Pitchstone Publishing.

Decamp, W. and J.M. Smith (2019), "Religion, Nonreligion, and Deviance: Comparing Faith's and Family's Relative Strength in Promoting Social Conformity," *Journal of Religion and Health*, 58: 206–20.

Einolf, C.J. (2011), "Gender Differences in the Correlates of Volunteering and Charitable Giving," *Nonprofit and Voluntary Sector Quarterly*, 40 (6): 1092–112.

Galen, L.W. and J. Kloet (2011), "Personality and Social Integration Factors Distinguishing Non-Religious from Religious Groups: The Importance of Controlling for Attendance and Demographics," *Archive for the Psychology of Religion*, 33: 205–28.

Galen, L.W., M. Sharp, and A. McNulty (2015), "The Role of Nonreligious Group Factors versus Religious Belief in the Prediction of Prosociality," *Social Indicators Research*, 122: 411–32.

Galen, L.W., T.J. Williams, and A.L. Ver Wey (2014), "Personality Ratings Are Influenced by Religious Stereotype and Ingroup Bias," *International Journal for the Psychology of Religion*, 24: 282–97.

Gebauer, J.E., D.L. Paulhus, and W. Neberich (2013), "Big Two Personality and Religiosity across Cultures: Communals as Religious Conformists and Agentics as Religious Contrarians," *Social Psychological and Personality Science*, 4: 21–30.

Gebauer, J.E., C. Sedikides, and A. Schrade (2017), "Christian Self Enhancement," *Journal of Personality and Social Psychology*, 113: 786–809.

Gervais, W.M., A.F. Shariff and A. Norenzayan (2011), "Do You Believe in Atheists? Distrust Is Central to Anti-atheist Prejudice," *Journal of Personality and Social Psychology*, 101: 1189–206.

Gore, R., L.W. Galen, P. Zuckerman, D. Pollock, and F.L. Shults (2019), "Good without God? Connecting Religiosity, Affiliation and Pro-sociality Using World Values Survey Data and Agent-based Simulation," *SocArXiv*. https://doi.org/10.31235/osf.io/jnpe9.

Graham, J. and J. Haidt (2010), "Beyond Beliefs: Religions Bind Individuals into Moral Communities," *Personality and Social Psychology Review*, 14: 140–50.

Guo, Q., Z. Liu, and Q. Tian (2018), "Religiosity and Prosocial Behavior at National Level," *Psychology of Religion and Spirituality*, 12 (1): 55–65.

Hermann, A. and R. Fuller (2017), "Trait Narcissism and Contemporary Religious Trends," *Archive for the Psychology of Religion*, 39: 99–117.

Hood, R.W., P.C. Hill, and B. Spilka (2009), *The Psychology of Religion: An Empirical Approach*, 4th edn., New York: Guilford Press.

Jackson, J.C. and K. Gray (2019), "When a Good God Makes Bad People: Testing a Theory of Religion and Immorality," *Journal of Personality and Social Psychology*, 117: 1203–30.

Johnson, M.K., W.C. Rowatt, L.M. Barnard-Brak, J.P. Patock-Peckham, J.P. LaBouff, and R.D. Carlisle (2011), "A Mediational Analysis of the Role of Right-Wing Authoritarianism and Religious Fundamentalism in the Religiosity–Prejudice Link," *Personality and Individual Differences*, 50: 851–6.

Koleva, S.P., J. Graham, R. Iyer, P.H. Ditto, and J. Haidt (2012), "Tracing the Threads: How Five Moral Concerns (Especially Purity) Help Explain Culture War Attitudes," *Journal of Research in Personality*, 46: 184–94.

Langer, E. (2012), "Saved 100 Jews from the Nazis in Amsterdam," *The Washington Post*, March 1. https://www.washingtonpost.com/national/tina-strobos-dutch-student-who-rescued-100-jews-during-the-holocaust-dies-at-91/2012/02/29/gIQAfalKjR_story.html (accessed September 13, 2020).

Lim, C. and C.A. MacGregor (2012), "Religion and Volunteering in Context: Disentangling the Contextual Effects of Religion on Voluntary Behavior," *American Sociological Review*, 77: 747–79.

Loveland, M.T., A.G. Capella, and I. Maisonet (2017), "Prosocial Skeptics: Skepticism and Generalized Trust," *Critical Research on Religion*, 5 (3): 251–65.

Maclean, A.M., L.J. Walker, and M.K. Matsuba (2004), "Transcendence and the Moral Self: Identity Integration, Religion, and Moral Life," *Journal for the Scientific Study of Religion*, 43: 429–37.

Malka, A., C.J. Soto, A.B. Cohen, and D.T. Miller (2011), "Religiosity and Social Welfare: Competing Influences of Cultural Conservatism and Prosocial Value Orientation," *Journal of Personality*, 79: 763–92.

Manning, L.K. (2010), "Gender and Religious Differences Associated with Volunteering in Later Life," *Journal of Women & Aging*, 22: 125–35.

Manesi, Z., P.A.M. Van Lange, N.J. Van Doesum, and T.V. Pollet (2018), "What Are the Most Powerful Predictors of Charitable Giving to Victims of Typhoon Haiyan: Prosocial Traits, Socio-demographic Variables, or Eye Cues?," *Personality and Individual Differences*, 146: 217–25.

Marshall, R. (1991), *In the Sewers of Lvov: A Heroic Story of Survival from the Holocaust*, New York: Scribner.

McCullough, M.E. and B.L.B. Willoughby (2009), "Religion, Self-regulation, and Self-control: Associations, Explanations, and Implications," *Psychological Bulletin*, 135: 69–93.

Merino, S. (2013), "Religious Social Networks and Volunteering: Examining Recruitment via Close Ties," *Review of Religious Research*, 55: 509–27.

Middleton, R. and S. Putney (1962), "Religion, Normative Standards and Behavior," *Sociometry*, 25: 141–52.

Midlarsky, E., S.F. Jones, and R.P. Corley (2005), "Personality Correlates of Heroic Rescue during the Holocaust," *Journal of Personality*, 73: 907–34.

Myers, D.G. (2012), "Reflections on Religious Belief and Prosociality: Comment on Galen (2012)," *Psychological Bulletin*, 138: 913–17.

Oliner, S.P. and P.M. Oliner (1988), *The Altruistic Personality: Rescuers of Jews in Nazi Europe*, New York: Free Press.

Paul, G. (2009), "The Chronic Dependence of Popular Religiosity Upon Dysfunctional Psychological Conditions," *Evolutionary Psychology*, 7: 398–441.

Petrinovich, L., P. O'Neill, and M.J. Jorgensen (1993), "An Empirical Study of Moral Intuitions: Toward an Evolutionary Ethics," *Journal of Personality and Social Psychology*, 64: 467–78.

Pew Research Center (2009), "The Religious Dimensions of the Torture Debate," April 29. http://www.pewforum.org/2009/04/29/the-religious-dimensions-of-the-torture-debate/ (accessed September 13, 2020).

Pew Research Center (2012), "'Nones' on the Rise: One in Five Adults Has No Religious Affiliation," October 9. https://www.pewforum.org/2012/10/09/nones-on-the-rise/ (accessed September 13, 2020).

Pew Research Center (2015), "Religious Landscape Study," November 3. https://www.pewforum.org/2015/11/03/chapter-1-importance-of-religion-and-religious-beliefs/ (accessed September 13, 2020).

Pew Research Center (2018), "How Religious Commitment Varies by Country among People of All Ages," June 13. https://www.pewforum.org/2018/06/13/how-religious-commitment-varies-by-country-among-people-of-all-ages/ (accessed September 13, 2020).

Piazza, J. (2012), "'If You Love Me Keep My Commandments': Religiosity Increases Preference for Rule-based Moral Arguments," *International Journal for the Psychology of Religion*, 22: 285–302.

Public Religion Research Institute (PRRI) (2012), *The 2012 American Values Survey: How Catholics and the Religiously Unaffiliated Will Shape the 2012 Election and Beyond*, October. http://publicreligion.org/site/wp-content/uploads/2012/10/AVS-2012-Pre-election-Report-for-Web.pdf (accessed September 13, 2020).

Putnam, R.D. and D.E. Campbell (2010), *American Grace: How Religion Divides and Unites Us*, New York: Simon & Schuster.

Saroglou, V. (2010), "Religiousness as a Cultural Adaptation of Basic Traits: A Five-Factor Model Perspective," *Personality and Social Psychology Review*, 14: 108–25.

Saroglou, V., V. Delpierre, and R. Dernelle (2004), "Values and Religiosity: A Meta-Analysis of Studies using Schwartz's Model," *Personality and Individual Differences*, 37: 721–34.

Saroglou, V., I. Pichon, L. Trompette, M. Verschueren, and R. Dernelle (2005), "Prosocial Behavior and Religion: New Evidence Based on Projective Measures and Peer Ratings," *Journal for the Scientific Study of Religion*, 44: 323–48.

Saslow, L.R., R. Willer, M. Feinberg, P.K. Piff, K. Clark, D. Keltner, and S.R. Saturn (2013), "My Brother's Keeper? Compassion Predicts Generosity among Less Religious Individuals," *Social Psychological and Personality Science*, 41: 31–8.

Schwartz, S.H. and S. Huismans (1995), "Value Priorities and Religiosity in Four Western Religions," *Social Psychology Quarterly*, 58: 88–107.

Sedikides, C. and J.E. Gebauer (2010), "Religiosity as Self-enhancement: A Meta-Analysis of the Relation between Socially Desirable Responding and Religiosity," *Personality and Social Psychology Review*, 14: 17–36.

Smith, G.A. (2017), "A Growing Share of Americans Say It's Not Necessary to Believe in God to Be Moral," Pew Research Center, October 16. https://www.pewresearch.org/fact-tank/2017/10/16/a-growing-share-of-americans-say-its-not-necessary-to-believe-in-god-to-be-moral/ (accessed September 13, 2020).

Smith, J.M. (2017), "Communal Secularity: Congregational Work at the Sunday Assembly," in R. Cragun, C. Manning, and L. Fazzino (eds.), *Organized Secularism*, 151–70, Berlin: De Gruyter Press.

Stavrova, O. and P. Siegers (2014), "Religious Prosociality and Morality across Cultures: How Social Enforcement of Religion Shapes the Effects of Personal Religiosity on Prosocial and Moral Attitudes and Behaviors," *Personality and Social Psychology Bulletin*, 40: 315–33.

Storm, I. (2015), "Civic Engagement in Britain: The Role of Religion and Inclusive Values," *European Sociological Review*, 31: 14–29.

Tarrant, M., N.R. Branscombe, R.H. Warner, and D. Weston (2012), "Social Identity and Perceptions of Torture: It's Moral When We Do It," *Journal of Experimental Social Psychology*, 48: 513–18.

Weeden, J. and R. Kurzban (2013), "What Predicts Religiosity? A Multinational Analysis of Reproductive and Cooperative Morals," *Evolution and Human Behavior*, 34: 440–5.

Wilcox, W.B., A.J. Cherlin, J.E. Uecker, and M. Messel (2012), "No Money, No Honey, No Church: The Deinstitutionalization of Religious Life among the White Working Class," *Research in the Sociology of Work*, 23: 227–50.

Yilmaz, O. and H.G. Bahçekapili (2016), "Supernatural and Secular Monitors Promote Human Cooperation only if They Remind of Punishment," *Evolution and Human Behavior*, 37 (1): 79–84.

Zell, A. and R.F. Baumeister (2013), "How Religion Can Support Self-control and Moral Behavior?," in R.F. Paloutzian and C.L. Park (eds.), *Handbook of the Psychology of Religion and Spirituality*, 2nd edn., 498–518, New York: Guilford Press.

Zuckerman, P. (2008), *Society Without God: What the Least Religious Nations Can Tell Us about Contentment*, New York: New York University Press.

Glossary Terms

Asceticism Personal restraint, discipline, and self-denial.

Authoritarianism The tendency to value obedience and conformity to traditional social norms and figures of authority.

Consequentialism A view that ethical or moral judgments are determined by the objective outcome of the action.

Deontology A view that the morality of judgments or actions is determined by rules or obligations.

Ecological fallacy An incorrect inference made about individuals based on information about the group to which they belong.

Metaethics The underlying nature of ethical and moral judgments.

Parochialism A limited or narrow outlook.

Prosociality Actions that benefit others.

Worldview A commitment to a particular coherent philosophy of life or conception of the world.

9

The Politics of Nonreligion

Jonathan Simmons

Introduction

The nonreligious are a growing demographic in many Western countries, which has implications for understanding the changing religious landscape (Scheitle, Corcoran, and Halligan 2018). Some estimates suggest that the number of nonreligious people in the United States could reach almost half of its population in twenty-five years (Coleman III et al. 2018; Stinespring and Cragun 2015). Similarly, Canada experienced over a 100 percent increase in religious nones between 1985 and 2010 (Wilkins-Laflamme 2015).

Some types of nonreligious individuals (such as atheists) are becoming more vocal and public about their lack of religion (Galen 2009; Kettell 2015; Taira 2016). These two trends—the growth of the nonreligious and the increased political visibility of atheists—suggest a major sociocultural shift with political implications. This chapter seeks to describe some key issues and debates regarding the relationship between nonreligion and politics, focusing on how the nonreligious view social and political issues and how they engage in politics and activities intended to influence or to change existing power structures within the public sphere.

The growth of the nonreligious or the religiously unaffiliated reflects the decline in organized religion in the West (Voas and Chaves 2016). Within the last fifteen to twenty years, scholars from a variety of fields including sociology, psychology, anthropology, and political science have taken an interest in the diversity of nonreligious worldviews, perspectives, and commitments (Bowman et al. 2017; Coleman III et al. 2018; Silver 2013). Scholarly interest in the religiously unaffiliated corresponds with disputes about the role that religion plays in motivating "religious terrorism," the saliency of vocal public intellectuals dubbed the "New Atheists" (who released a series of best-selling books), and concerns about the impact of nonreligious growth on the changing religious landscape (Cragun 2016).

Although interest in nonreligion and atheism has flourished in recent decades, scholars of nonreligion have been slow to examine the relationship between nonreligion, atheism, and politics. We cannot say the same for religion. Sociologists of religion have long appreciated the various elements that make up the dynamic relationship between religion and politics, that is, the relationship between democratic political institutions and religious communities and authorities. Recently, however, because of the growth of the nonreligious and increasingly visible and public examples of atheist activism, this lack of attention to nonreligion and politics has changed, with more scholars taking an interest in the political attitudes and behaviors of the nonreligious.

Before I discuss the politics of nonreligion and atheism, it may be helpful to discuss some key terms, namely nonreligion, politics, and the public sphere. Although the term "nonreligion" may seem self-explanatory, it encompasses a variety of dispositions and a broad range of viewpoints and behaviors (Coleman III et al. 2018; Silver et al. 2014). As discussed in the series introduction, those who identify as nonreligious may self-identify as "atheist," "agnostic," or "secular humanist," varied terms that highlight individuals' orientations regarding the existence of God (Hwang and Cragun 2017). We associate the nonreligious with atheists, but the nonreligious also may include believers who reject organized religion and/or individuals who prefer to describe themselves as spiritual (Lee 2014). Because of the diversity of nonreligious identities, we should avoid treating nonreligion as a homogeneous reference group (Schnell 2015).

Politics refers to many processes, but with an emphasis on the acquisition or use of authority and how a society should be organized. Typically, when we talk about politics, we highlight the formal practices associated with state power, but more broadly conceived, politics can refer to informal activities taken by citizens to address their concerns within the public sphere. The public sphere refers to a realm of social life where people can speak about public matters, deliberate, and settle disagreements on how to best organize civil society. Politics is an important dimension of public life and the public sphere.

This chapter is organized as follows: First, I discuss the relation between nonreligion and the public sphere. Second, I describe the politics of nonreligion, summarizing the political attitudes of the nonreligious, including political party affiliation. Third, I introduce nonreligious political grievances, focusing on the discrimination and *marginalization* of self-disclosed atheists. Fourth, I describe the politics of atheism, highlighting the emergence of an atheist genre of literature, atheist celebrities, and the growth of atheist organizations starting in the early 2000s and continuing to the present day. Finally, I examine internal controversies about organized nonreligion, focusing on gender imbalances and inequalities within the atheist movement.

Nonreligion and the Public Sphere

The recent rise in the number of people categorized as nonreligious has received a lot of attention. In the United States, the nonreligious are becoming a larger percentage of the American population. Nearly a third of adults claim no religious affiliation (Campbell and

Layman 2017; Campbell et al. 2018; Thiessen and Wilkins-Laflamme 2017). In Canada, the story is similar. Between 1985 and 2010, the number of Canadians identifying as nonreligious grew from 10.5 percent to 23.8 percent, making the "nones" the second largest "religious group" in the country after all Christian groups combined (Wilkins-Laflamme 2015; Zuckerman et al. 2016).

Along with observing that the nonreligious are a growing segment of the population, scholars have identified variation within the nonreligious, including those who do not reject belief in God (Woodhead 2014). Some categories to describe varying levels of religiosity among the nonreligious include active or convinced atheists, believing without belonging (those who believe in God or gods but do not attend churches or other worship groups), and those who move back and forth between religiously affiliated and unaffiliated states (Wilkins-Laflamme 2015). Although not all nonreligious individuals are entirely without belief, the nonreligious as a whole are less religious than those who affiliate with a religion.

Demographically as depicted in figure 9.1, the nonreligious are more likely to be male, white, from the upper strata of education, and more common in developed countries (Cragun 2015). Younger adults (those under thirty years old) also are more likely to identify as nonreligious (Beit-Hallahmi 2007). In the United States, atheists are more likely to live in the Northeast or West, are more likely to be individualistic, and are more egalitarian than the religious (Crandall and Cunningham 2016; Doane and Elliott 2015; Schnabel 2016). These demographic factors, coupled with the growth of the nonreligious, are inherently interesting as a sociological phenomenon, but one

FIGURE 9.1 *The nonreligious have historically been disproportionately white and male, but that is changing in North America.* Source: *SOPA Images / Getty Images.*

FIGURE 9.2 *The sign in this photograph with the suggestion, "Get religion out of my underwear," illustrates that the nonreligious are increasingly organized and pushing against religious intrusions into secular spheres.* Source: *Brendan Smialowski / Getty Images.*

reason scholars have paid so much attention to this trend is the potential political consequences of increasing nonreligious identification.

As figure 9.2 illustrates," the nonreligious vote, take part in a variety of community-based and political organizations, involve themselves in formal political processes, and are increasingly vocal and public about their secularity (Zuckerman, Galen, and Pasquale 2016). Besides being vocal about their secularity, the nonreligious have distinct worldviews (Coleman III et al. 2018). For example, the nonreligious especially value self-constructed morality (Coleman III et al. 2018). These values may affect the construction of nonreligious political identities and electoral behavior. For example, some evidence exists of a value-conflict between the nonreligious and religious minorities (especially Muslims) because of atheists' expectations regarding privatized religion—that religion should retreat to the private sphere in contrast with many religious people who still see a role for religious reasoning in public discourse (Ribberink, Achterberg, and Houtman 2017).

The limits of the legitimate public role of religion is a recurring topic of debate among the nonreligious. One concern the nonreligious may have is that when religion becomes public, religious convictions may take priority in political debate, leading to the coercion of religious minorities. Related issues include the reasonable accommodation of religious differences (Bilodeau et al. 2018). Regarding nonreligion, scholars argue that as the numbers of the nonreligious continue to increase, tensions will emerge

FIGURE 9.3 *Nonreligious individuals have taken to debating religious fundamentalists when fundamentalists attempt to proselytize in public.* Source: *Brendan Smialowski / Getty Images.*

between the nonreligious and the religious over what is appropriate in the public sphere (Beaman, Steele, and Pringnitz 2018) Figure 9.3 illustrates one of the forms this tension can take.

Incorporating the nonreligious in the public sphere is a question of diversity (Lee 2017). For the nonreligious, the social world is religious by default (Beaman, Steele, and Pringnitz 2018). How can the nonreligious take part in the public sphere free of coercive religion? Whether there is space for the nonreligious in the public sphere is an ongoing concern for the nonreligious, some of whom look to secularize public space and privatize religion (Blankholm 2014; Gorski 2019). Although this approach to the public sphere may not seem inclusive of religion, religious people have often marginalized the nonreligious (Cragun and Hammer 2011; Fisher 2017). For example, religious hegemony in the public sphere includes "God talk," which refers to the use of religious justifications for political argument. The nonreligious are especially averse to God talk, suggesting that they are impatient with the public role for religion and perhaps supportive of the commitment to state neutrality in religious matters (Beaman 2017; Evans 2017).

Politics of Nonreligion

To understand the impact of the nonreligious on the public sphere, it is important to have a solid understanding of the political attitudes of the nonreligious. Research has shown that the nonreligious are open-minded and low on authoritarian characteristics (Hunsberger and Altemeyer 2006). They also are socially liberal. For example, the nonreligious are more pro-choice regarding abortion issues than their religious counterparts, and they are supportive of liberal positions on a host of other issues including gay marriage and cannabis legalization. Why the nonreligious are more likely to be politically liberal is an ongoing question. One popular if controversial explanation about the politically liberal nature of the nonreligious is that their left-leaning beliefs, attitudes, and behaviors are reactions to the conservatism of the Christian right (Djupe, Neiheisel, and Conge 2018; Hout and Fischer 2002).

In the United States, many members of the Republican Party share with the Christian right the most extreme positions on issues such as opposition to lesbian, gay, bisexual, transgender, queer/questioning and related (LGTBQ+) rights (Campbell et al. 2018). Those Americans, therefore, who hold more moderate or liberal political attitudes, often associate conservative politics with religiosity. This explanation is consistent with research showing that increasingly, religion divides American political party coalitions. For example, most unaffiliated voters align themselves with the Democratic Party. This growth of the nonreligious among active Democrats furthers the religious-secular divide between the Democrats and Republicans, with the latter

FIGURE 9.4 *Evangelical Americans have been among the most reliable of President Donald Trump's supporters.* Source: *Mark Wallheiser/Stringer/Getty.*

party courting committed Evangelicals and other religious traditionalists as figure 9.4 illustrates (Campbell et al. 2018; Layman and Weaver 2016).

Although Democratic Party affiliation tells us something important about nonreligious political views and values, political party affiliation does not map perfectly to individual conservative or liberal political views, which is why examining political attitudes may shed light on more fundamental values or perhaps clarify the nature of relations between political ideology and nonreligion. One approach to examining political attitudes is to categorize people along a liberal-conservative continuum (Schieman, Bierman, and Upenieks 2019). Liberals prefer social progress over tradition, whereas conservatives prefer stability and tradition (Lassetter and Neel 2019). Whether people are liberal or conservative may suggest how they view the world and the kinds of social and political issues that they find important. But, just as a political party affiliation is an imperfect representation of political views, not all who self-identify as liberal or conservative always endorse liberal and conservative positions on sociopolitical issues (Morgan and Wisneski 2017).

The labels "liberal" and "conservative" can have various meanings, depending on geography and historical context. For example, a conservative in one state may not be the same as a conservative in another state (Robertson and Cardon 2003). Despite some limitations, the labels "liberal" and "conservative" (or "left" and "right") can serve as a useful shorthand for ideological proclivities (Jones et al. 2018). Another term that can serve as a useful shorthand is "progressive." The term progressive refers to those on the political left who highly value increased egalitarianism in social and economic relations (Fuist 2018). For example, the nonreligious are more likely than their religious peers to support egalitarian ideas such as fairness and equality of opportunity (Schnabel 2016).

If the nonreligious are liberal, then atheists are even more socially liberal and open to diversity (McCaffree 2017; Minton, Kahle, and Kim 2015). Atheists, who are mostly a subset of the nonreligious, are individuals who do not believe in a god or gods. Although atheists may be the most visible political subgroup, some describe themselves as culturally religious while not believing in gods. For example, we can see examples of atheism in religious traditions such as Buddhism and Hinduism, and many secular Jews are atheists (Cheng, Pagano, and Shariff 2018; Decosimo 2018; Zuckerman, Galen, and Pasquale 2016).

Atheists are more likely to engage in activism to promote their secularity than are other types of nonreligious people. Although now it is common to speak of an "atheist movement," several scholars have debated the "movementness" of more visibly political forms of atheism (Stahl 2010). Although these early debates made sense when nonreligion research was still emerging as an identifiable field, it is now clear that various secular organizations collaborate in a rich social movement space. In particular, American secularism is a dynamic and healthy social movement (Cimino and Smith 2014; Cragun and Fazzino 2017; LeDrew 2015).

Political Grievances and Activism

Grievances play a vital role in nonreligious activism (Kettell 2014). Grievances are real or imagined wrongs that serve as important preconditions for the emergence of a social movement (LeFebvre and Armstrong 2016; Snow 2013). Although not all grievances lead to activism, they supply a compelling backdrop to past and emerging forms of activism (Simmons 2018). The nonreligious enjoy immense freedoms in the Western world, but they have grievances about the ubiquity of religion in the public sphere and the marginalization of nonreligious identities (Smith 2013a). Some scholars even argue that the public sphere coerces the nonreligious into religious behavior because of the default assumption of religiousness (Beaman, Steele, and Pringnitz 2018).

One could easily see how the assumption of religiousness leads to conflict, especially in the United States, where politics and religion are inexorably linked (Campbell and Layman 2017). More concretely, surveys show that Americans remain uncomfortable with voting atheists into office and many would disapprove of their children marrying atheists (Edgell, Gerteis, and Hartmann 2006; Kalkan, Layman, and Green 2018; Weber et al. 2012). Although we are likely to see improvements in these as the nonreligious grow in number, the nonreligious are one of the least trusted minority groups in America. As a result, the nonreligious are likely to face stigma and discrimination for the foreseeable future (Cheng, Pagano, and Shariff 2018; Loren and Rambo 2018).

Atheists are cultural outsiders in many countries, including the United States (Edgell et al. 2016). By a cultural outsider, I mean that atheists do not receive full acceptance in American society. Other examples of cultural outsiders include racial and sexual minorities (Braunstein 2019). By not embracing a religious identity, Americans see this subset of the nonreligious as having rejected core political and cultural values associated with the United States and its national identity. Christian religious identity has long been a symbolic marker for Americans invested in distinguishing between those who have moral worth and non-Christian groups (including the nonreligious) who have often faced decreased trust and discrimination because of a pervasive Christian symbolic boundary marker (Whitehead and Scheitle 2017).

Because atheists remain cultural outsiders in the United States, they face perceived and actual discrimination and marginalization, especially when they are open about their nonbelief (Cragun et al. 2012). Some of the most common forms of marginalization include minor insults, harassment, exclusion, and physical abuse (Brewster et al. 2016; Cragun et al. 2012). Self-disclosing or "coming out" as an atheist is subject to resistance from one's social group, especially within religious communities. Although "out" atheists can face significant consequences for being out, many nonreligious people who have not yet self-disclosed expect resistance to their nonreligious identities, leading to psychological distress and lower physical well-being (Abbott and Mollen 2018).

Nonreligious responses to grievances, including perceived and actual discrimination and marginalization, involve challenging religion and its perceived imposition in the marketplace of ideas (Kettell 2015). Many of these challenges focus on equal rights, such as confronting communities that may infringe on nonreligious rights. Nonreligious activists have challenged government funding of religious organizations, sought to remove Ten Commandments monuments from public spaces, and tried to end prayer in public schools (Beaman 2015). The nonreligious also have been engaged in efforts to develop a sense of community around a shared *collective identity*, that is, a sense of "we-feeling," or sense of belonging that individuals feel because of their participation in social movement activities (Milan 2015).

Social movements build a collective identity through in-group/out-group relationships—the distinction between "us" and "others"—though sometimes those boundaries may be permeable. Collective identity plays a vital role in supporting group consciousness within social movements and organizations, especially when we consider the crucial role identity construction plays in raising awareness of shared grievances (Smith 2013b).

Nonreligious organizations such as the Council for Secular Humanism (CSH), the American Humanist Association (AHA), and the Atheist Alliance International (AAI) position themselves in opposition to religion and religious believers, mainly because they see both as threats to political and civil society. These strategies provide mechanisms that motivate nonreligious people to act on their grievances, that is, to "mobilize" around a nonreligious identity, destigmatizing that identity (e.g., atheism), and challenging religious beliefs in the public sphere (Guenther and Mulligan 2014; Smith 2013b).

Politics of New Atheism

I have so far discussed the political attitudes and affiliations of the nonreligious. In this section, I will discuss the sociopolitical impacts of atheist activism in the United States. I am focusing on atheism in this volume because atheism continues to dominate our public conversations about nonreligion and politics. Also, much of the scholarly attention regarding the nonreligious and their political activities concerns the emergence of New Atheism in the early twenty-first century.

Gary Wolf coined the term "New Atheism" to describe the politically charged books of public intellectuals in the aftermath of the September 11, 2001, terrorist attacks that took place in New York City, Washington, DC, and the sky above Pennsylvania (Kettell 2013). Four books by prominent atheists are relevant here: *The End of Faith: Religion, Terror, and the Future of Reason* by American neuroscientist Sam Harris in 2004; *Breaking the Spell: Religion as a Natural Phenomenon* by American philosopher Daniel Dennett in 2006; *The God Delusion* by British biologist Richard Dawkins in 2006; and *God Is Not Great: How Religion Poisons Everything* by British journalist Christopher Hitchens in 2007 (Dawkins 2016; Dennett 2007; Harris 2005; Hitchens 2008).

This emergent atheist "genre" of literature focuses on the scientific implausibility of religious claims while highlighting the sociopolitical consequences of those beliefs. Tonally, the New Atheists aim to treat religion like any other subject—with transparent critique (LeDrew 2012; McAnulla et al. 2018). New Atheism has been subject to criticism, with scholarly debates focusing on the politics of the movement. Although one should not confuse criticisms of New Atheism with criticisms of the broader category of nonreligious activism, sometimes it is difficult to separate the two, largely because of the impact of New Atheist intellectuals on organized atheist activism in recent years.

The politics of New Atheism focuses on the use of identity politics among atheist activists. Identity politics refers to politics whereby people relate to one another as members of groups based upon characteristics such as religion, race, gender, and sexual orientation (Kettell 2013; Smith 2013b; Taira 2016). Other scholarship focuses on the atheist movement's political aims, and the strategies "movement atheism" uses to achieve its goals or address the grievances of its supporters (McAnulla et al. 2018; Tomlins 2016). Still other approaches focus on New Atheism's public policy dimensions, especially its opposition to religious influence over public policy (Clements and Gries 2017; Franks 2017; Kettell 2013).

A central debate regarding New Atheism is whether the movement is liberal. One view is that New Atheism follows a long-standing liberal tradition of peaceful opposition to religion. For example, Marcus Schulzke argues that New Atheists' critique of religion raises necessary and important questions about the role of religion in the public sphere. According to this view, New Atheism is consistent with a liberal politics that shows that "absolutist systems of values" such as religion are harmful to the public sphere (Schulzke 2013: 790).

The dominant view, however, emphasizes New Atheism's intolerance and insensitivity toward cultural pluralism. For example, Amarasingam and Brewster argue that popular New Atheist authors hold views that do not mix well with multiculturalism (Amarasingam and Brewster 2016). Some critics also argue that New Atheism is Islamophobic (Clements and Gries 2017; Geissbühler 2002), a criticism that some New Atheist authors, for instance Sam Harris, reject.

Another major concern for critics of New Atheism is that it may contribute to a culture war over the position of religion in the public square. Scholars argue that New Atheism's differential treatment of Islam may fuel the *Clash of Civilizations* thesis, which argues that future conflicts will be between Western and Islamic civilizations. Several scholars argue that New Atheism's more strident form of atheist activism is contributing to the growth of right-wing anti-immigration sentiments (Amarasingam and Brewster 2016). Others link New Atheism with alt-right and anti-Muslim attitudes (Bradley and Tate 2010; Stahl 2010; Taira 2016; Torres 2017). Responses to these criticisms are rare outside of atheist communities, however, some scholars have added nuance to the discussion by highlighting the voices of ex-Muslims who embrace diversity but reject multiculturalism as a policy (Orenstein and Weismann 2016).

Political Tensions and Conflicts

Many nonreligious organizations focus on social events, often prioritizing community spaces for members. Recently, the failure of those safe spaces, that is, nonreligious organizations' unwillingness to address the needs of all members or potential members has introduced some social and political fault lines to the atheist movement. One of the primary fault lines that has appeared in recent years concerns gender inequality and related issues tied to diversity within nonreligious organizations (Guenther 2019).

The increased visibility of nonreligious political activism (especially the growth of atheist organizations) has raised questions about the composition of the nonreligious community (Schnabel et al. 2016). In particular, scholars have increasingly called for greater attention to the relationship between gender and nonreligion (Baker and Whitehead 2016; Edgell, Frost, and Stewart 2017; Stinson et al. 2013; Trzebiatowska 2018). They have also tried to shine a light on the imbalanced ethnic/racial composition of nonreligious organizations and how ethnicity/race impact nonreligious identification (Hutchinson 2018; Kolysh 2017; Taylor 2017). But most recent work in this area focuses on the gender imbalance among the nonreligious and the "sexism problem" with organized nonreligion (Schnabel et al. 2016).

On the one hand, nonreligious individuals are liberal and progressive about gender attitudes. On the other hand, women are underrepresented in nonreligious organizations (Schnabel et al. 2016). This apparent contradiction is frustratingly at odds with the goals of nonreligious activism because atheist activists frequently critique religion for its patriarchal gender norms, that is, norms that disproportionately favor men and masculinity over women and femininity (Baker and Whitehead 2016; Nyhagen 2017).

Many concerns about the gender imbalance within nonreligious organizations overlap with the broader consensus that men are more likely to be atheists. Explanations vary for why women are less likely to be atheists than men, but a promising area of research focuses on the intersection of social categories, including gender, education, and political identity, and how those categories shape the experiences of both men and women (Baker and Whitehead 2016). For example, being nonreligious may be less socially risky for men because they are more likely to have resources to avoid stigma. Because women's atheism violates certain gender expectations, nonreligious women may face greater discrimination (Edgell, Frost, and Stewart 2017). Because of the politicization of religion, politics and political positioning may affect one's likelihood of leaving organized religion and potentially identifying as an atheist. For example, those who are politically conservative are unlikely to claim no religion (Baker and Whitehead 2016).

Although accounting for intersecting social statuses when looking at gender differences in nonreligiosity is important, it is also worth noting that the nonreligious community shares features that privilege male voices over female voices (Amarasingam and Brewster 2016). Organized nonreligion emphasizes the values of rationality and objectivity. Some scholars argue that these values are masculine traits and potentially exclude women who may not share the same values (Guenther 2019). For example, women have expressed feelings of exclusion within the nonreligious community because of the pressure to hide or turn away from their emotions in favor of a more rational and scientific mode of behavior. For women who are not interested in science, reason, and critical thinking, organized nonreligion may be uninviting (Guenther 2019).

The privileging of science and rationality is not the only exclusionary tendency within organized nonreligion. Some members of nonreligious organizations have expressed hostility toward feminism. Because both atheism and feminism are devalued identities, several scholars have taken an interest in the relationship between atheism and feminism. Along with the contradictions regarding the gender representation with organized nonreligion, male atheists may claim to support women's rights while using science to reinforce their own sexist assumptions (Trzebiatowska 2018). Of course, some male atheists explicitly distance themselves from feminism, seeing humanism as sufficiently egalitarian despite the absence of gender equality within the nonreligious social movement space (Stinson et al. 2013; Trzebiatowska 2018).

Conclusion

The growth of nonreligious organizations, such as the American Atheists and the Freedom From Religion Foundation, and atheists' increased political participation has gained the attention of scholars. Although the political dimensions of nonreligion remain under-studied compared to other areas of inquiry, a growing body of research has painted a picture of nonreligious individuals' political attitudes, their political affiliations, and how they engage in political activities to address their grievances with religion in the public sphere. This chapter has introduced some themes and issues related to nonreligion and politics, including atheists' political mobilization. The nonreligious are ideologically left-wing and often progressive regarding social issues. Likewise, the nonreligious, especially those who are "out" as atheists, face stigma and discrimination, leading to political grievances. Nonreligious activism is a response to actual and perceived grievances. There are debates regarding the politics of atheism, including controversies regarding New Atheism and its goal of removing religion from the marketplace of ideas. In the United States, the nonreligious have increasingly mobilized around a collective identity that opposes religious beliefs in the public sphere, and we can expect future challenges with the continued growth of the nonreligious. Although the central premise of this chapter concerns the politics of nonreligion in relation to religious hegemony, there is also internal political conflict related to gender inequalities within organized nonreligion.

Further Reading and Online Resources

Quack, J., C. Schuh, and S. Kind (2019), *The Diversity of Nonreligion: Normativities and Contested Relations*, New York: Routledge.

Zuckerman, P., L.W. Galen, and F.L. Pasquale (2016), *The Nonreligious: Understanding Secular People and Societies*, New York: Oxford University Press.

References

Abbott, D.M. and D. Mollen (2018), "Atheism as a Concealable Stigmatized Identity: Outness, Anticipated Stigma, and Well-Being," *Counseling Psychologist*, 46 (6): 685–707. https://doi.org/10.1177/0011000018792669.

Amarasingam, A. and M.E. Brewster (2016), "The Rise and Fall of the New Atheism: Identity Politics and Tensions within US Nonbelievers," in R. Cipriani and F. Garelli (eds.), *Annual Review of the Sociology of Religion: Sociology of Atheism*, 118–36, Leiden: Brill.

Baker, J.O. and A.L. Whitehead (2016), "Gendering (Non)Religion: Politics, Education, and Gender Gaps in Secularity in the United States," *Social Forces*, 94 (4): 1623–45. https://doi.org/10.1093/sf/sov119.

Beaman, L.G. (2015), "Freedom of and Freedom from Religion: Atheist Involvement in Legal Cases," in G. Beaman and S. Tomlins (eds.), *Atheist Identities: Spaces and Social Contexts*, 39–52, Cham: Springer. https://doi.org/10.1007/978-3-319-09602-5_3.

Beaman, L.G. (2017), "Religious Diversity in the Public Sphere: The Canadian Case," *Religions*, 8 (12): 259. https://doi.org/10.3390/rel8120259.

Beaman, L.G., C. Steele, and K. Pringnitz (2018), "The Inclusion of Nonreligion in Religion and Human Rights," *Social Compass*, 65 (1): 43–61. https://doi.org/10.1177/0037768617745480.

Beit-Hallahmi, B. (2007), "Atheists: A Psychological Profile," in M. Martin (ed.), *Cambridge Companions to Philosophy, The Cambridge Companion to Atheism*, 300–17, New York: Cambridge University Press. https://doi.org/10.1017/CCOL0521842700.019.

Bilodeau, A., L. Turgeon, S. White, and A. Henderson (2018), "Strange Bedfellows? Attitudes toward Minority and Majority Religious Symbols in the Public Sphere," *Politics and Religion*, 11 (2): 309–33. https://doi.org/10.1017/S1755048317000748.

Blankholm, J. (2014), "The Political Advantages of a Polysemous Secular," *Journal for the Scientific Study of Religion*, 53 (4): 775–90. https://doi.org/10.1111/jssr.12152.

Bowman, N.A., A.N. Rockenbach, M.J. Mayhew, T.A. Riggers-Piehl, and T.D. Hudson (2017), "College Students' Appreciative Attitudes toward Atheists," *Research in Higher Education*, 58 (1): 98–118. https://doi.org/10.1007/s11162-016-9417-z.

Bradley, A. and A. Tate (2010), *The New Atheist Novel: Philosophy, Fiction and Polemic after 9/11*, London: Bloomsbury.

Braunstein, R. (2019), "Muslims as Outsiders, Enemies, and Others: The 2016 Presidential Election and the Politics of Religious Exclusion," in J.L. Mast and J.C. Alexander (eds.), *Politics of Meaning/Meaning of Politics: Cultural Sociology of the 2016 U.S. Presidential Election*, 185–206, Cham: Springer. https://doi.org/10.1007/978-3-319-95945-0_11.

Brewster, M.E., J. Hammer, J.S. Sawyer, A. Eklund, and J. Palamar (2016), "Perceived Experiences of Atheist Discrimination: Instrument Development and Evaluation," *Journal of Counseling Psychology*, 63 (5): 557–70. https://doi.org/10.1037/cou0000156.

Campbell, D.E. and G.C. Layman (2017), "The Politics of Secularism in the United States," in R.A. Scott and S.M. Kosslyn (eds.), *Emerging Trends in the Social and Behavioral Sciences*, Chichester: John Wiley. https://doi.org/10.1002/9781118900772.etrds0423.

Campbell, D.E., G.C. Layman, J.C. Green, and N.G. Sumaktoyo (2018), "Putting Politics First: The Impact of Politics on American Religious and Secular Orientations," *American Journal of Political Science*, 62 (3): 551–65. https://doi.org/10.1111/ajps.12365.

Cheng, Jr. Z.H., L.A. Pagano, and A.F. Shariff (2018), "The Development and Validation of the Microaggressions against Non-religious Individuals Scale (MANRIS)," *Psychology of Religion and Spirituality*, 10 (3): 254–62. https://doi.org/10.1037/rel0000203.

Cimino, R. and C. Smith (2014), *Atheist Awakening: Secular Activism and Community in America*, New York: Oxford University Press.

Clements, B. and P. Gries (2017), "'Religious Nones' in the United Kingdom: How Atheists and Agnostics Think about Religion and Politics," *Politics and Religion*, 10 (1): 161–85. https://doi.org/10.1017/S175504831600078X.

Coleman III, T.J., R.W. Hood Jr., H. Streib, J. Stinespring, and R. Cragun (2018), "An Introduction to Atheism, Agnosticism, and Nonreligious Worldviews," *Psychology of Religion and Spirituality*, 10 (3): 203–6. https://doi.org/10.1037/rel0000213.

Cragun, R.T. (2015), "Who Are the 'New Atheists'?," in G. Beaman and S. Tomlins (eds.), *Atheist Identities: Spaces and Social Contexts*, 195–211, Cham: Springer. https://doi.org/10.1007/978-3-319-09602-5_12.

Cragun, R.T. (2016), "Nonreligion and Atheism," in D. Yamane, (ed.), *Handbook of Religion and Society*, 301–20, Cham: Springer. https://doi.org/10.1007/978-3-319-31395-5_16.

Cragun, R. and L. Fazzino (2017), "'Splitters!': Lessons from Monty Python for Secular Organizations in the US," in R. Cragun, C. Manning, and L. Fazzini (eds.), *American Secularism*, 57–85, Berlin: DeGruyter. https://doi.org/10.1515/9783110458657-005.

Cragun, R.T. and J.H. Hammer (2011), "'One Person's Apostate Is Another Person's Convert': What Terminology Tells Us about Pro-Religious Hegemony in the Sociology of Religion," *Humanity & Society*, 35 (1–2): 149–75. https://doi.org/10.1177/016059761103500107.

Cragun, R.T., B. Kosmin, A. Keysar, J.H. Hammer, and M. Nielsen (2012), "On the Receiving End: Discrimination toward the Non-Religious in the United States," *Journal of Contemporary Religion*, 27 (1): 105–27. https://doi.org/10.1080/13537903.2012.642741.

Crandall, H. and C.M. Cunningham (2016), "Media Ecology and Hashtag Activism: #Kaleidoscope," *Explorations in Media Ecology*, 15 (1): 21–32. https://doi.org/10.1386/eme.15.1.21_1.

Dawkins, R. (2016), *The God Delusion*, London: Black Swan.

Decosimo, D. (2018), "For Big Comparison: Why the Arguments against Comparing Entire Religious Traditions Fail," *Religion Compass*, 12 (5–6): e12265. https://doi.org/10.1111/rec3.12265.

Dennett, D.C. (2007), *Breaking the Spell: Religion As a Natural Phenomenon*, New York: Penguin Books.

Djupe, P.A., J.R. Neiheisel, and K.H. Conger (2018), "Are the Politics of the Christian Right Linked to State Rates of the Nonreligious? The Importance of Salient Controversy," *Political Research Quarterly*, 71 (4): 910–22. https://doi.org/10.1177/1065912918771526.

Doane, M.J. and M. Elliott (2015), "Perceptions of Discrimination among Atheists: Consequences for Atheist Identification, Psychological and Physical Well-being," *Psychology of Religion and Spirituality*, 7 (2): 130–41. https://doi.org/10.1037/rel0000015.

Edgell, P., J. Gerteis, and D. Hartmann (2006), "Atheists as 'Other': Moral Boundaries and Cultural Membership in American Society," *American Sociological Review*, 71 (2): 211–34. https://doi.org/10.1177/000312240607100203.

Edgell, P., J. Frost, and E. Stewart (2017), "From Existential to Social Understandings of Risk: Examining Gender Differences in Nonreligion," *Social Currents*, 4 (6): 556–74. https://doi.org/10.1177/2329496516686619.

Edgell, P., D. Hartmann, E. Stewart, and J. Gerteis (2016), "Atheists and Other Cultural Outsiders: Moral Boundaries and the Non-Religious in the United States," *Social Forces*, 95 (2): 607–38. https://doi.org/10.1093/sf/sow063.

Evans, J.H. (2017), "Aversion to and Understanding of God Talk in the Public Sphere: A Survey Experiment," *Journal for the Scientific Study of Religion*, 56 (3): 459–80. https://doi.org/10.1111/jssr.12368.

Fisher, A.R. (2017), "A Review and Conceptual Model of the Research on Doubt, Disaffiliation, and Related Religious Changes," *Psychology of Religion and Spirituality*, 9 (4): 358–67. https://doi.org/10.1037/rel0000088.

Franks A.S. (2017), "Improving the Electability of Atheists in the United States: A Preliminary Examination," *Politics and Religion*, 10 (3): 597–621. https://doi.org/10.1017/S1755048317000293.

Fuist, T.N. (2018), "'Not Left-Wing, Just Human': The Integration of Personal Morality and Structural Critique in Progressive Religious Talk," *Politics and Religion*, 11 (1): 169–91. https://doi.org/10.1017/S1755048317000402.

Galen, L.W. (2009), "Profiles of the Godless," *Free Inquiry*, 29 (5): 41–5.

Geissbühler, S. (2002), "No Religion, No (Political) Values? Political Attitudes of Atheists in Comparison," *Journal for the Study of Religions and Ideologies*, 1 (2): 114–22.

Gorski, P.S. (2019), "The Politics of Religion and Language: Similar or Different?," *Social Science History*, 43 (2): 393–7. https://doi.org/10.1017/ssh.2019.11.

Guenther, K.M. (2019), "Secular Sexism: The Persistence of Gender Inequality in the US New Atheist Movement," *Women's Studies International Forum*, 72: 47–55. https://doi.org/10.1016/j.wsif.2018.11.007.

Guenther, K.M. and K. Mulligan (2014), "From the Outside in: Crossing Boundaries to Build Collective Identity in the New Atheist Movement," *Social Problems*, 60 (4): 457–75. https://doi.org/10.1525/sp.2013.60.4.457.

Harris, S. (2005), *The End of Faith: Religion, Terror, and the Future of Reason*, New York: W.W. Norton.

Hitchens, C. (2008), *God Is Not Great: How Religion Poisons Everything*, New York: Emblem Editions.

Hout, M. and C.S. Fischer (2002), "Why More Americans Have No Religious Preference: Politics and Generations," *American Sociological Review*, 67 (2): 165–90. https://doi.org/10.2307/3088891.

Hunsberger, B.E. (2010), *Atheists: A Groundbreaking Study of America's Nonbelievers*, Amhurst, NY: Prometheus Books.

Hutchinson, S. (2018), "Respectability among Heathens: Black Feminist Atheist Humanists," in A.B. Pinn (ed.), *Humanism and the Challenge of Difference*, 37–50, Cham: Springer. https://doi.org/10.1007/978-3-319-94099-1_3.

Hwang, K. and R.T. Cragun (2017), "Agnostic, Atheistic, and Nonreligious Orientations," in D.D. VonDras (ed.), *Better Health through Spiritual Practices: A Guide to Religious Behaviors and Perspectives that Benefit Mind and Body*, 309–33, Santa Barbara, CA: Praeger.

Jones, K.L., S. Noorbaloochi, J.T. Jost, R. Bonneau, J. Nagler, and J.A. Tucker (2018), "Liberal and Conservative Values: What We Can Learn from Congressional Tweets," *Political Psychology*, 39 (2): 423–43. https://doi.org/10.1111/pops.12415.

Kalkan, K.O., G.C. Layman, and J.C. Green (2018), "Will Americans Vote for Muslims? Cultural Outgroup Antipathy, Candidate Religion, and U.S. Voting Behavior," *Politics and Religion*, 11 (4): 798–829. https://doi.org/10.1017/S1755048318000342.

Kettell, S. (2013), "Faithless: The Politics of New Atheism," *Secularism and Nonreligion*, 2: 61–72.

Kettell, S. (2014), "Divided We Stand: The Politics of the Atheist Movement in the United States," *Journal of Contemporary Religion*, 29 (3): 377–91. https://doi.org/10.1080/13537903.2014.945722.

Kettell, S. (2015), "Non-religious Political Activism: Patterns of Conflict and Mobilisation in the United States and Britain," *Journal of Religion in Europe*, 8 (3–4): 365–91. https://doi.org/10.1163/18748929-00804007.

Kolysh, S. (2017), "Straight Gods, White Devils: Exploring Paths to Non-Religion in the Lives of Black LGBTQ People," *Secularism and Nonreligion*, 6 (2). https://doi.org/10.5334/snr.83.

Lassetter, B. and R. Neel (2019), "Malleable Liberals and Fixed Conservatives? Political Orientation Shapes Perceived Ability to Change," *Journal of Experimental Social Psychology*, 82: 141–51. https://doi.org/10.1016/j.jesp.2019.01.002.

Layman, G.C. and C.L. Weaver (2016), "Religion and Secularism among American Party Activists," *Politics and Religion*, 9 (2): 271–95. https://doi.org/10.1017/S1755048316000079.

LeDrew, S. (2012), "The Evolution of Atheism: Scientific and Humanistic Approaches," *History of the Human Sciences*, 25 (3): 70–87. https://doi.org/10.1177/0952695112441301.

LeDrew, S. (2015), "Atheism versus Humanism: Ideological Tensions and Identity Dynamics," in S. Tomlins and L. Beaman (eds.), *Atheist Identities: Spaces and Social Contexts*, 53–68, Cham: Springer. https://doi.org/10.1007/978-3-319-09602-5.

Lee, L. (2014), "Secular or Nonreligious? Investigating and Interpreting Generic 'Not Religious' Categories and Populations," *Religion*, 44 (3): 466–82. https://doi.org/10.1080/0048721X.2014.904035.

Lee, L. (2017), "What of Nonreligion in the Public Sphere?." http://eprints.lse.ac.uk/76424/ (accessed August 25, 2019).

LeFebvre, R.K. and C. Armstrong (2016), "Grievance-based Social Movement Mobilization in the #Ferguson Twitter Storm," *New Media & Society*, 20 (1): 8–28. https://doi.org/10.1177/1461444816644697.

Loren, D. and C. Rambo (2018), "'God Smites You!': Atheists' Experiences of Stigma, Identity Politics, and Queerness*," *Deviant Behavior*, 40 (4): 445–60. https://doi.org/10.1080/01639625.2018.1431039.

McAnulla, S., S. Kettell, M. Schulzke, S. Kettell, and M. Schulzke (2018), *The Politics of New Atheism*, 1st edn., Routledge Studies in Religion and Politics, New York: Routledge. https://doi.org/10.4324/9781315560465.

McCaffree, K. (2017), "American Nones," in K. McCaffree (ed.), *The Secular Landscape: The Decline of Religion in America*, 203–48, Cham: Springer. https://doi.org/10.1007/978-3-319-50262-5_5.

Milan, S. (2015), "From Social Movements to Cloud Protesting: The Evolution of Collective Identity," *Information, Communication & Society*, 18 (8): 887–900. https://doi.org/10.1080/1369118X.2015.1043135.

Minton, E.A., L.R. Kahle, and C.-H. Kim (2015), "Religion and Motives for Sustainable Behaviors: A Cross-Cultural Comparison and Contrast," *Journal of Business Research*, Elsevier, 68 (9): 1937–44. https://doi.org/10.1016/J.JBUSRES.2015.01.003.

Morgan, G.S. and D.C. Wisneski (2017), "The Structure of Political Ideology Varies between and within People: Implications for Theories about Ideology's Causes," *Social Cognition*, 35 (4): 395–414. https://doi.org/10.1521/soco.2017.35.4.395.

Nyhagen, L. (2017), "The Lived Religion Approach in the Sociology of Religion and Its Implications for Secular Feminist Analyses of Religion," *Social Compass*, 64 (4): 495–511. https://doi.org/10.1177/0037768617727482.

Orenstein, Z. and I. Weismann (2016), "Neither Muslim nor Other: British Secular Muslims," *Islam and Christian–Muslim Relations*, 27 (4): 379–95. https://doi.org/10.1080/09596410.2016.1148892.

Ribberink, E., P. Achterberg, and D. Houtman (2017), "Secular Tolerance? Anti-Muslim Sentiment in Western Europe," *Journal for the Scientific Study of Religion*, 56 (2): 259–76. https://doi.org/10.1111/jssr.12335.

Robertson, J. and S. Cardon (2003), "Political Perceptions among a Peculiar People: Conservatism in Committed vs. Less Committed Latter-day Saints," *Sigma: Journal of Political and International Studies*, 21 (6): 70–81.

Scheitle, C.P., K.E. Corcoran, and C. Halligan (2018), "The Rise of the Nones and the Changing Relationships between Identity, Belief, and Behavior," *Journal of Contemporary Religion*, 33 (3): 567–79. https://doi.org/10.1080/13537903.2018.1535379.

Schieman, S., A. Bierman, and L. Upenieks (2019), "Beyond 'Heartless Conservative' and 'Bleeding Heart Liberal' Caricatures: How Religiosity Shapes the Relationship between Political Orientation and Empathy," *Journal for the Scientific Study of Religion*, 58 (2): 360–77. https://doi.org/10.1111/jssr.12595.

Schnabel, L. (2016), "Religion and Gender Equality Worldwide: A Country-Level Analysis," *Social Indicators Research*, 129 (2): 893–907. https://doi.org/10.1007/s11205-015-1147-7.

Schnabel, L., M. Facciani, A. Sincoff-Yedid, and L. Fazzino (2016), "Gender and Atheism: Paradoxes, Contradictions, and an Agenda for Future Research," in R. Cipriani and F. Garelli (eds.), *Annual Review of the Sociology of Religion: Sociology of Atheism*, 75–97, Leiden: Brill.

Schnell, T. (2015), "Dimensions of Secularity (DoS): An Open Inventory to Measure Facets of Secular Identities," *International Journal for the Psychology of Religion*, 25 (4): 272–92. https://doi.org/10.1080/10508619.2014.967541.

Schulzke, M. (2013), "The Politics of New Atheism," *Politics and Religion*, 6 (4): 778–99. https://doi.org/10.1017/S1755048313000217.

Sherkat, D.E. (2008), "Beyond Belief: Atheism, Agnosticism, and Theistic Certainty in the United States," *Sociological Spectrum*, 28 (5): 438–59. https://doi.org/10.1080/02732170802205932.

Silver, C.F. (2013), "Atheism, Agnosticism, and Nonbelief: A Qualitative and Quantitative Study of Type and Narrative," PhD diss., University of Tennessee at Chattanooga.

Silver, C.F., T.J. Coleman, R.W. Hood, and J.M. Holcombe (2014), "The Six Types of Nonbelief: A Qualitative and Quantitative Study of Type and Narrative," *Mental Health, Religion & Culture*, 17 (10): 990–1001. https://doi.org/10.1080/13674676.2014.987743.

Simmons, E.S. (2018), "Targets, Grievances, and Social Movement Trajectories," *Comparative Political Studies*, published online October 29. https://doi.org/10.1177/0010414018806532.

Smith, J.M. (2013a), "Atheists in America: Investigating Identity, Meaning, and Movement," PhD thesis, University of Colorado at Boulder.

Smith, J.M. (2013b), "Creating a Godless Community: The Collective Identity Work of Contemporary American Atheists," *Journal for the Scientific Study of Religion*, 52 (1): 80–99. https://doi.org/10.1111/jssr.12009.

Snow, D.A. (2013), "Grievances, Individual and Mobilizing," in D.A. Snow, D. Della Porta, B. Klandermans, and D. McAdam (eds.), *The Wiley Blackwell Encyclopedia of Social and Political Movements*, Chichester: Wiley-Blackwell. https://doi.org/10.1002/9780470674871.wbespm100.

Stahl, W.A. (2010), "One-Dimensional Rage: The Social Epistemology of the New Atheism and Fundamentalism," in Amarnath Amarasingam (ed.), *Religion and the New Atheism: A Critical Approach*, 95–108, Leiden: Brill. https://doi.org/10.1163/ej.9789004185579.i-253.38.

Stinespring, J. and R. Cragun (2015), "Simple Markov Model for Estimating the Growth of Nonreligion in the United States," *Science, Religion and Culture*, 2: 96–103.

Stinson, R., K. Goodman, C. Bermingham, and S. Ali (2013), "Do Atheism and Feminism Go Hand-in-Hand?: A Qualitative Investigation of Atheist Men's Perspectives about Gender Equality," *Secularism and Nonreligion*, 2: 39–60. http://doi.org/10.5334/snr.ak.

Taira, T. (2016), "New Atheism as Identity Politics," in M. Guest and E. Arweck (eds.), *Religion and Knowledge: Sociological Perspectives*, 113–30, London: Routledge.

Taylor, K.D. (2017), "Beyond Atheism: An Intersectional Approach to Exploring Secular Identity and Religion among Black Women," MA diss., University of Texas at San Antonio.

Thiessen, J. and S. Wilkins-Laflamme (2017), "Becoming a Religious None: Irreligious Socialization and Disaffiliation," *Journal for the Scientific Study of Religion*, 56 (1): 64–82. https://doi.org/10.1111/jssr.12319.

Tomlins, S. (2016), "Navigating Atheist Identities: An Analysis of Nonreligious Perceptions and Experiences in the Religiously Diverse Canadian City of Ottawa," PhD thesis, University of Ottawa.

Torres, P. (2017), "From the Enlightenment to the Dark Ages: How 'New Atheism' Slid into the Alt-right," *Salon*, July 29. https://www.salon.com/2017/07/29/from-the-enlightenment-to-the-dark-ages-how-new-atheism-slid-into-the-alt-right/ (accessed January 28, 2019).

Trzebiatowska, M. (2018), "'Atheism Is Not the Problem. The Problem Is Being a Woman': Atheist Women and Reasonable Feminism," *Journal of Gender Studies*, 28 (4): 475–87. https://doi.org/10.1080/09589236.2018.1523053.

Voas, D. and M. Chaves (2016), "Is the United States a Counterexample to the Secularization Thesis?," *American Journal of Sociology*, 121 (5): 1517–56. https://doi.org/10.1086/684202.

Weber, S.R., K.I. Pargament, M.E. Kunik, J.W. Lomax, and M.A. Stanley (2012), "Psychological Distress among Religious Nonbelievers: A Systematic Review," *Journal of Religion and Health*, 51 (1): 72–86. https://doi.org/10.1007/s10943-011-9541-1.

Whitehead, A.L. and C.P. Scheitle (2017), "We the (Christian) People: Christianity and American Identity from 1996 to 2014," *Social Currents*, 5 (2): 157–72. https://doi.org/10.1177/2329496517725333.

Wilkins-Laflamme, S. (2015), "How Unreligious Are the Religious 'Nones'? Religious Dynamics of the Unaffiliated in Canada," *Canadian Journal of Sociology*, 40 (4): 477–500.

Woodhead, L. (2014), "Launch Series: The 'Fuzzy' Nones," [Blog] NSRN, March 7. http://faithdebates.org.uk/wp-content/uploads/2014/04/Linda-Woodhead-the-fuzzy-nones_.pdf (accessed August 26, 2019).

Zuckerman, P., L.W. Galen, and F.L. Pasquale (2016), *The Nonreligious: Understanding Secular People and Societies*, New York: Oxford University Press.

Glossary Terms

Collective identity A shared definition of a group, founded on members' interests, experiences, and feelings of solidarity with the social group, organization, or social movement. A strong collective identity involves cultural, emotional, and psychological connections with an imagined or active community.

Grievances Perceived or actual wrongs that may motivate activist mobilization. Grievances are necessary but not sufficient conditions for participation in social movements.

Marginalization A process by which an individual or social group is excluded from the dominant community and social institutions. Marginalization often involves a disconnect from institutions as well as the disadvantages this distancing incurs such as unequal access to social, political, or economic resources.

New Atheism A twenty-first-century nonreligious movement that is known for its strident critique of religion in the public sphere. Some characteristics of New Atheism include a privileging of science, rationality, and its expansive political activities including legal cases, protests, and rallies.

Public sphere The community space that facilitates democratic practice, contention, and debate. The public sphere includes public opinion, political activities, public spaces, for instance libraries, and mechanisms of communication such as the mass media.

10

Nonreligion and Health

David Speed

A goal of this chapter is to "push back" against the erroneous conclusion that *nones* are somehow less healthy than those who are religious, believe in god(s), or who are spiritual. Although there are tens of millions of nones within Canada, Mexico, and the United States (see Figure 10.1), studies addressing this growing body of "religious minorities" are rare. It is somewhat ironic that, in an article devoted to *non*religion and health, much of the discussion will address religion and health. This inclusive approach is not to promote a "fair and balanced debate," rather, it is born purely of necessity. If one wants to understand the nonreligion–health relationship, they must have a broader view of the religion–health puzzle. There is a widely promulgated notion that *religion and spirituality* (R/S) promote well-being, and that to not pray or to be an *atheist* or to not attend church has dire consequences with respect to health. These misconceptions about the nonreligion–health relationship illustrate why a discussion on this topic is warranted. To be clear, there is not *a* relationship between these constructs there are *many* relationships. The discussion of research throughout this chapter is careful but frank. However, it is important to remember that generalizations may not capture the full nuance of the field (see Further Reading and Online Resources).

Religion/Spirituality Goes Mainstream

Prior to the mid-1970s, research in general and psychological research especially held a dim view toward religion and its impact on wellness (see Ellis 1962). This attitude was fueled by the poorly tested assertion that religion was indicative of stunted mental growth, and there was a widespread belief that religious people would be less healthy than the nonreligious. However by the mid-1980s, an accumulation of research studies began to suggest that there were no health differences between the religious and

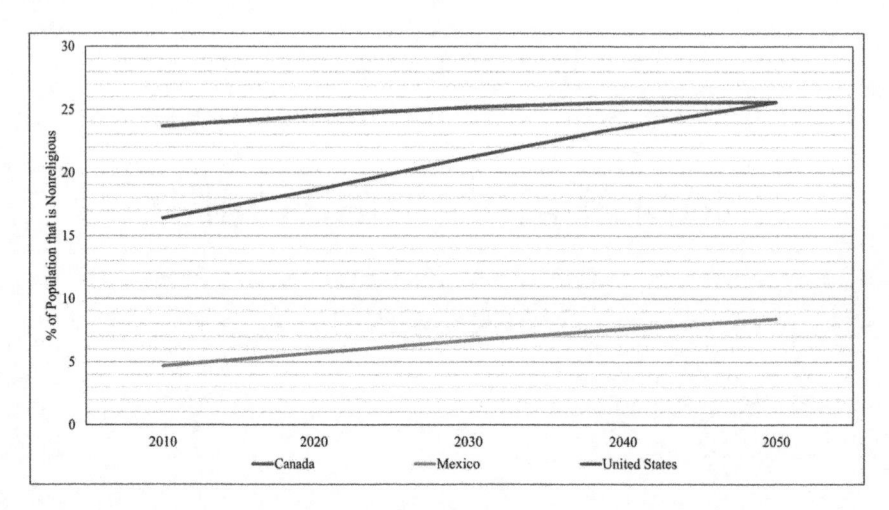

FIGURE 10.1 *Projected growth of the religiously unaffiliated populations in Canada, Mexico, and the United States.* Source: *Created by author from Pew Research Center (2015) data.*

nonreligious (Sharkey and Malony 1986: 641), while literature reviews suggested that there may be a *positive* relationship between religion and health (Levin and Schiller 1987). Around this time, research addressing religion and health grew exponentially and within thirty years there were thousands of studies, many of which concluded that religion (and eventually spirituality) was an important part of human well-being. Religion/spirituality was eventually implicated in decreased rates of mental illness (Koenig 2009: 285–8), increased rates of mental flourishing (Myers 2008), diminished substance abuse (Desmond, Ulmer, and Bader 2013; Koenig 2009: 288–9), delayed mortality (Jarvis and Northcott 1987: 817–20), and greater happiness (Francis, Robbins, and White 2003: 52), among other findings.

Scientific research does not happen in a vacuum, it is often incorporated into policies and practices. Over time there were calls from various researchers to incorporate R/S into an increasing number of traditionally secular areas. This advocacy manifested in a variety of ways: encouraging R/S to be incorporated into therapy (Koenig 2008; Masters 2010; Ventis 1995; Whitley 2012), encouraging R/S to be incorporated into patient care (Callister et al. 2004; Greenstreet 1999; O'Brien 2017), encouraging R/S to be incorporated into screening soldiers (Hufford, Fritts, and Rhodes 2010; Pargament and Sweeney 2011; Peterson, Park, and Castro 2011), among other policies and practices. The push for including religion (and spirituality) into these domains was not necessarily problematic. If something is healthy then it makes sense to investigate its adoption in health-relevant areas. But this push toward applying this research was done against a backdrop of little to no research on the health of the nones (Brewster et al. 2014; Hwang, Hammer, and Cragun 2011; Zuckerman 2009). To put it bluntly, researchers were aggressively including R/S in numerous arenas but were not fully cognizant of the negative impact of those efforts on irreligious and nonreligious groups. Eventually there was pushback against these intrusions by different researchers working independently (e.g., Hammer, Cragun, and Hwang 2013; Poole, Cook, and Higgo 2019), but this did not substantially change the inertia of how many scholars and policy makers adopted elements of R/S research.

Determining the Boundaries of the Religion–Health Relationship

At its heart, science is all about knockdown, dragged out arguments. Careful, dedicated scientists relish in debating ideas not because they enjoy tearing down other people's work (well, some of us do) but because it is an effective method to determine what is true. During the decades' long elevation of R/S research on health, there were sporadic research papers that noted unusually absent findings within the R/S–health field. The crux of the issue was this: if R/S promotes health, then it would stand to reason that groups such as the nones should be less healthy. In other words, if you compare your average religious person and your average none, the former should be healthier. However, much of the literature that had emerged in the few decades since the 1980s had a difficult time establishing consistent, *meaningful* differences between these groups. While the literature could confirm that R/S was often associated with health—the logically convergent finding (i.e., the nones were less healthy) could not be established, which raised several red flags.

An important clue to these suspiciously absent findings was the observation that the R/S–health relationship changed, sometimes quite significantly, based on who participated in research studies. Researchers who used large or nationally representative general samples tended to find a muted R/S–health relationship, while smaller studies that recruited from churches or had predominantly religious samples, tended to report stronger "pro-R/S" findings (e.g., Benjamins, Trinitapolli, and Ellison 2006: 600; Ellison et al. 2011: 124; Gauthier et al. 2006: 143; Krause and Wulff 2004: 141; Ryan and Francis 2012: 777). Basically, studies that excluded nones were different from the ones that included them. When researchers began to expand the scope of their investigation to include nones, the "robust R/S–health relationship" became noticeably attenuated (i.e., it ceased to matter). Researchers still sporadically found positive connections between R/S–health in large-scale samples, but the majority of these relationships were weak, absent, or even sporadically in favor of the nones (e.g., Benjamins 2005: 488; Hayward et al. 2016: 1032; Levin and Markides 1985: 66; Nowakowski and Sumerau 2017: 5).

Part of the reason that this nonreligion–health connection had been missed was that the R/S–health literature was concerned with the presence of R/S in individuals and not its *absence*. In other words, scholars were studying how specific religious activities (e.g., attending church on Sunday) or being religious in certain ways (e.g., using a belief in the afterlife to cope with challenging situations) were beneficial, but there was virtually no consideration for how not doing these things may be beneficial or detrimental. Even when national studies included nones within their samples—which was an important step in resolving the conflicts within the literature—there was no substantive exploration of this group's experience with R/S. For example, several studies that sampled nones also established that specific religious beliefs and behaviors (e.g., attending church, prayer, religiosity) had salutary effects. Researchers then went on to conclude that the health benefits of these religious beliefs and behaviors must be true of everyone—and because nones were included within samples—religious beliefs and behaviors were assumed to benefit nones as well (Krause 2003, 2005; Krause and Hayward 2012; Levin and Markides 1985; Park Lee et al. 2013; Schnall et al. 2010).

The assumption that the relationship between R/S–health exists and is positive for nones is stunning for several reasons. First, nonreligious groups are less likely to report having religious beliefs and behaviors (Baker and Smith 2009: 726); atheists, not surprisingly, go to church less frequently than believers do. But, and this is important, some atheists do attend religious services. Atheists who attend religious services are, not surprisingly, often motivated to do so for very different reasons than are theists who attend religious services. At the very least this would suggest that atheists attending church should be treated differently than *theists* attending church. Second, the nonreligious *intentionally* indicate that they are not a part of a religious tradition. This group of respondents is literally indicating that they would not like to be identified as religious—suggesting that their relationship with religion may be outside of the norm. Third, there is no theoretical model within the R/S–health field that suggests that religious beliefs and behaviors are *intrinsically* beneficial (Cragun et al. [2016] make this point clearly). Even if the first two points were somehow rendered irrelevant, the assumption *still* would not fit within the theoretical framework of the R/S–health field. In summary, researchers implicitly assumed that a group that was *actively disengaged* from R/S would still benefit from R/S. It is difficult to draw a parallel example that does justice to this assumption, but it would be on par with assuming that because many people generally like eating steak, *vegans* specifically would be happier if they ate more steak as well.

Readers should note that, individually, these studies had done nothing wrong on a case-by-case basis. Authors of these research studies often provided defensible rationales for why they chose to approach a research question the way that they did. However, the sum of the R/S–health field is comprised of the thousands of analytical decisions made by hundreds of individual studies, all of which tended to not substantively address the nonreligion–health question. Unsurprisingly, later research revealed that several of the health benefits associated with religious beliefs and behaviors were indeed contingent on a person's R/S identity, and when atheists and nones engaged in R/S activities they actually reported *poorer* health (Speed 2017: 247–52; Speed and Fowler 2016: 993–6, 2017: 302–3). This is a microcosm of the nonreligion–health field; researchers are often fighting an uphill battle to "defend" the health of nones against overreaching statements about the benefits of religion and spirituality.

Explanations for the Religion–Health Link

Despite the R/S–health relationship being hit-and-miss, it should be acknowledged that researchers sporadically find *some* salutary relationships. So, what of these? Are nones at a health disadvantage because of these scattered positive associations? Within the R/S–health field there are several theories that have been proffered to account for why "more R/S = better health." I will address two of these explanations (George, Ellison, and Larson 2002; Koenig and Larson 2002). One of the more intuitive reasons why R/S might promote health is that it encourages social support, which is the friends and family that an individual has in their personal network. Social support is a widely studied area of social science and encompasses not only the people one can rely on but also memberships within organizations (Jacobson 1986). Given that humans evolved as a social species, it is unsurprising to find that humans with higher levels of social support tend to be mentally and physically healthier (Antonucci, Fuhrer, and Jackson 1990; Cobb 1976; Uchino 2009).

If you were to list the benefits associated with social support and compare it to the list of benefits associated with R/S, beyond both of them acting as a "stress buffer" in bad times (Wills, Yaeger, and Sandy 2003), you would find a high degree of overlap. Both social support and R/S promote psychological wellness, both are associated with a lowered prevalence of mental illness, and both are associated with lowered substance abuse. In a twist that *really* muddles things up, researchers repeatedly note that one of the benefits of R/S is that it promotes social support (Morton, Lee, and Martin 2017: 17; Steffen, Masters, and Baldwin 2017: 165). Given the connection between R/S and social support, researchers have theorized that different health benefits associated with R/S are achieved in part *through* social support (Fenelon and Danielsen 2016: 56; Lim and Putnam 2010: 924; Salsman et al. 2005: 529). People high on R/S will have highly structured weekly meeting times where they get regular social support (e.g., mosque, synagogue, church attendance), while people low on R/S generally do not have these regular activities. Consequently, some research has found that when you control for social support, the relationship between church attendance and health is attenuated (Ai et al. 2013: 83; Fenelon and Danielsen 2016). Basically, R/S is legitimately predicting well-being, but only because it is so strongly associated with promoting social support.

A separate theoretical explanation for the R/S–health relationship is that people who are higher in R/S may adopt a behavior or avoid a behavior because they are religious or spiritual. This encouragement (*prescription*) or discouragement (*proscription*) can have health implications, but depends on which behaviors are being targeted. For example, there are proscriptions in Judaism about wearing clothing of mixed fibers, and some groups of observant Jews will make efforts to live up to these standards. In this case there is a religious proscription that influences behavior, but not one that affects a *health* behavior (polyester-cotton blends are perhaps fatal to a sense of fashion, but little else). However, Judaism also has proscriptions against intoxicants, which has implications for health. Consequently, if a researcher were to find that religious adherents are less likely to experience cirrhosis, heart disease, stroke, and early mortality (Jarvis and Northcott 1987; Seybold and Hill 2001: 22), this could be plausibly linked to behavioral proscriptions.

One of the more consistent findings within R/S–health research is that R/S is positively associated with reduced substance use and dependence (i.e., alcohol, cigarettes, illegal drugs). This relationship has likely drawn the largest amount of cross-cultural support in North America (Canada [Baetz et al. 2006: 658; Tuck et al. 2017: 2033], Mexico [De Santis et al. 2016: 22; Hodge, Marsiglia, and Nieri 2011: 142; Marsiglia et al. 2005: 591], and the United States [Michalak, Trocki, and Bond 2007: 273–4; Neymotin and Downing-Matibag 2013: 560–3; Smith and Farias 2002: 12–13]), and other researchers have reported a persistent effect within the broader international community (cf. DeCamp and Smith 2019: 215–17; Tonigan, Miller, and Schermer 2002: 537–9). Because nones are not prohibited from partaking in drugs or alcohol and are therefore more likely to imbibe these substances, this may be construed as a health penalty for nonreligion. But, even this finding is not as simple as it sounds. For instance, people higher on R/S may lie about drug and alcohol use because of social desirability. Or, people may drift away from R/S because of the belief–behavior inconsistency of consuming drugs/alcohol while being religiously affiliated (Uecker, Regnerus, and Vaaler 2007). So, the R/S–substance use connection may be a genuine (albeit small) and probably indirect relationship—but it also may be a product of other processes that are tied into being religious or spiritual.

Researchers in the R/S–health field will also note that R/S is associated with delayed sexual debut (Sprecher and Treger 2015: 939), negative attitudes toward premarital sex (Petersen and Donnenwerth 1997: 1081), greater reported intentions to avoid risky sex (McNamara et al. 2010: 32), and reduced abortion rates (Adamczyk and Felson 2008: 31–2). Ignoring that R/S is only a minor predictor of these things (Adamczyk and Felson 2008: 27, 33; Holway and Hernandez 2017: 405–6) and that there are complex processes that are tied to decision-making regarding sex (e.g., substance use [Caldeira et al. 2009: 14]; nonreligious social factors [Neymotin and Downing-Matibag 2013: 560–3]), it is important to note that several of these outcomes are irrelevant to health. Youth having *consensual and informed* sex is not detrimental to health; the notions of "virginal purity" or "waiting until marriage" are subjectively important to some but not others. Even so, there is no empirical evidence that they improve health. Pointing out that religious or spiritual youth adhere to R/S ideals is *only* relevant if those prescriptions or proscriptions are empirically salutary, and in the case of abstinence before marriage, the evidence suggests it is not salutary.

The objective health issues arising from youth having sex, namely unwanted pregnancy and sexually transmitted infections, are reducible with safe sex practices (see Figure 10.2). However, people reporting higher levels of R/S report *fewer* parental discussions about contraception (Regnerus 2005: 94–5) and *less knowledge* about contraception (Crosby and Yarber 2001: 419; Lindberg, Maddow-Zimet, and Boonstra 2016: 624). State-level research suggests that religiosity is correlated with higher teen birthrates even when controlling for abortion and income (Strayhorn and Strayhorn

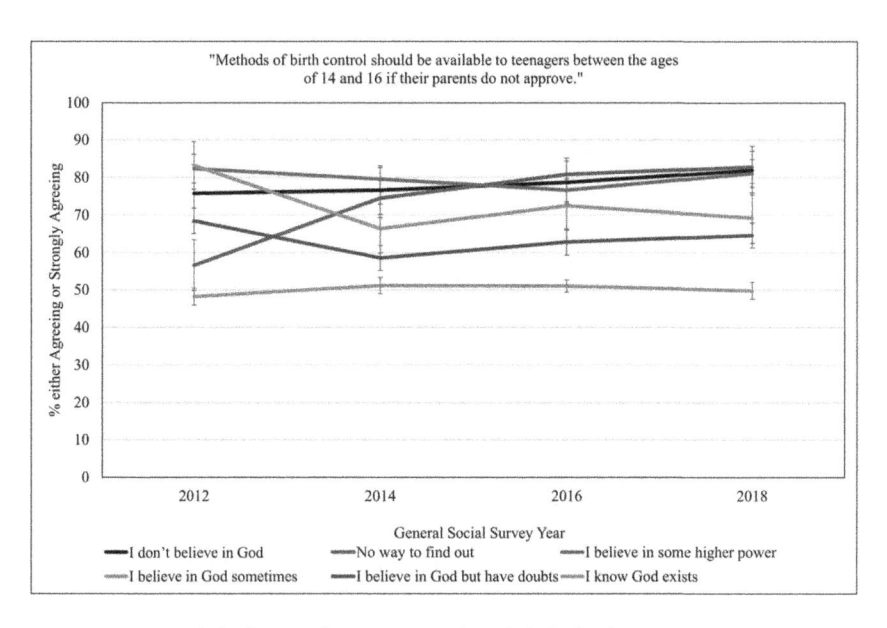

FIGURE 10.2 *How belief in God is associated with beliefs about teenagers' access to birth control (with linearized error bars).* Source: *Created by author from General Social Survey data for 2012, 2014, 2016, and 2018.*

2009), which has substantial impacts on adolescent developmental trajectories. Abstinence-only sexual education programs, which tend to be religiously motivated (Baker, Smith, and Stoss 2015: 242–3; Waxman 2004: 15–16), do not work (Stanger-Hall and Hall 2011: 4–5; Trenholm et al. 2007: 33) and are rife with misinformation about HIV prevention, condom effectiveness, abortion risks (Ott and Santelli 2007; Waxman 2004), and exclude lesbian, gay, bisexual, transgender, and queer/questioning (LGBTQ) youth (Elia and Eliason 2010). This is an unambiguous case in which not only is R/S *not* healthy, it has a substantial likelihood of causing harm.

Is Religion/Spirituality Special?

To recap, the two most prominent explanations to account for the R/S–health relationship are social support and behavioral prescriptions or proscriptions; in basic terms, "friends" and "health choices." These explanations are both logical, simple, and empirically supported—and they also happen to not be unique to religion. While people can build friendships, and socialize because they are religious or spiritual, the same thing is true of people playing on sports teams (Babiss and Gangwisch 2009: 379–82) or being involved with chess clubs on the internet (Ginsburg and Weisband 2002: 2233). Yes, R/S is a relatively easy way to meet people and to cultivate a social support network, but the benefits extracted from R/S vis-à-vis social support are not something only attainable through religious or spiritual views. While this is admittedly a somewhat reductionist perspective on a large and complex field, there is a real chance that much of the R/S–health relationship is just a repackaged benefit of social participation. Functionally, researchers are agog over R/S promoting a bevy of positive health outcomes, while simultaneously ignoring that R/S is structurally identical to any number of activities that promote identical positive outcomes. In other words, friendship and supportive networks are great for health, irrespective of their source.

In a similar fashion, it is entirely plausible that many listed benefits of R/S are a product of the prescriptions and proscriptions that are embedded within the complex structure of disparate ideologies. It is evident that not drinking, not smoking, and not doing drugs because of religious or spiritual concerns will produce better health outcomes. But it is also equally evident that not drinking, not smoking, and not doing drugs because you are trying to win a $20 wager *will also produce better health outcomes*. To be clear: the *belief* that produces the abstention is irrelevant to the *benefits* of that abstention. While R/S certainly has the "metaphysical infrastructure" to encourage teetotalling within its more devout followers (Meyers et al. 2017: 107–9), the benefits are not intrinsically tied to religion and spirituality. The benefits are tied to the abstention from intoxicating and harmful substances. It should also be acknowledged that R/S is associated with fewer unwanted pregnancies because its adherents are not having sex, not because R/S is doing something specifically health-promoting. Celibacy is an effective method in which to avoid pregnancy, but this is true regardless of the motivating factors. Proponents of R/S, who would boast of the reduced pregnancy rate associated with R/S viewpoints, are akin to Montana bragging about its lack of tsunami deaths. Yes, the claim is true in an absolute sense, but one only need to look at the absence of an ocean on the state's border to be dubious of the statement's virtues.

Nonreligion and Health

So, what *is* the relationship between nonreligion and health? Besides the somewhat-consistent findings between R/S and diminished substance use, the nonreligion–health field is a mixture of a few positive results, a few negative results, and a whole lot of *null results*. The term "null results" is the academic way of saying that two statistical values are within each other's error of the estimate 95 percent of the time—which is a complicated way of saying, "We can't find a difference between Group A and Group B." Every time researchers *fail to establish* that nones are less healthy, that religiosity is good, or that going to church protects against some health condition these are counted as null results. For example, a study that looks at three R/S predictors and five health outcomes will be looking to find a relationship for *fifteen different comparisons*; given that studies often only find limited support for R/S–health, it means that the bulk of results are often null. Null results are tricky to interpret within academia because we

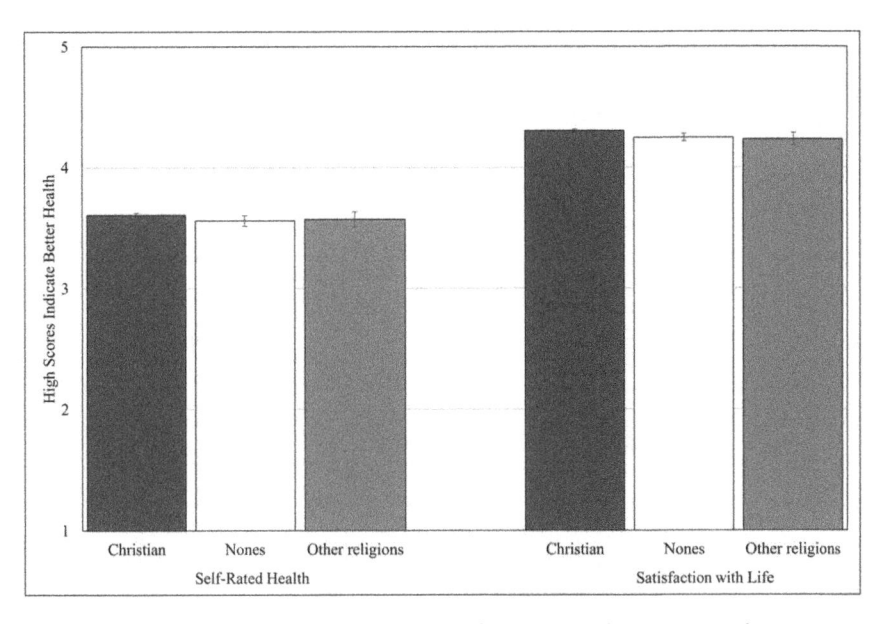

FIGURE 10.3 *Self-reported health data from the 2011 and 2012 Canadian Community Health Survey by religious affiliation (with standard error bars).*

are not always sure if there is *genuinely* no difference between groups or whether researchers have done a poor job looking for differences. Because of this ambiguity we're going to skip discussing the large field of null results within the R/S–health field. Overall, however, there are *few* differences between nones and R/S groups (e.g., Figure 10.3 shows that while Christians and nones report *literally* different scores for self-rated health and satisfaction with life, these scores are *statistically* equivalent), and when differences emerge they tend to be small and not super important (Figure 10.4 shows that people who attend church report statistically higher levels of satisfaction with life and somewhat better self-rated health, but the differences are tiny).

Nonreligion's salutary effects

Mexico has a relatively small number of nonreligious citizens, even when grouping atheists and agnostics in with the religiously unaffiliated, only 7 percent of the population are nones (Duro 2018: 4; though this estimate varies by survey and study). In some circumstances, nonreligion is associated with *better* health. Mexican and Hispanic respondents who are nones are more likely to perceive mental illness as having a biological basis and not having a spiritual etiology (De Santis et al. 2016: 22). In other words, when confronted by a person claiming to be an agent of Satan, nonreligious people are more likely to call a psychiatrist than a priest. While not a health outcome

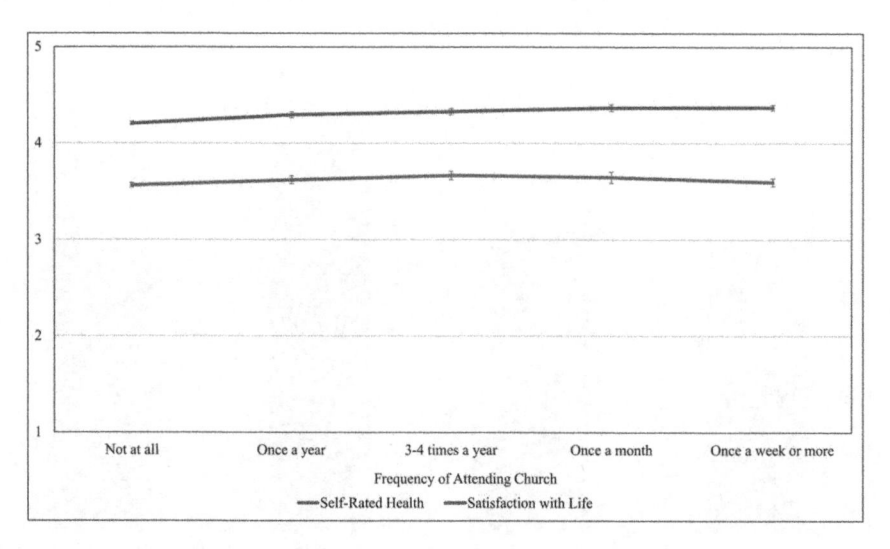

FIGURE 10.4 *Church attendance predicting self-rated health and satisfaction with life in the combined 2011 and 2012 Canadian Community Health Survey (with standard error bars).*

per se, attitudes toward health are important because they predict the response that an individual will make. Arguably, perceiving mental health as a medical issue—as opposed to a metaphysical one—is important.

From an American perspective, data from the 2010 Baylor Religion Survey (BRS) revealed that, when controlling for level of community participation (including religious participation) and other covariates, self-identified American atheists reported less general anxiety, less social anxiety, less paranoia, less obsession, and less compulsion than (at different times) evangelical Protestants, mainline Protestants, black Protestants, Catholics, Jews, other religions, and nones who believed in God (Baker, Stroope, and Walker 2018: 52). Data from the Landmark Spirituality and Health Survey (LSHS) indicated that atheists, when compared to the religiously affiliated, have a lower BMI, fewer chronic conditions, and fewer daily limitations (Hayward et al. 2016: 1032). Basically, not only were American atheists not "doing poorly," they were thriving with respect to several assessed health outcomes. Research into the health of religiously unaffiliated Americans also shows a small number of positive findings with respect to preventative care (e.g., vaccination rates [Bodson et al. 2017: 7]).

Nationally representative data for Canadians reveal that people with lower levels of spirituality are less likely to report depression, mania, past personality disorders, and social phobias (Baetz et al. 2006: 657–8), while other findings suggest that nonspirituality is associated with less depression (Baetz et al. 2004: 820–1). Using data from New Brunswick and Manitoba, Speed (2017: 375) found that women who did not value religion or were not religiously affiliated were more likely to have gone for cervical cancer screening in their lifetime. Data from the Canadian General Social Survey suggested that the nones reported higher levels of mastery (i.e., feeling more empowered), which is an important predictor of psychological wellness (Speed and Fowler 2017: 6–8). These findings from Canada are of interest because they came from representative data sets that can be *generalized* to the wider Canadian population.

Nonreligion's deleterious effects

With respect to health penalties associated with nonreligion, Mexicans who are not religious are less likely to seek out preventative screening in *some* circumstances but not others (Benjamins 2007: 229–30); and Mexicans who go to church, and presumably derive social support from this action, were less likely to think they were a burden to their family and think about killing themselves (Hoffman and Marsiglia 2014: 261). With respect to biological markers for wellness, church attendance was negatively associated with waist-to-hip ratio, diastolic blood pressure, and pulse rates in Mexicans (Hill, Rote, and Ellison 2017: 262–3)—outcomes that tend to be used as proxy indicators for other health conditions. While it is true that Mexicans who do not go to church are purportedly less healthy, it would also suggest in a more basic sense that people who are able to go out and socialize regularly are healthier than those who do not or *cannot*.

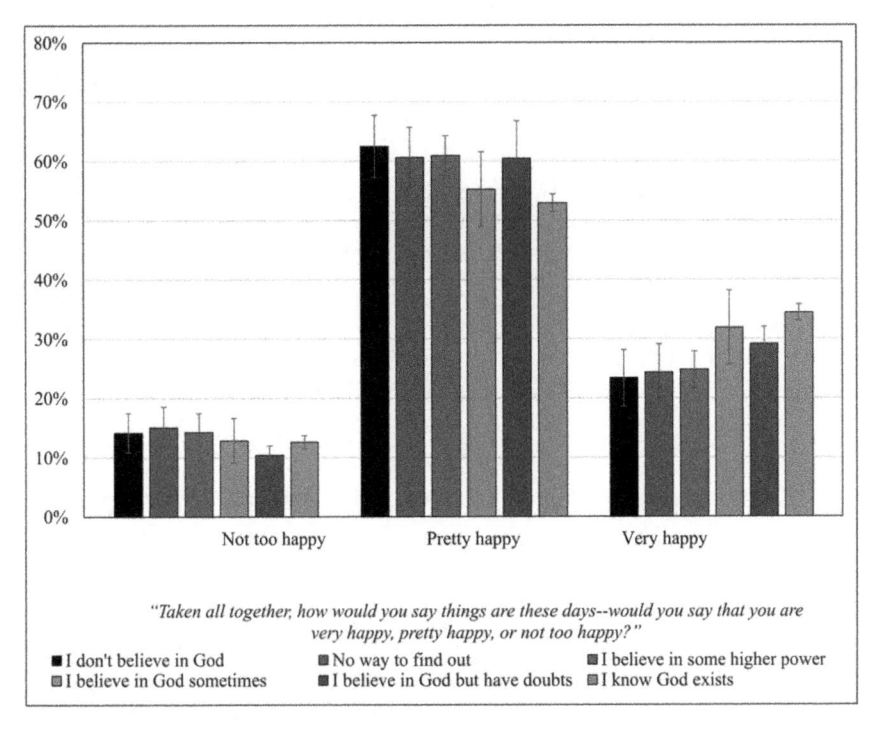

FIGURE 10.5 *Confidence in God's existence predicting happiness category in the 2018 General Social Survey (with standard error bars).*

Atheism is also sporadically associated with poorer health outcomes or health penalties. Some research suggests that American atheists are more likely to engage in non-suicidal self-injury compared to religiously affiliated people (Kuentzel et al. 2012: 293–4). While this finding may be the product of a small-scale, non-generalizable study, it could also reflect that some religious norms may discourage self-harm. Other research using the LSHS indicated that, when compared to the religiously affiliated, atheists reported lower levels of happiness, lower levels of gratitude (also found by Moore and Leach [2015: 58]), lower levels of optimism, lower levels of meaning in life (cf. Speed, Coleman III, and Langston 2018: 5–6), and lower levels of forgiveness of self (Hayward et al. 2016: 1032). However, one of the major issues confounding this area of research is that atheists are perceived negatively within North American society (Gervais, Shariff, and Norenzayan 2011: 1200), which is partially driven by religious factors (Edgell, Gerteis, and Hartmann 2006: 219–27). The upshot of this negativity is that when researchers investigate mental well-being and purpose within atheists, they are receiving responses from a group of people who are aware that they are the focal point of intense social dislike. Consequently, it's unclear if differences in happiness are attributable to the *nature* of nonbelief or the *environment* in which nonbelief is persecuted (see Figure 10.5).

Canadians who report lower levels of religiousness and church attendance are more likely to score highly on problematic gambling measures (Mutti-Packer et al. 2017: 5–7). Similarly, more frequent church attendance was associated with reduced depression (Baetz et al. 2006: 657–8; Baetz et al. 2004: 820–1), mania, social phobia, and fewer personality disorders in a separate sample of Canadians (Baetz et al. 2006: 657–8). Dilmaghani (2018: 125) notes that individuals lower in R/S are less likely to endorse items about community membership and personal growth, which would be consistent with the general finding that individuals who are engaged with R/S report better social support. Speed and Fowler (2017: 996–8) note that while religiously unaffiliated individuals are less healthy than Christians, this is only true when the unaffiliated engage in religious activities (e.g., church attendance). This is not so much a negative finding with respect to nonreligion, as it is an emphasis that R/S does not have a uniformly positive relationship for everyone. In fact, some research suggests that the relationship between R/S and health isn't *linear* at all, it's *curvilinear*.

Rethinking the R/S–Health Relationship

While the notion of a curvilinear (i.e., quadratic) relationship had been around since the beginning of the R/S–health research surge (predating even Ross [1990: 239–42]), it took some time for the prospect to be investigated with seriousness. As researchers became more circumspect about the R/S–health relationship, they realized that the least healthy people within studies were often the ones without firm theological perspectives, ones without particular orthodoxies, or ones with a wishy-washy type of religious affiliation. This could be represented graphically with a u-shape (see Figure 10.6).

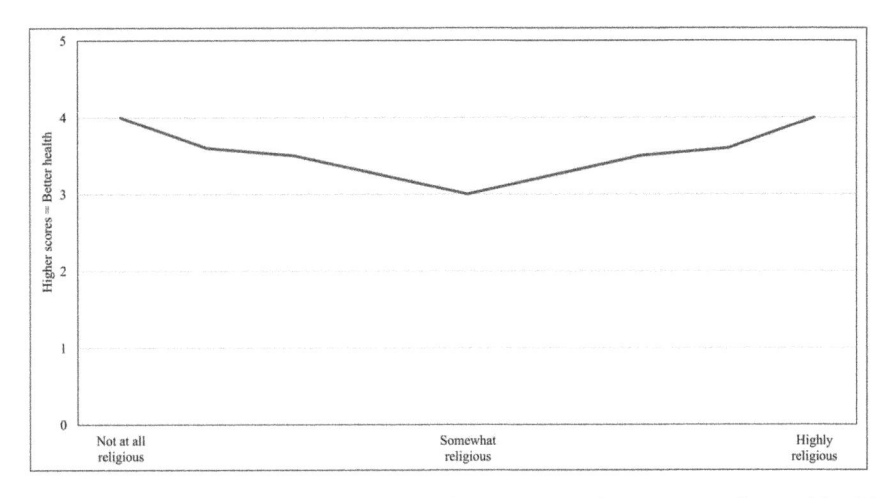

FIGURE 10.6 *Simulated curvilinear relationship between religion/spirituality and health.*

Basically, the über-nonreligious and the über-religious are healthier because they are more "committed" to their perspectives.

A curvilinear relationship is fascinating because it accounts for several of the discrepancies within the R/S–health literature. Recall that studies using *exclusively* religious samples found a positive relationship between R/S and health—this makes sense because the lowest level of religion in those studies is likely going to be somewhere in the middle of a religiosity scale. Recall that studies comparing atheists and Christians tend to find few health differences between the groups—this makes sense too because the study may be comparing "committed" individuals on both sides of that u-shaped curve. A curvilinear relationship has been acknowledged in both the Canadian literature (Dilmaghani [2018: 128]; it is also consistent with Speed and Fowler [2017: 992–8]) and the US literature (Eliassen, Taylor, and Lloyd 2005: 192–6; Galen and Kloet 2011: 679; Mochon, Norton, and Ariely 2011: 8–10; Speed 2017: 248–53), and has a much more nuanced understanding than the simplistic "more R/S = more health" perspective. While a curvilinear relationship solves several known issues with the R/S–health literature, it does so at a "terrible" cost.

If the R/S–health relationship is curvilinear, this calls into question the specific relevance of religion or spirituality in the promotion of health, which if you have been paying attention, is a major theme of this chapter. It is important to think of *why* the relationship between R/S–health is likely curvilinear—and it deals with *coherency* (Antonovsky 1993; Ellison 1991: 86; Galen and Kloet 2011: 686). The upshot of coherency is that people will understand the world to work in a predictable manner, and this predictability lends itself to better psychological well-being. This is not to suggest commitment to a *specific* worldview is health promoting, it is that *any* worldview that allows an individual to make sense of the environment is health promoting. A breast cancer diagnosis could be "made sense of" because of a trust in God's judgment, or it could be "made sense of" because of an understanding of genetic factors in developing neoplasms. Provided a person can make sense of their world's events, they are better off for it irrespective of their chosen lens. While R/S is certainly a *popular* way of imparting meaning, there are other viable approaches to achieving the same degree of coherence. The upshot of this is that R/S may provide meaning, which produces better health, but at the same time any meaning-giving philosophy is bound to do the same.

Summary

As noted at the beginning of this chapter, nonreligon does not have *a* relationship with health, it has numerous relationships with health. While there are certainly some instances in which an R/S viewpoint is associated with small health gains for an individual, there are counterexamples where having lower R/S is also associated with better health. This is because religion and spirituality are not intrinsically good or bad, and their absence is not necessarily deleterious or salutary. The effect that R/S has on well-being is affected by interpersonal, intrapersonal, cultural, and contextual factors that are as varied as the people who hold R/S viewpoints. Consequently, it should be no surprise that atheists, the unaffiliated, the nonspiritual, deists, agnostics, and many other nonreligious and nonbelieving individuals are able to achieve fulfillment and enjoyment from life. While the nonreligion–health field has a way to go still, we have reached an important milestone in which we can talk about a person being a none without simultaneously assuming they have a damning health liability.

Further Reading and Online Resources

Baker, J.O., S. Stroope, and M.H. Walker (2018), "Secularity, Religiosity, and Health: Physical and Mental Health Differences between Atheists, Agnostics, and Nonaffiliated Theists Compared to Religiously Affiliated Individuals," *Social Science Research*, 75: 44–57.

de Jager Meezenbroek, E., B. Garssen, M. van den Berg, D. Van Dierendonck, A. Visser, and W.B. Schaufeli (2012), "Measuring Spirituality as a Universal Human Experience: A Review of Spirituality Questionnaires," *Journal of Religion and Health*, 51 (2): 336–54.

Galen, L.W. and J.D. Kloet (2011), "Mental Well-being in the Religious and the Non-religious: Evidence for a Curvilinear Relationship," *Mental Health, Religion & Culture*, 14 (7): 673–89.

Hammer, J.H., R.T. Cragun, and K. Hwang (2013), "Measuring Spiritual Fitness: Atheist Military Personnel, Veterans, and Civilians," *Military Psychology*, 25 (5): 438–51.

Nowakowski, A. and J. Sumerau (2017), "Health Disparities in Nonreligious and Religious Older Adults in the United States: A Descriptive Epidemiology of 16 Common Chronic Conditions," *Secularism and Nonreligion*, 6: 4. https://doi.org/10.5334/snr.85.

Speed, D., T.J. Coleman III, and J. Langston (2018), "What Do You Mean, 'What Does It All Mean?' Atheism, Nonreligion, and Life Meaning," *Sage Open*, 8 (1). https://doi.org/10.1177/2158244017754238.

References

Adamczyk, A. and J. Felson (2008), "Fetal Positions: Unraveling the Influence of Religion on Premarital Pregnancy Resolution," *Social Science Quarterly*, 89 (1): 17–38.

Ai, A.L., B. Huang, J. Bjorck, and H.B. Appel (2013), "Religious Attendance and Major Depression among Asian Americans from a National Database: The Mediation of Social Support," *Psychology of Religion and Spirituality*, 5 (2): 78–89. https://doi.org/10.1037/a0030625.

Antonovsky, A. (1993), "The Structure and Properties of the Sense of Coherence Scale," *Social Science & Medicine*, 36 (6): 725–33.

Antonucci, T.C., R. Fuhrer, and J.S. Jackson (1990), "Social Support and Reciprocity: A Cross-ethnic and Cross-national Perspective," *Journal of Social and Personal Relationships*, 7 (4): 519–30.

Babiss, L.A. and J.E. Gangwisch (2009), "Sports Participation as a Protective Factor against Depression and Suicidal Ideation in Adolescents as Mediated by Self-Esteem and Social Support," *Journal of Developmental & Behavioral Pediatrics*, 30 (5): 376–84. https://doi.org/10.1097/dbp.0b013e3181b33659.

Baetz, M., R. Griffin, R. Bowen, H.G. Koenig, and E. Marcoux (2004), "The Association between Spiritual and Religious Involvement and Depressive Symptoms in a Canadian Population," *Journal of Nervous and Mental Disease*, 192 (12): 818–22. https://doi.org/10.1097/01.nmd.0000146735.73827.85.

Baetz, M., R. Bowen, G. Jones, and T. Koru-Sengul (2006), "How Spiritual Values and Worship Attendance Relate to Psychiatric Disorders in the Canadian Population," *Canadian Journal of Psychiatry*, 51 (10): 654–61.

Baker, J.O. and B. Smith (2009), "None Too Simple: Examining Issues of Religious Nonbelief and Nonbelonging in the United States," *Journal for the Scientific Study of Religion*, 48 (4): 719–33.

Baker, J.O., K.K. Smith, and Y.A. Stoss (2015), "Theism, Secularism, and Sexual Education in the United States," *Sexuality Research and Social Policy*, 12 (3): 236–47. https://doi.org/10.1007/s13178-015-0187-8.

Baker, J.O., S. Stroope, and M.H. Walker (2018), "Secularity, Religiosity, and Health: Physical and Mental Health Differences between Atheists, Agnostics, and Nonaffiliated Theists Compared to Religiously Affiliated Individuals," *Social Science Research*, 75: 44–57. https://doi.org/10.1016/j.ssresearch.2018.07.003.

Benjamins, M.R. (2005), "Social Determinants of Preventive Service Utilization: How Religion Influences the Use of Cholesterol Screening in Older Adults," *Research on Aging*, 27 (4): 475–97. https://doi.org/10.1177/0164027505276048.

Benjamins, M.R. (2007), "Predictors of Preventive Health Care Use among Middle-Aged and Older Adults in Mexico: The Role of Religion," *Journal of Cross-Cultural Gerontology*, 22 (2): 221–34. https://doi.org/10.1007/s10823-007-9036-4.

Benjamins, M.R., J. Trinitapoli, and C.G. Ellison (2006), "Religious Attendance, Health Maintenance Beliefs, and Mammography Utilization: Findings from a Nationwide Survey of Presbyterian Women," *Journal for the Scientific Study of Religion*, 45 (4): 597–607. https://doi.org/10.1111/j.1468-5906.2006.00330.x.

Bodson, J., A. Wilson, E.L. Warner, and D. Kepka (2017), "Religion and HPV Vaccine-Related Awareness, Knowledge, and Receipt among Insured Women Aged 18–26 in Utah," *PloS One*, 12 (8): e0183725. https://doi.org/10.1371/journal.pone.0183725.

Brewster, M.E., M.A. Robinson, R. Sandil, J. Esposito, and E. Geiger (2014), "Arrantly Absent: Atheism in Psychological Science from 2001 to 2012," *The Counseling Psychologist*, 42 (5): 628–63.

Caldeira, K.M., A.M. Arria, K.E. O'Grady, E.M. Zarate, K.B. Vincent, and E.D. Wish (2009), "Prospective Associations between Alcohol and Drug Consumption and Risky Sex among Female College Students," *Journal of Alcohol and Drug Education*, 53 (2): nihpa115858.

Callister, L.C., A.E. Bond, G. Matsumura, and S. Mangum (2004), "Threading Spirituality throughout Nursing Education," *Holistic Nursing Practice*, 18 (3): 160–6.

Chevrette, M. and H.A. Abenhaim (2015), "Do State-Based Policies Have an Impact on Teen Birth Rates and Teen Abortion Rates in the United States?," *Journal of Pediatric and Adolescent Gynecology*, 28 (5): 354–61. https://doi.org/10.1016/j.jpag.2014.10.006.

Cobb, S. (1976), "Social Support as a Moderator of Life Stress," *Psychosomatic Medicine*, 38 (5): 300–14.

Cragun, D., R.T. Cragun, B. Nathan, J.E. Sumerau, and A.C.H. Nowakowski (2016), "Do Religiosity and Spirituality Really Matter for Social, Mental, and Physical Health?: A Tale of Two Samples," *Sociological Spectrum*, 36 (6): 359–77.

Crosby, R.A. and W.L. Yarber (2001), "Perceived Versus Actual Knowledge about Correct Condom Use among US Adolescents: Results from a National Study," *Journal of Adolescent Health*, 28 (5): 415–20.

DeCamp, W. and J.M. Smith (2019), "Religion, Nonreligion, and Deviance: Comparing Faith's and Family's Relative Strength in Promoting Social Conformity," *Journal of Religion and Health*, 58 (1): 206–20.

De Santis, J.P., E. Provencio-Vasquez, B. Mancera, and H.J. Mata (2016), "Health Risk and Protective Factors among Hispanic Women Living in the US–Mexico Border Region," *Hispanic Health Care International*, 14 (1): 17–25. https://doi.org/10.1177/1540415316629679.

Desmond, S.A., J.T. Ulmer, and C.D. Bader (2013), "Religion, Self Control, and Substance Use," *Deviant Behavior*, 34 (5): 384–406.

Dilmaghani, M. (2018), "Importance of Religion or Spirituality and Mental Health in Canada," *Journal of Religion and Health*, 57 (1): 120–35.

Duro, C.N.M. (2018), "Agnostics and Atheists in Mexico," in H.P.P. Gooren (ed.), *Encyclopedia of Latin American Religions*, 1–6, Mexico City: Springer.

Edgell, P., J. Gerteis, and D. Hartmann (2006), "Atheists as 'Other': Moral Boundaries and Cultural Membership in American Society," *American Sociological Review*, 71 (2): 211–34.

Elia, J.P. and M.J. Eliason (2010), "Dangerous Omissions: Abstinence-Only-until-Marriage School-Based Sexuality Education and the Betrayal of LGBTQ Youth," *American Journal of Sexuality Education*, 5 (1): 17–35. https://doi.org/10.1080/15546121003748848.

Eliassen, A.H., J. Taylor, and D.A. Lloyd (2005), "Subjective Religiosity and Depression in the Transition to Adulthood," *Journal for the Scientific Study of Religion*, 44 (2): 187–99.

Ellis, A. (1962), *The Case against Religion: A Psychotherapists's View*, Austin, TX: Institute for Rational Living.

Ellison, C.G. (1991), "Religious Involvement and Subjective Well-being," *Journal of Health and Social Behavior*, 32 (1): 80–99.

Ellison, C.G., J.D. Boardman, D.R. Williams, and J.S. Jackson (2001), "Religious Involvement, Stress, and Mental Health: Findings from the 1995 Detroit Area Study," *Social Forces*, 80 (1): 215–49.

Ellison, C.G., M. Bradshaw, J. Storch, J.P. Marcum, and T.D. Hill (2011), "Religious Doubts and Sleep Quality: Findings from a Nationwide Study of Presbyterians," *Review of Religious Research*, 53 (2): 119–36.

Espinosa-Hernández, G., J. Bissell-Havran, and A. Nunn (2015), "The Role of Religiousness and Gender in Sexuality among Mexican Adolescents," *Journal of Sex Research*, 52 (8): 887–97. https://doi.org/10.1080/00224499.2014.990951.

Fenelon, A. and S. Danielsen (2016), "Leaving My Religion: Understanding the Relationship between Religious Disaffiliation, Health, and Well-Being," *Social Science Research*, 57: 49–62. https://doi.org/10.1016/j.ssresearch.2016.01.007.

Fernández-Niño, J.A., I. Bojorquez, C. Becerra-Arias, and C.I. Astudillo-Garcia (2019), "Religious Affiliation and Major Depressive Episode in Older Adults: A Cross-Sectional Study in Six Low-and Middle-Income Countries," *BMC Public Health*, 19 (1): 460. https://doi.org/10.1186/s12889-019-6806-1.

Francis, L.J., M. Robbins, and A. White (2003), "Correlation between Religion and Happiness: A Replication," *Psychological Reports*, 92 (1): 51–2.

Galen, L.W. and J.D. Kloet (2011), "Mental Well-Being in the Religious and the Non-Religious: Evidence for a Curvilinear Relationship," *Mental Health, Religion & Culture*, 14 (7): 673–89. https://doi.org/10.1080/13674676.2010.510829.

Gauthier, K.J., A.N. Christopher, M.I. Walter, R. Mourad, and P. Marek (2006), "Religiosity, Religious Doubt, and the Need for Cognition: Their Interactive Relationship with Life Satisfaction," *Journal of Happiness Studies*, 7 (2): 139–54. https://doi.org/10.1007/s10902-005-1916-0.

George, L.K., C.G. Ellison, and D.B. Larson (2002), "Explaining the Relationships between Religious Involvement and Health," *Psychological Inquiry*, 13 (3): 190–200. https://doi.org/10.1207/S15327965PLI1303_04.

Gervais, W.M., A.F. Shariff, and A. Norenzayan (2011), "Do You Believe in Atheists? Distrust Is Central to Anti-Atheist Prejudice," *Journal of Personality and Social Psychology*, 101 (6): 1189. https://doi.org/10.1037/a0025882.

Ginsburg, M. and S. Weisband (2002), "Social Capital and Volunteerism in Virtual Communities: The Case of the Internet Chess Club," in *Proceedings of the 35th Annual Hawaii International Conference on System Sciences*, 2225–34. IEEE.

Greenstreet, W.M. (1999), "Teaching Spirituality in Nursing: A Literature Review," *Nurse Education Today*, 19 (8): 649–58.

Hammer, J.H., R.T. Cragun, and K. Hwang (2013), "Measuring Spiritual Fitness: Atheist Military Personnel, Veterans, and Civilians," *Military Psychology*, 25 (5): 438–51. https://doi.org/10.1037/mil0000010.

Hayward, R.D., N. Krause, G. Ironson, P.C. Hill, and R. Emmons (2016), "Health and Well-Being among the Non-Religious: Atheists, Agnostics, and No Preference Compared with Religious Group Members," *Journal of Religion and Health*, 55 (3): 1024–37. https://doi.org/10.1007/s10943-015-0179-2.

Hill, T.D., S.M. Rote, and C.G. Ellison (2017), "Religious Participation and Biological Functioning in Mexico," *Journal of Aging and Health*, 29 (6): 951–72. https://doi.org/10.1177/0898264317716244.

Hodge, D.R., F.F. Marsiglia, and T. Nieri (2011), Religion and Substance Use among Youths of Mexican Heritage: A Social Capital Perspective," *Social Work Research*, 35 (3): 137–46.

Hoffman, S. and F.F. Marsiglia (2014), "The Impact of Religiosity on Suicidal Ideation among Youth in Central Mexico," *Journal of Religion and Health*, 53 (1): 255–66. https://doi.org/10.1007/s10943-012-9654-1.

Holway, G.V. and S.M. Hernandez (2018), "Oral Sex and Condom Use in a US National Sample of Adolescents and Young Adults," *Journal of Adolescent Health*, 62 (4): 402–10. https://doi.org/10.1016/j.jadohealth.2017.08.022.

Hufford, D.J., M.J. Fritts, and J.E. Rhodes (2010), "Spiritual Fitness," *Military Medicine*, 175 (suppl. 8): 73–87.

Hwang, K., J.H. Hammer, and R.T. Cragun (2011), "Extending Religion-Health Research to Secular Minorities: Issues and Concerns," *Journal of Religion and Health*, 50 (3): 608–22. https://doi.org/10.1007/s10943-009-9296-0.

Jacobson, D.E. (1986), "Types and Timing of Social Support," *Journal of Health and Social Behavior*, 27 (3): 250–64.

Jarvis, G.K. and H.C. Northcott (1987), "Religion and Differences in Morbidity and Mortality," *Social Science & Medicine*, 25 (7): 813–24.

Kelly, P.E., J.R. Polanin, S.J. Jang, and B.R. Johnson (2015), "Religion, Delinquency, and Drug Use: A Meta-Analysis," *Criminal Justice Review*, 40 (4): 505–23. https://doi.org/10.1177/0734016815605151.

Koenig, H.G. (2008), "Religion and Mental Health: What Should Psychiatrists Do?," *Psychiatric Bulletin*, 32 (6): 201–3.

Koenig, H.G. (2009), "Research on Religion, Spirituality, and Mental Health: A Review," *Canadian Journal of Psychiatry*, 54 (5): 283–91.

Koenig, H.G. and D.B. Larson (2001), "Religion and Mental Health: Evidence for an Association," *International Review of Psychiatry*, 13 (2): 67–78.

Krause, N. (2003), "Religious Meaning and Subjective Well-Being in Late Life," *Journals of Gerontology Series B: Psychological Sciences & Social Sciences*, 58B (3): S160.

Krause, N. (2005), "God-Mediated Control and Psychological Well-Being in Late Life," *Research on Aging*, 27 (2): 136–64. https://doi.org/10.1177/0164027504270475.

Krause, N. and K. Wulff (2004), "Religious Doubt and Health: Exploring the Potential Dark Side of Religion (English)," *Sociology of Religion*, 65 (1): 35–56.

Krause, N. and R.R. Hayward (2012), "Humility, Lifetime Trauma, and Change in Religious Doubt among Older Adults," *Journal of Religion and Health*, 51 (4): 1002–16. https://doi.org/10.1007/s10943-012-9576-y.

Kuentzel, J.G., A. Eamonn, N. Boutros, D. Chugani, and D. Barnett (2012), "Nonsuicidal Self-Injury in an Ethnically Diverse College Sample," *American Journal of Orthopsychiatry* 82: 291–7. https://doi.org/10.1111/j.1939-0025.2012.01167.x.

Levin, J.S. and K.S. Markides (1985), "Religion and Health in Mexican Americans," *Journal of Religion and Health*, 24 (1): 60–9.

Levin, J.S. and P.L. Schiller (1987), "Is There a Religious Factor in Health?," *Journal of Religion and Health*, 26 (1): 9–36.

Lim, C. and R.D. Putnam (2010), "Religion, Social Networks, and Life Satisfaction," *American Sociological Review*, 75: 914–33. https://doi.org/10.1177/0003122410386686.

Lindberg, L.D., I. Maddow-Zimet, and H. Boonstra (2016), "Changes in Adolescents' Receipt of Sex Education, 2006–2013," *Journal of Adolescent Health*, 58 (6): 621–7. https://doi.org/10.1016/j.jadohealth.2016.02.004.

Marsiglia, F.F., S. Kulis, T. Nieri, and M. Parsai (2005), "God Forbid! Substance Use among Religious and Nonreligious Youth," *American Journal of Orthopsychiatry*, 75 (4): 585–98. https://doi.org/10.1037/0002-9432.75.4.585.

Masters, K.S. (2010), "The Role of Religion in Therapy: Time for Psychologists to Have a Little Faith?," *Cognitive and Behavioral Practice*, 17 (4): 393–400.

McNamara, P., J.P. Burns, P. Johnson, and B.H. McCorkle (2010), "Personal Religious Practice, Risky Behavior, and Implementation Intentions among Adolescents," *Psychology of Religion and Spirituality*, 2 (1): 30. https://doi.org/10.1037/a0017582.

Meyers, J.L., Q. Brown, B.F. Grant, and D. Hasin (2017), "Religiosity, Race/Ethnicity, and Alcohol Use Behaviors in the United States," *Psychological Medicine*, 47 (1): 103–14. https://doi.org/10.1017/S0033291716001975.

Michalak, L., K. Trocki, and J. Bond (2007), "Religion and Alcohol in the US National Alcohol Survey: How Important Is Religion for Abstention and Drinking?," *Drug and Alcohol Dependence*, 87 (2–3): 268–80. https://doi.org/10.1016/j.drugalcdep.2006.07.013.

Mochon, D., M.I. Norton, and D. Ariely (2011), "Who Benefits from Religion?," *Social Indicators Research*, 101 (1): 1–15. https://doi.org/10.1007/s11205-010-9637-0.

Moore, J.T. and M.M. Leach (2016), "Dogmatism and Mental Health: A Comparison of the Religious and Secular," *Psychology of Religion and Spirituality* 8: 54–64. https://doi.org/10.1037/rel0000028.

Morton, K.R., J.W. Lee, and L.R. Martin (2017), "Pathways from Religion to Health: Mediation by Psychosocial and Lifestyle Mechanisms," *Psychology of Religion and Spirituality*, 9 (1): 106.

Mutti-Packer, S., D.C. Hodgins, R.J. Williams and B.K. Thege. 2017. "The Protective Role of Religiosity against Problem Gambling: Findings from a Five-Year Prospective Study," *BMC Psychiatry* 17: 1–10. https://doi.org/10.1186/s12888-017-1518-5.

Myers, D.G. (2008), "Religion and Human Flourishing," in M. Eid and R.J. Larsen (eds.), *The Science of Subjective Well-Being*, 323–43, New York: Guilford Press.

Neymotin, F. and T.M. Downing-Matibag (2013), "Religiosity and Adolescents' Involvement with Both Drugs and Sex," *Journal of Religion and Health*, 52 (2): 550–69. https://doi.org/10.1007/s10943-011-9507-3.

Nowakowski, A. and J. Sumerau (2017), "Health Disparities in Nonreligious and Religious Older Adults in the United States: A Descriptive Epidemiology of 16 Common Chronic Conditions," *Secularism and Nonreligion*, 6 (4): 1–15. https://doi.org/10.5334/snr.85.

O'Brien, M.E. (2017), *Spirituality in Nursing*, Burlington, MA: Jones & Bartlett Learning.

Ott, M.A. and J.S. Santelli (2007), "Abstinence and Abstinence-Only Education," *Current Opinion in Obstetrics & Gynecology*, 19 (5): 446.

Pargament, K.I. and P.J. Sweeney (2011), "Building Spiritual Fitness in the Army: An Innovative Approach to a Vital Aspect of Human Development," *American Psychologist*, 66 (1): 58–64. https://doi.org/10.1037/a0021657.

Park, N., B. Lee, F. Sun, D. Klemmack, L. Roff, and H. Koenig (2013), "Typologies of Religiousness/Spirituality: Implications for Health and Well-Being," *Journal of Religion and Health*, 52 (3): 828–39. https://doi.org/10.1007/s10943-011-9520-6.

Peterson, C., N. Park, and C.A. Castro (2011), "Assessment for the US Army Comprehensive Soldier Fitness Program: The Global Assessment Tool," *American Psychologist*, 66 (1): 10. https://doi.org/10.1037/a0021658.

Petersen, L.R. and G.V. Donnenwerth (1997), "Secularization and the Influence of Religion on Beliefs about Premarital Sex," *Social Forces*, 75 (3): 1071–88.

Pew Research Center (2015), "Religious Composition by Country, 2010–2050," April 5. https://www.pewforum.org/2015/04/02/religious-projection-table/2010/number/all/ (accessed September 14, 2020).

Poole, R., C.C. Cook, and R. Higgo (2019), "Psychiatrists, Spirituality and Religion," *British Journal of Psychiatry*, 214 (4): 181–2. https://doi.org/10.1192/bjp.2018.241.

Regnerus, M.D. (2005), "Talking about Sex: Religion and Patterns of Parent–Child Communication about Sex and Contraception," *Sociological Quarterly*, 46 (1): 79–105. https://doi.org/10.1111/j.1533-8525.2005.00005.x.

Ross, C.E. (1990), "Religion and Psychological Distress," *Journal for the Scientific Study of Religion*, 29: 236–45.

Ryan, M. and A. Francis (2012), "Locus of Control Beliefs Mediate the Relationship between Religious Functioning and Psychological Health," *Journal of Religion and Health*, 51 (3): 774–85. https://doi.org/10.1007/s10943-010-9386-z.

Salsman, J.M., T.L. Brown, E.H. Brechting, and C.R. Carlson (2005), "The Link between Religion and Spirituality and Psychological Adjustment: The Mediating Role of Optimism and Social Support," *Personality and Social Psychology Bulletin*, 31: 522–35. https://doi.org/10.1177/0146167204271563.

Schnall, E., S. Wassertheil-Smoller, C. Swencionis, V. Zemon, L. Tinker, M. O'Sullivan, and M. Goodwin (2010), "The Relationship between Religion and Cardiovascular Outcomes and All-Cause Mortality in the Women's Health Initiative Observational Study," *Psychology & Health*, 25 (2): 249–63. https://doi.org/10.1080/08870440802311322.

Seybold, K.S. and P.C. Hill (2001), "The Role of Religion and Spirituality in Mental and Physical Health," *Current Directions in Psychological Science*, 10 (1): 21–4.

Sharkey, P.W. and H.N. Malony (1986), "Religiosity and Emotional Disturbance: A Test of Ellis's Thesis in His Own Counseling Center," *Psychotherapy: Theory, Research, Practice, Training*, 23 (4): 640.

Smith, C. and R. Faris (2002), *Religion and American Adolescent Delinquency, Risk Behaviors and Constructive Social Activities*, A Research Report of the National Study of Youth and Religion, no. 1, Chapel Hill, NC: National Study of Youth and Religion.

Speed, D. (2017), "Unbelievable?! Theistic/Epistemological Viewpoint Affects Religion-Health Relationship," *Journal of Religion and Health*, 56: 238–57. https://doi.org/10.1007/s10943-016-0271-2.

Speed, D., T.J. Coleman III, and J. Langston (2018), "What Do You Mean, 'What Does It All Mean?' Atheism, Nonreligion, and Life Meaning," *Sage Open*, 8 (1): https://doi.org/10.1177/2158244017754238.

Speed, D. and K. Fowler (2016), "What's God Got to Do with It? How Religiosity Predicts Atheists' Health," *Journal of Religion and Health*, 55: 296–308. https://doi.org/10.1007/s10943-015-0083-9.

Speed, D. and K. Fowler (2017), "Good for All? Hardly! Attending Church Does Not Benefit Religiously Unaffiliated," *Journal of Religion and Health*, 56: 986–1002. https://doi.org/10.1007/s10943-016-0317-5.

Sprecher, S. and S. Treger (2015), "Virgin College Students' Reasons for and Reactions to Their Abstinence from Sex: Results from a 23-Year Study at a Midwestern US University," *Journal of Sex Research*, 52 (8): 936–48. https://doi.org/10.1080/00224499.2014.983633.

Stack, S. and A.J. Kposowa (2011), "Religion and Suicide Acceptability: A Cross-National Analysis," *Journal for the Scientific Study of Religion*, 50 (2): 289–306.

Stanger-Hall, K.F. and D.W. Hall (2011), "Abstinence-Only Education and Teen Pregnancy Rates: Why We Need Comprehensive Sex Education in the US," *PloS One*, 6 (10): e24658. https://doi.org/10.1371/journal.pone.0024658.

Steffen, P.R., K.S. Masters, and S. Baldwin (2017), "What Mediates the Relationship between Religious Service Attendance and Aspects of Well-Being?," *Journal of Religion and Health*, 56: 158–70. https://doi.org/10.1007/s10943-016-0203-1.

Strayhorn, J.M. and J.C. Strayhorn (2009), "Religiosity and Teen Birth Rate in the United States," *Reproductive Health*, 6 (1): 14. https://doi.org/10.1186/1742-4755-6-14.

Tonigan, J.S., W.R. Miller, and C. Schermer (2002), "Atheists, Agnostics and Alcoholics Anonymous," *Journal of Studies on Alcohol*, 63 (5): 534–41.

Trenholm, C., B. Devaney, K. Fortson, K. Quay, J. Wheeler, and M. Clark (2007), *Impacts of Four Title V, Section 510 Abstinence Education Programs*, Final Report, Mathematica Policy Research, Inc.

Tuck, A., M. Robinson, B. Agic, A.R. Ialomiteanu, and R.E. Mann (2017), "Religion, Alcohol Use and Risk Drinking among Canadian Adults Living in Ontario," *Journal of Religion and Health*, 56: 2023–38.

Uchino, B.N. (2009), "Understanding the Links between Social Support and Physical Health: A Lifespan Perspective with Emphasis on the Separability of Perceived and Received Support," *Perspectives in Psychological Science*, 4: 236–55. https://doi.org/10.1111/j.1745-6924.2009.01122.x.

Uecker, J.E., M.D. Regnerus, and M.L. Vaaler (2007), "Losing My Religion: The Social Sources of Religious Decline in Early Adulthood," *Social Forces*, 85 (4): 1667–92. https://doi.org/10.1353/sof.2007.0083.

Ventis, W.L. (1995), "The Relationships between Religion and Mental Health," *Journal of Social Issues*, 51 (2): 33–48.
Waxman, H. (2004), *The Content of Federally Funded Abstinence-Only Education Programs*, Washington, DC: US House of Representatives Committee on Government Reform—Minority Staff Special Investigations Division. https://spot.colorado.edu/~tooley/HenryWaxman.pdf (accessed October 21, 2020).
Whitley, R. (2012), "Religious Competence as Cultural Competence," *Transcultural Psychiatry*, 49 (2): 245–60.
Wills, T.A., A.M. Yaeger, and J.M. Sandy (2003), "Buffering Effect of Religiosity for Adolescent Substance Use," *Psychology of Addictive Behaviors*, 17 (1): 24. https://doi.org/10.1037/0893-164X.17.1.24.
Yang, Z. and L.M. Gaydos (2010), "Reasons for and Challenges of Recent Increases in Teen Birth Rates: A Study of Family Planning Service Policies and Demographic Changes at the State Level," *Journal of Adolescent Health*, 46 (6): 517–24.
Yeung, J.W., Y.C. Chan, and B.L. Lee (2009), "Youth Religiosity and Substance Use: A Meta-Analysis from 1995 to 2007," *Psychological Reports*, 105 (1): 255–66. https://doi.org/10.2466/PR0.105.1.255-266.
Zuckerman, P. (2009), "Atheism, Secularity, and Well-Being: How the Findings of Social Science Counter Negative Stereotypes and Assumptions," *Sociology Compass*, 3: 949–71.

Glossary Terms

Atheists People who do not believe in God(s). Provided a person would *not* agree with the statement, "I believe in God(s)," they are definitionally an atheist. Data from the 2018 General Social Survey suggest that 15.6 percent of Americans indicate that they do not believe in God, and therefore qualify as atheist. Somewhat confusingly, atheism is offered as a religious affiliation option in some research projects, which produces a situation where a person may be *culturally* religious but not believe in God(s). Think of parents who bring their children to church a few times a year (e.g., Christmas and Easter) because they enjoy being a part of a religious tradition but also don't really believe in God. These people would *identify* as being religiously affiliated but would also *qualify* as atheist. This isn't uncommon: data from the 2018 General Social Survey suggest that 3.7 percent of Protestants don't believe in God, 3.4 percent of Catholics don't believe in God, 26.5 percent of Jews don't believe in God, and 4.8 percent of generic Christians don't believe in God. This lack of boundaries with religious and spiritual definitions can make the discussion of atheism demographics difficult because individuals may straddle several groups, but likely "default" to being religiously affiliated.

Coherency The way the world behaves in a predictable manner or an underlying perceived structure to one's life experiences. Humans tend to report better psychological well-being when the world is orderly (as opposed to chaotic) and predictable (as opposed to unpredictable). Coherency can be achieved via R/S: people who have trust in God(s) or "the universe" may feel comfort that *seemingly* random events are a part of a plan that carefully accounts for them as individuals. Coherency can also be achieved via non-R/S: people may believe the universe is random and that good or bad events that happen to them are not necessarily a product of their own actions. Coherency is one of the theories to explain why R/S is healthy, but it also lends itself to explain why more "committed" nones report similar health outcomes as "committed" R/S people.

Generalized results Scenarios where research findings can be applied to a large number of people within the population. Research that uses data that is nationally representative (e.g., General Social Survey, Baylor Religion Study, Landmark Spirituality and Health Survey) has collected information from a wide cross-section of the population and is generally applicable to a larger number of people than research that only used people from a single site or a handful of sites. For example, research that samples people only from one Baptist church in Louisiana may be applicable to other Baptist churches in Louisiana, but certainly not *all* churches in Louisiana let alone atheists in Wisconsin. When researchers use large nationally representative surveys of Canadians and Americans, they tend to either find a weak R/S–health relationship, or no R/S–health relationship. When researchers use smaller nonrepresentative surveys of religious sites, they tend to find a somewhat stronger relationship between R/S and health. This suggests that the effects of R/S may be restricted or more pronounced for religious or spiritual groups, and not necessarily applicable to nones.

Nones A catchall term for a group of individuals who would be considered "removed" from religion. This group consists of the religiously unaffiliated, atheists, agnostics, deists, apatheists, antitheists, etc. Nones is kept as a deliberately broad term as it encompasses anyone who is not part of a religious or spiritual tradition. Because boundaries surrounding these traditions are often vague or ambiguous, it is possible that a person could be described as a none but also be described as a part of a religious tradition. This is surprisingly common and illustrates the difficulty in defining "what" religious is. A good example of this incongruity would be people who do not believe in God(s) but who identify as culturally Catholic or Jewish. These people often have more in common with nonreligious groups than with religious groups.

Null results Situations where one cannot reasonably say that one variable can be consistently related to another variable. Imagine a study in which you have a group of 100 people and you randomly assign them into two groups based on the flip of a coin. If you were to take the average height of the "heads" group and the average height of the "tails" group, it is unlikely that the two values would be *exactly* the same. Let's say that the average height of the "heads" group was 160.0 centimeters and the average height of the "tails" group was 161.0 centimeters. These values are admittedly not the same, but does that mean that we should always expect that any group randomly sorted into a "tails" group to be taller than any group randomly sorted into the "heads" group? Well, probably not—after all, there's no reason to suspect that people randomly sorted into the "tails" group would be consistently automatically taller. Differences between the "heads" group and the "tails" group can emerge randomly despite there not being an underlying difference between the groups. This is because random sampling produces *approximately* equal scores, but rarely will it produce *precisely* equal scores. When we say that two scores are "statistically equivalent" it means that they are so close to each other that it makes more sense to describe the differences as a product of random chance as opposed to an underlying difference. Null results are when researchers cannot reasonably say that there is a genuine underlying difference, or that the differences we observe are functionally meaningless. More colloquially speaking, null results suggest that two groups are pretty much the same.

Prescriptions and proscriptions Behaviors that a person is instructed to do (prescriptions) or to not do (proscriptions). Within the context of religion and spirituality, people may feel compelled to do or not do specific behaviors (e.g., not eating shellfish, treating one's body well) and these decisions may have health implications. Prescriptions and proscriptions are functionally "dos" and "do nots" and are a potential mechanism to explain why people higher on R/S may report better health outcomes. Specifically, if people higher on R/S are more likely to believe that they should not smoke, it would make sense that people higher on R/S are less likely to get smoking-related illnesses (e.g., cancer). However in these cases, it is important to note that R/S is merely an intermediary mechanism to better health: secular people who do not smoke would reap the same benefits.

Religion/spirituality (R/S) A variety of beliefs, behaviors, and identities that would be associated with religious or spiritual traditions. Briefly, the term R/S could describe church attendance, prayer, meditation, belief in God(s), religious affiliation, religiosity, religious importance, spiritual fulfillment, spiritual valuation, etc.; as you can see there are many potential topics covered under the R/S umbrella. Consequently, the term "R/S–health literature" is used as a shorthand to describe any research that has assessed religion or spirituality in any context, with any concept that is directly or indirectly related to health. The term "R/S" is used repeatedly as a shorthand for a general set of findings rather than a specific finding. For example, the phrase "R/S is associated with reduced depression" is a convenient way of saying "in Study X church attendance was associated with reduced depression, in Study Y being Christian or Buddhist was associated with lower depression, in Study Z reporting higher religiosity was associated with reduced depression." It is not that *all* things related to R/S have been tied to reduced depression, but at least one R/S-related thing has been tied to depression.

11

Secular Parenting

Christel Manning

Introduction

The religious landscape in North America is changing, and perhaps the biggest change is the move away from organized religion. For much of the twentieth century, over 90 percent of Americans claimed a religious affiliation. But starting in the 1970s those numbers began to drop, and today the so-called *nones* comprise nearly a quarter of the adult population and well over one-third of the *millennial* and post-millennial generations (Lipka 2015; Longhurst 2019). Until about a decade ago, the main path to becoming a none was defection: individuals were raised with religion and decided to leave it as adults. In recent years, however, increasing numbers of parents are actively raising their children secular (Bengtson et al. 2018; Thiessen and Laflamme 2017). The growth in secular parenting is significant because religion has been seen as a primary mode of transmitting meaning and value to children, and because religions have depended on socialization of the next generation to maintain institutional continuity. What happens when that is no longer the norm? What does secular parenting look like, and how is it different (or not) from religious parenting? Figure 11.1 shows the increasingly likelihood that children will be raised without religion. What traditions and values are secular parents transmitting to their children, and what impact does this have on individuals and society?

Defining Secularity

There is considerable debate over what it means to be secular, and depending on how you define it, secular parenting may not look all that different from religious parenting. The term "none" comes from survey research asking people what is their religious preference or affiliation: if they say, Catholic or Jewish or Buddhist, respondents are

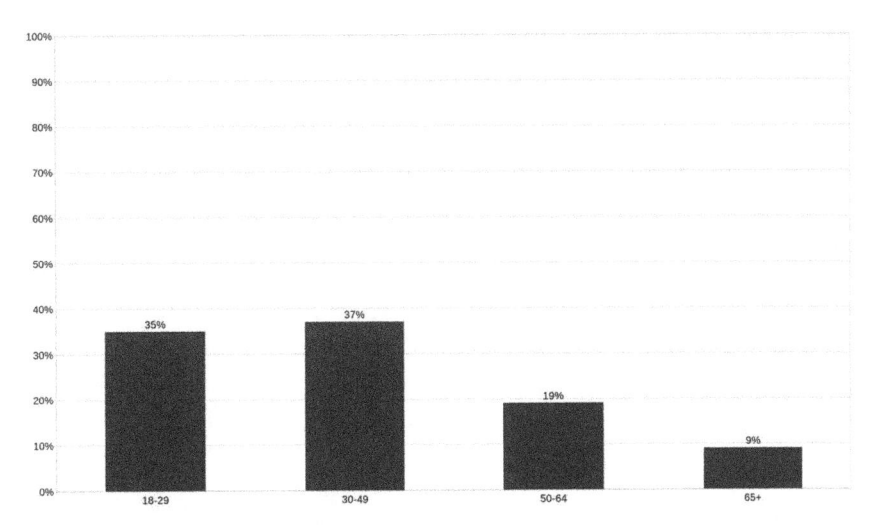

FIGURE 11.1 *People starting families now are more likely to be nonreligious.* Source: *Pew, 2014.*

counted as religious; if they say *atheist*, or *agnostic*, or nothing in particular, they are dubbed none. But those answer choices often hide a more complex picture. Many of the so-called nones are better described as unaffiliated believers (Manning 2015). They believe in God, frequently pray, and even read scripture, but they identify as none because they don't like organized religion. While they may have a deep personal faith, they are alienated by religion's public institutional face: the priest sex scandals in the Catholic Church, the anti-gay messages of some conservative Protestant churches, the use of religion to justify white supremacy or women's oppression or terrorism, or the opposition of some religious leaders to science and climate change have all contributed to people disaffiliating from religions. Jefferson Bethke of YouTube fame is a vivid example of this type of none (Jeff & Alyssa 2012).

The statistics on nones may overstate secularity in America but the reverse is also true. Many people are counted as religious when really they are not. Often dubbed *marginal affiliates* or *culturally religious*, some individuals identify with a religion even though their participation is minimal (Thiessen 2015). Saying their religious affiliation is Catholic or Hindu can be a way of affirming their Irish or Indian heritage, the foods they eat, and the holidays they like to celebrate with family, even though they don't believe in God(s), never pray, and think church or temple is boring or a waste of time. Furthermore, of course, claiming a religious affiliation can be a useful tool in business or electoral politics. This begs the question: how do we know who the real secular individuals are?

Distinguishing between belief, behavior, and belonging, as widely used measures of religion, can be helpful here (Manning 2016). Rejection of God or the supernatural may be thought of as secular belief, never attending services or openly flouting religious rules as secular behavior, and disaffiliating from church or joining an atheist organization is the inverted equivalent of belonging (i.e., not belonging). What complicates the picture is that secular belief, behavior, and belonging do not always coincide. An atheist who attends church with his Baptist wife and children is secular in terms of belief but appears religious in his behavior. Jefferson Bethke, noted above, is religious in belief but secular in belonging. Catholics who claim belief in God but don't attend Mass and have premarital sex while using condoms are secular in behavior. So one way out of this quandary is to count as secular those who are nonreligious on more than one dimension.

Another helpful distinction is between affirmative and passive secularity. Secularity is generally conceptualized in terms of what people are *not* believing, or doing, or joining. This kind of passive secularity is widespread (Putnam and Campbell 2010) and can be difficult to disentangle from religion. So-called Christmas and Easter Catholics, the culturally Jewish, the marginal affiliates mentioned above are all variations of passive secularity. It may be more useful to think about secularity in terms of what people come to believe or do or join in place of religion. When families identify as atheist or freethinkers, when they raise their children to believe in science and the natural order of the universe or the ethical principles of the Humanist Association, when they practice meditation, or gather with other secularists for a ceremony to mark the death of a loved one, we might call this affirmative secularity. When people actively affirm a worldview, they are more likely to pass it on to their children. But, as we will see below, there is considerable variation in traditions and values, even among the affirmatively secular.

Meaning and Values

Religion has long been viewed as a primary source of meaning and moral values. So people who don't have religion may seem morally suspect, and parents who choose to raise their children without it seem to be putting them at risk for not having a moral foundation. Surveys show that three-quarters of Americans (including more than half the nones and about a third of atheists) agree that churches and other religious institutions protect and strengthen morality in society (McClure 2017). Atheists in particular continue to face social stigma despite the increase in nones and their resulting visibility in society (Edgell et al. 2016; Villa 2019). More than a third of Americans think atheists lack a moral center. Atheism is associated with materialism and elitism on the one hand and with criminality on the other, and Americans are less likely to vote for atheist candidates or to offer them employment. These prejudices carry over into the perception of all nonreligious people: those who see atheism as a problem tend to view growth in secularity as bad for America.

The negative prejudice against secular individuals is rooted, like many prejudices, in ignorance. If religion is where you learn right from wrong, it is easy to assume that people without religion won't know the difference. If church is where most children learn basic moral teachings such as honoring your parents, don't kill, don't steal, keep your promises, then they will often be inclined to assume that's where everybody learns to be a good person. If religion is one's source of meaning in life, not having religion would seem to imply a lack of meaning. The label nones, which defines people in terms of what they lack, only reinforces these prejudices.

The so-called nones usually do have deeper meaning systems that are expressed in distinctive beliefs, practices, and sometimes even communities. Further, while those meaning systems are diverse, there are also some common values that inform nonreligious parenting.

Meaning is found in this world

George Jacob Holyoke, who first coined the term "secularism," defined it as a positive, this worldly orientation (Zuckerman 2014). The sense of awe and reverence for something greater than we are, a feeling of love and connectedness to others, a passion to contribute to a better world are not unique to religion, and secular individuals find meaning in nature, in their relationships, at work, and in social activism (Manning 2019). The emphasis on this world encourages a practical, empirical attitude that encourages experimentation and cautions individuals not to believe without evidence or practice without benefits. In this view, the universe has no inherent purpose but each of us can create one for ourselves.

FIGURE 11.2 *Many secular individuals find meaning in nature.* Source: *bombuscreative / Getty Images.*

Personal Choice and Accountability

Secular individuals embrace the value of personal choice, that every individual has the right, if not the duty, to choose their own worldview and to freely express that worldview (Manning 2015; Thiessen 2015). Related to the emphasis on choice is an affirmation of pluralism: that wisdom can be found in multiple religious and philosophical traditions and that it's okay to combine ideas and practices from various sources. The emphasis on choice leads to personal accountability. Secular morality is not about abstaining from sex or alcohol, or doing what some authority tells you to do, or not doing something because you fear otherworldly consequences. Rather it's about developing your own inner moral compass (Zuckerman 2014).

The Golden Rule

At the core of secular morality is the Golden Rule, to treat others as you would like to be treated. Following this rule, most secular individuals believe it is wrong to harm others and it is right to help those in need (Zuckerman 2014). While the Golden Rule is incorporated into many religions, it is not inherently religious. Avoiding harm and helping others does not require belief in God(s) but human empathy. And the rule is best learned not from sermons but in our interactions in day-to-day life.

Influences on Secular Parenting

Secular parents, like religious ones, want to pass on values and traditions to their children. But there is a great deal of variation in both what they choose to transmit (content) and how they go about doing that (process). Research suggests that the content and process of secular parenting are shaped by at least three factors: the parent's own secular worldview, where they live, and family structure.

The Diversity of Secular Worldviews

When we exclude unaffiliated believers and marginal affiliates, there is still diversity among nones. Some follow a distinctly secular philosophy. Some are eclectic or pluralist, weaving their own personal meaning system from a variety of sources including religious traditions. And some do not espouse any particular worldview.

Philosophical secularism

Many *secular* individuals follow an explicitly secular philosophy, such as humanism, freethought, or Ethical Culture, that is often associated with a larger movement or literature. While some find a home in a secular organization such as the American Humanist Association, only a minority of followers affiliate with such institutions (Cragun, Manning, and Fazzino 2017). Instead, they often read key texts and may communicate online with other followers or contribute to political causes. Philosophical secularists are affirmatively secular, self-consciously choosing what they consider to be rational beliefs and proven practices. They believe that our lives are shaped by natural/material forces and by human decisions. They may engage in meditation or yoga because they feel it provides mental or physical benefits. They may also engage in social justice work as an expression of secular philosophy. They identify as none because they have replaced religion with a secular philosophy. As with secular worldviews, some secular people adopt a explicitly secular identities, as suggested by figure 11.3.

Spiritual but not religious or SBNR (aka Pluralists or Seeker Spirituality)

Other individuals identify as having no religion because they do not think any single tradition or life philosophy has a corner on truth. They feel all religions and secular philosophies contain wisdom (and all have problems) and we must combine what we

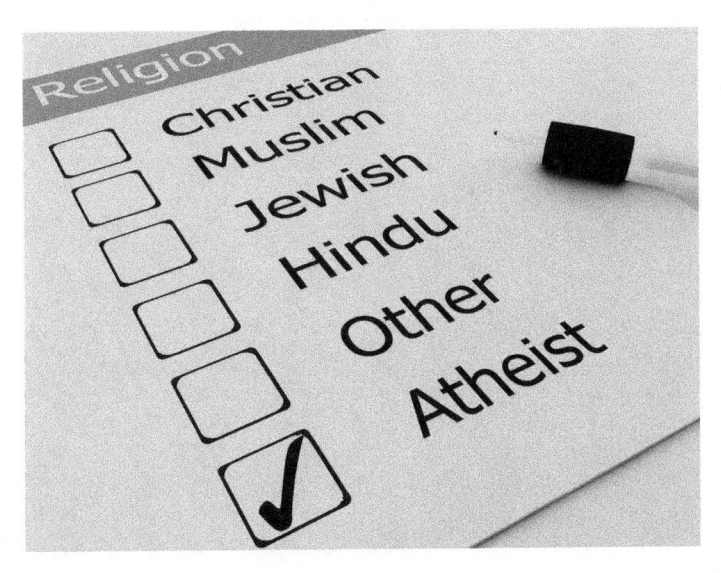

FIGURE 11.3 *Some nones have a distinct nonreligious identity.* Source: *castillodominici/ Getty/iStock Images Plus.*

like from among them. Since SBNR worldviews are both eclectic and personal, there is tremendous variation. Most reject the idea of a personal god(s) in favor of a higher power, energy, or life force that may influence nature or human life. Practices include prayer, meditation, yoga, and rituals from various religions that have been reinterpreted to fit individual sensibilities (e.g., celebrating Christmas as a festival of nature that marks the return of the sun).

Indifferent

Finally, many people have no religion because they are simply indifferent to it. They don't reject religion (as philosophical secularists do) but they are not searching for spiritual meaning either (as many SBNRs are). They find questions about God(s) or an afterlife or whether any particular scriptures are true to be irrelevant to their lives, and they do not participate in spiritual practice because they are too busy with other things such as work, family, or sports. There is obviously no organization for indifferents though some are still nominal members of organized religion.

It should not be surprising that what secular parents transmit to their children will depend on what type of none they are and on their reasons for adopting that identity. An atheist who comes to that worldview after rejecting his own fundamentalist Christian upbringing may feel more strongly about raising his own children without religion than an atheist parent who grew up without religion. Although they value freedom of choice

FIGURE 11.4 *Some nones are better described as spiritual but not religious. Source: fizkes / Getty Images.*

and may seek to expose their children to a variety of perspectives, the parent's own worldview is likely to have an outside influence because it is modeled on a day-to-day basis.

Location

Secular parenting also depends on where the family lives, the role of religion in the local public culture, and the social acceptance of nonreligious people in the wider community. In both the United States and Canada, religious affiliation is the cultural norm, making secular families a minority who sometimes have to deal with negative stigma. But how much they feel like a minority varies.

Although the percentage of nones is about the same in both nations, it may be easier to be nonreligious in Canada. More people in Canada are only marginally religious, plus Evangelicalism is more widespread in the United States (Longhurst 2019). But there are also variations in the number of secular people living in any given region. The US Bible Belt has a significantly smaller percentage of nones (about 15 percent) than the New England region and the Pacific Northwest (26 percent). There is even more regional polarization in Canada, ranging from nones constituting 44 percent of the population in British Columbia and Western Canada to only 12 percent in Quebec (Bibby 2012; Pew Research Center 2013).

These numbers can shape the experience of secular families (Garcia and Blankholm 2016). For example, in the US South, where Evangelicalism predominates, religion is very much part of public conversation. Public officials invoke their faith to support their political agenda; people will offer to pray over you when you're having a bad day; and if you've moved into a new neighborhood they may ask what church you attend. So an atheist family can feel put on the spot. By contrast, in New England where religion is more privatized and such talk is considered impolite, nobody would know the family is atheist. There is some evidence that location and the real or anticipated stigma that secular parents face influences their parenting choices. Manning (2015) found secular parents living in the Bible Belt more likely to affiliate with an organization that supports their worldview and to enroll their children in educational programming they offer. McClure (2017) found atheist parents in that region mitigate stigma by avoiding the label atheist and instead identifying their worldview as a secular form of spirituality.

Family Structure

Finally, secular child-rearing is shaped by the larger family structure. In making decisions about what worldview to transmit to a child and how to do so, there are many stakeholders: not just the father and mother but also stepparents, grandparents, and others.

Religious intermarriage has become increasingly common over the twentieth century, and many seculars are married to someone who is religiously affiliated. How such couples will raise their children can be a matter of contention. The religious parent will often push for some exposure to a family tradition, for example by enrolling the child in a Sunday school program or taking them to church. The secular parent may not want the children to be indoctrinated and may model a questioning attitude. Research shows children raised by parents who have different religious preferences are less likely to be raised with any religion at all (Kosmin and Keysar 2006; Phillips 2005). This may be because parents seek to avoid conflict, or it may be that people who marry someone of a different religion tend to be less religious themselves.

Divorce is commonplace, and many children grow up in single parent or blended families. If the custodian parent is secular they will obviously have a strong influence on worldview transmission, but the visiting parent may seek to exert influence, for example by taking children to church or synagogue. Research on religious transmission shows the mother to have a strong influence, but one recent study found that fathers had a more important role in secular parenting (Bengtson et al. 2018).

Grandparents may also influence what children are being taught, either encouraging or pushing back against secular parenting. Pushing religion may be overt, for example by asking when a child will be baptized or bar mitzvahed. Or it may be more indirect,

FIGURE 11.5 *Grandparents may influence the transmission of secular worldviews.* Source: *eclipse_images / Getty Images.*

such as sending religious themed children's books or grandma praying with a child when she is babysitting. Some grandparents actively encourage the transmission of a secular worldview, and there are longitudinal studies documenting multigenerational secular families (Bengtson et al. 2018).

Secular Parenting Strategies

The above discussion has argued that secular parenting is influenced by more than the parent's own worldview. Being part of what is still a minority, nonreligious parents may have to negotiate religious influences from extended family members and the religious culture where they live. What further complicates both the content and process of secular worldview transmission is a relative lack of cultural resources to support it. The socialization of children, whether religious or secular, may occur in the home or with the help of institutions. Religious parents may display symbols such as a crucifix or a menorah in the home, and the family may celebrate important holidays such as Christmas or Passover by saying prayers, reading scripture, or eating a ceremonial meal together. But there are few distinctly secular symbols and holidays that atheist or SBNR parents can make use of. While religious parents take their kids to church and send them to Sunday school, most secular individuals are not affiliated with religious institutions and the organizations available often don't offer activities oriented to children (there are important exceptions, which are discussed below). Perhaps more importantly, because many secular parents care deeply about choice, they often want to expose their children to more than one option. The result is a great deal of variation in secular parenting strategies. Manning (2015) identified five different approaches: conventional, outsourcing, alternative, self-provision, or non-provision.

The conventional approach

Readers may be surprised to learn that many secular parents raise their children within a religious community. It's usually because one parent is religious but sometimes grandparents exert some influence. The children may attend a weekly religious education program or go to services with the religious parent, and the family engages in at least a nominal celebration of major holidays in the home. These parents often see practical value in religion even when they have left it behind: it's a good way to teach morality and values, learn about the Bible as part of cultural literacy, or religious congregations offer youth programming they like (e.g., afternoon care, summer camps, volunteer opportunities). Parents also often feel an obligation to impart a traditional family heritage, especially when religion expresses a particular culture or ethnicity (e.g., Jews, Irish Catholics, Hindus, etc.). While they are wary of religious indoctrination, these parents feel that because they are secular, questioning and doubt are encouraged, as is allowing children to make their own choices.

Outsourcing

Some parents seek to pass on tradition but still keep their distance. They can do this by enrolling their children in a religious education program provided by a church or synagogue, while the parents remain outside. They do not join or attend services with their child and do not intentionally engage in any religious activity in the home. For instance, a secular Jewish family might send their son or daughter to Hebrew school on Sunday mornings but they don't maintain membership in a temple or attend even on high holidays. They might celebrate Hanukkah with presents and sweets but they view this as a secular holiday that affirms their family history and cultural identity. Some outsourcing parents choose this option in response to a child's apparent interest in spiritual matters. But most do so for similar reasons as those who choose the conventional route. Outsourcing mitigates the problem of indoctrination because it creates a boundary between secular home life and religious education, making clear that religion is a choice.

The alternative approach

A growing number of parents are raising their children affirmatively secular and want to be part of a community that supports this choice. They can find that by affiliating with organizations such as the American Humanist Association, the Unitarian Universalist Association (UUA), or more recently the Sunday Assembly. These families may read books to children that invite reflection on spiritual or ethical questions, engage them in conversations about social issues, or they might celebrate holidays from traditions that are meaningful to them (e.g., a secular Hanukkah, a pagan summer solstice, and Darwin's birthday). Those values are reinforced through communal engagement with a secular congregation. UUA offers formal "worldview education" programs, a kind of secular Sunday school that teaches kids about many different religions as well as humanist and atheist philosophies and encourages the child to explore. The program was established decades ago and is quite comprehensive, offering various age-appropriate levels, and is available in most of their local chapters. Other organizations have started such programs more recently; the availability of these other programs varies. Secular organizations may provide summer camps, afterschool care, and weekend social justice work. Parents see these pluralistic programs as well suited for today's world (it fosters tolerance of diversity, provides cultural literacy, and expands the pool of wisdom a young person can draw on). Given the minority status of secular people, they also appreciate having a community of like-minded secular families. As figure 11.6 illustrates, secular parents often what their children exposed to a broader array of ideas and values.

FIGURE 11.6 *Secular parents want to expose their children to diverse worldviews.* Source: FatCamera / Getty Images.

Self-providers

Other parents want to provide an affirmatively secular upbringing but do so alone. They will often buy parenting books or go explore blogs to get help teaching their kids about various religions or about secular morality. Their strategies are very similar to those employed by parents who join alternative communities: reading books and watching videos with children, conversations, and creating and celebrating unique family rituals in the home. Without support from a wider community, these parents often struggle to maintain commitment to the process of worldview instruction. As their children enter adolescence, they may lose interest in these activities, and self-provider parents often feel they lack time or appropriate expertise to engage their children at a higher level. Yet many remain outside of organized community, either because they are suspicious of any organized philosophy, religious or secular, or because they are unable to find a suitable institution in their local area.

Non-providers

There are many parents who do not wish to transmit any particular worldview to their children. They do not enroll them in a secular or religious education program, and their home life does not involve any systematic effort to transmit a religious or secular philosophy to their children. They celebrate holidays but without reference to any particular "ism." There may be gifts at Christmas or Hanukkah, bunnies and eggs at Easter, but children learn nothing about the religious significance of these events, and parents don't substitute secular meaning such as solstices or mark explicitly secular events, for instance Darwin day. These families do impart moral values but they are grounded in universal principles such as the Golden Rule or personal accountability rather than adherence to a particular religious tradition or secular philosophy. Parents who are non-providers do not wish to impose any worldview on their child. They feel that when they are old enough, children will choose for themselves.

Which approach a family selects will depend on the various factors discussed earlier. If both parents identify with a secular philosophy they are more inclined to self-provide or affiliate with an alternative community than if parents are indifferent. Secular parents living in a highly religious region may be motivated to affiliate with an alternative institution so their kids can have a sense of belonging. Parents married to religious spouses are more likely to be conventional or to outsource religious education. In addition, families may move between the various options over time. A family may experiment with self-providing a humanist upbringing and only later join a humanist community. They may outsource religious instruction and after several years the secular parent could be persuaded by a religious spouse to attend religious services with her and the children. They may briefly rejoin organized religion to get a child baptized or circumcised, and soon get turned off and drop out again and do nothing with their children.

The variety of ways that secular families raise their children illustrate the difficulties in defining secularity. Religion and secularity are opposites in theory. But in real life, especially family life, the boundaries between religiousness and secularity are highly porous, and they are frequently shifting.

Impact of Secular Parenting

There is considerable debate over the impact of secular parenting. Is it better to raise children with or without religion? The available research does not give a clear answer.

Perhaps because most children in North America are raised with religion, it is widely assumed that doing so is good for them. There is substantial research literature that seems to support this (for a review, see Smith and Denton 2005). For example, studies comparing adolescents who are highly engaged in organized religion with those who are not, report that the former are less likely to use alcohol and drugs, engage in risky sexual behavior, and have lower rates of depression and suicide than the latter. Highly religious teens have closer ties to parents and siblings and do better in school. They have lower rates of media use (e.g., watching TV during the school week or downloading internet porn) and are more engaged in volunteer work to help others. Correlations, of course, do not prove causation. The studies control to varying degrees for other factors that may influence behavior, such as income and education. The differences between more and less religious teens are sometimes very small, but some scholars believe the sheer number of such positive correlations suggests religion may play a causal role (Smith and Denton 2005). They point out that organized religion has certain structural characteristics that facilitates these outcomes. It offers a clear framework to teach ethical values to children; there are compelling narratives that help them remember these messages; regular interaction with peers and adults who share the same values reinforces their plausibility; and a community of caring adults offer opportunities for positive mentoring and networking beyond the young person's immediate family.

But the fact that religion can have a positive impact on children does not mean secular children cannot do well without it. First, many of the supposed benefits of religion have more to do with being part of an organization or community than with particular theologies or practices, and the "structural characteristics" of organized religion that facilitate positive outcomes can also be found elsewhere. As we have seen earlier, secular philosophies can and do provide clear moral frameworks for teaching morality to children. Religion is not the only source of compelling narratives, and thanks to the internet and the rise of organized secularism, there is a growing body of resources (children's books, videos, etc.) that parents can draw on for inspiration. The growth of organized secularism and the creation of communities such as the Sunday Assembly provide support to families in similar ways that religion has. But there are other ways, such as environmental or social justice work, that secular parents can interact with other, like-minded families and provide their children with an extended community of caring adults.

A second reason to question claims that it is better to raise children with religion is that these studies do not adequately sample secular individuals. A closer examination of their research methodology finds that too many studies linking religion with health and well-being rely on volunteer samples who may or may not reflect the general population (Weber 2012). Worse, few studies include respondents who are affirmatively secular. They typically compare people who are highly engaged with organized religion with those who are disengaged from religion, ignoring those who have replaced religion with something they feel is better, such as a secular philosophy or a pluralistic non-theistic spirituality. Because there is a near universal absence of atheist control groups, we cannot draw valid conclusions about the impact of nonreligion (Hwang et al. 2011).

The few studies that do sample affirmatively secular individuals show that their children do just fine. One study (Bengston 2013) found nonreligious parents to be just as effective in imparting strong ethical standards as religious ones, and in teaching children to live a purpose filled life. Zuckerman (2014) has argued that a secular upbringing may actually be more likely to help kids grow up into ethical adults. Religion teaches children to obey a set of external rules given by a powerful authority, God(s), and sometimes enforced by corporal punishment. By contrast, secular families encourage children to think for themselves; they are encouraged to question authority, to solve problems rationally, and to empathize with others. As a result, secular teens are less likely than the religious to succumb to peer pressure, and grow up into adults who are less authoritarian, less racist, and more tolerant of others. A recent national study of young nones confirms that "religious identification is not necessary for meaning and moral values" (Clydesdale and Garces Foley 2019: 156). Like their religious peers, the majority of nones affirm that life has meaning and that to have a meaningful life you should help other people. The proportion who report that they spend a lot of time helping people in need, either individually or through organizations, is about the same as among religiously affiliated twentysomethings. Furthermore, more nones feel passionate about social justice compared to their religious peers.

Finally, the supposed benefits of raising children with religion must also be weighed against the costs. The positive outcomes such as lower alcohol or drug use attributed to religion are strongest for highly religious teens who are often raised in very conservative families such as fundamentalist Christians or Orthodox Jews. Some studies show children raised in such households are more likely to experience emotional and physical abuse and to suffer guilt and anxiety, especially over sexual feelings (Capps 1992; Cooper 2012). Secular parents must also consider what types of values are more important to them. Raising children with religion may help teens refrain from drinking alcohol and wait longer before having sex, but that only matters if you think temperance and chastity are virtues. The core values of nones tend to skew more progressive, for example supporting gender equality and diversity (Alper 2018). So if a secular upbringing helps a young person become less conformist and more tolerant of others, that is perceived to be a good outcome.

FIGURE 11.7 *Tolerance of diversity is a core value for many secular parents.* Source: *MixMike / Getty Images.*

Conclusion

In summary, it is difficult to generalize about secular parents. The line between religion and secularity is often unclear, and scholars have only recently begun to investigate the subject. Nonetheless, some patterns can be seen. Contrary to stereotype, secular parents have distinct value systems that lend meaning and moral order to life. Secular families hold diverse worldviews and their parenting choices will also be influenced by location and family structure. Like religious parents, secular parents desire to transmit their values and traditions to their children. But unlike religious parents, whose default is raising kids in their own tradition, secular parents are wary of indoctrinating their children and have limited options for joining a community. Research shows at least five different modes of transmission but these may not be unique to secular parents. There is some evidence that children benefit from being raised with organized religion, but research does not support the notion that secular parenting harms children. As the secular population grows, we will learn more about the impact of growing up without religion.

Further Reading and Online Resources

Bengtson, V.L. (2013), *Families and Faith: How Religion Is Passed Down across Generations*, New York: Oxford University Press.

Clydesdale, T. and K. Garces-Foley (2019), *The Twenty-Something Soul: Understanding the Religious and Secular Lives of American Young Adults*, New York: Oxford University Press.

Manning, C. (2015), *Losing Our Religion: How Unaffiliated Parents Are Raising Their Children*, New York: New York University Press.

Pew Research Center (2020), "Religiously Unaffiliated." https://www.pewresearch.org/topics/religiously-unaffiliated/ (accessed September 14, 2020).

Religion News Service (2020), "Search Results: Nones." https://religionnews.com/?s=nones (accessed September 14, 2020).

Zuckerman, P. (2014), *Living the Secular Life*, New York: Penguin Press.

References

Alper, R. (2018), "Why America's Nones Don't Identify with a Religion," Pew Research Center, August 8. https://www.pewresearch.org/fact-tank/2018/08/08/why-americas-nones-dont-identify-with-a-religion/ (accessed September 14, 2020).

Bengtson, V.L. (2013), *Families and Faith: How Religion Is Passed Down across Generations*, New York: Oxford University Press.

Bengtson, V.L., R.D. Hayward, P. Zuckerman, and M. Silverstein (2018), "Bringing Up Nones: Intergenerational Influences and Cohort Trends," *Journal for the Scientific Study of Religion*, 57 (2): 258–75.

Bibby, R. (2012), "Why Bother with Organized Religion? A Response to Thiessen," *Canadian Review of Sociology*, 49 (1): 91–101.

Capps, D. (1992), "Religion and Child Abuse: Perfect Together," *Journal for the Scientific Study of Religion*, 31 (1): 1–15.

Clydesdale, T. and K. Garces-Foley (2019), *The Twenty-Something Soul: Understanding the Religious and Secular Lives of American Young Adults*, New York: Oxford University Press.

Cooper, C. (2012), "Confronting Religiously Motivated Psychological Maltreatment of Children: A Framework for Policy Reform," *Virginia Journal of Social Policy & the Law*, 20 (1): 1–42.

Cragun, R.T., C. Manning, and L. Fazzino, eds. (2017), *Organized Secularism in the United States*, Berlin: DeGruyter Press.

Edgell, P., D. Hartmann, E. Stewart, and J. Gerteis (2016), "Atheists and Other Cultural Outsiders: Moral Boundaries and the Nonreligious in the United States," *Social Forces*, 95 (2): 607–38.

Garcia, A. and J. Blankholm (2016), "The Social Context of Organized Nonbelief: County-level Predictors of Nonbeliever Organizations in the United States," *Journal for the Scientific Study of Religion*, 55 (1): 75–90.

Hwang, K., J.H. Hammer, and R.T. Cragun (2011), "Extending Religion-Health Research to Secular Minorities: Issues and Concerns," *Journal of Religion and Health*, 50: 608–22.

Jeff and Alyssa (2012), "Why I Hate Religion, but Love Jesus || Spoken Word." YouTube, January 10. https://www.youtube.com/watch?v=1IAhDGYlpqY (accessed September 14, 2020).

Kosmin, B. and A. Keysar (2006), *Religion in a Free Market: Religious and Non-Religious Americans*, New York: Paramount Publishing.

Laflamme, S. and J. Thiessen (2017), "Becoming a Religious None: Irreligious Socialization and Disaffiliation," *Journal for the Scientific Study of Religion*, 56 (1): 64–82.

Lipka, M. (2015), "Millennials Increasingly Are Driving Growth of Nones," Pew Research Center, May 12. https://www.pewresearch.org/fact-tank/2015/05/12/millennials-increasingly-are-driving-growth-of-nones/ (accessed September 14, 2020).

Longhurst, J. (2019), "It's Easier to Be a None in Canada than in the U.S." Religion News Service, May 21. https://religionnews.com/2019/05/21/study-its-easier-to-be-a-none-in-canada-than-in-the-us/ (accessed September 14, 2020).

Manning, C. (2015), *Losing Our Religion: How Unaffiliated Parents Are Raising Their Children*, New York: New York University Press.

Manning, C. (2016), "Secularity and Family Life," in P. Zuckerman (ed.), *Beyond Religion*, ch. 6, Farmington Hills, MI: Gale-Cengage.

Manning, C. (2019), "Meaning Making Narratives among Non-Religious Individuals Facing the End of Life," in V.L. Bengtson and M. Silverstein (eds.), *New Dimensions in Spirituality, Religion, and Aging*, 59–85, New York: Routledge.

McClure, A.I. (2017), "Becoming a Parent Changes Everything: How Nonbeliever and Pagan Parents Manage Stigma in the U.S. Bible Belt," *Qualitative Sociology*, 40: 331–52.

Pew Research Center (2013), "Canada's Changing Religious Landscape," June 27. https://www.pewforum.org/2013/06/27/canadas-changing-religious-landscape/ (accessed September 14, 2020).

Phillips, B. (2005), "Assimilation, Transformation, and the Long Range Impact of Intermarriage," *Contemporary Jewry*, 25 (1): 50–84.

Putnam, R. and D. Campbell (2010), *American Grace: How Religion Divides and Unites Us*, New York: Simon & Schuster.

Smith, C. and M.L. Denton (2005), *Soul Searching: The Religious and Spiritual Lives of American Teenagers*, New York: Oxford.

Thiessen, J. (2015), *The Meaning of Sunday: The Practice of Belief in a Secular Age*, Montreal: McGill-Queen's University Press.

Thiessen, J. (2016), "Kids, You Make the Choice: Religious and Secular Socialization among Marginal Affiliates and Nonreligious Individuals," *Secularism and Nonreligion*, 5 (6): 1–16.

Villa, V. (2019), "Religiously Unaffiliated People Face Harassment in a Growing Number of Countries," Pew Research Center, August 12. https://www.pewresearch.org/fact-tank/2019/08/12/religiously-unaffiliated-people-face-harassment-in-a-growing-number-of-countries/ (accessed September 14, 2020).

Weber, S., K.I. Pargament, M.E. Kunik, J.W. Lomax II, and M.A. Stanley (2012), "Psychological Distress among Religious Nonbelievers: A Systematic Review," *Journal of Religion and Health*, 51 (1): 72–86.

Zuckerman, P. (2014), *Living the Secular Life*, New York: Penguin Press.

Glossary Terms

Agnostic A person who thinks it is impossible to know whether God exists or who is non-committal on the question.

Atheist A person who does not believe in God(s). The term is problematic because it identifies individuals only in terms of what they do not believe in (God[s]). Atheists find meaning in a variety of philosophies and traditions.

Culturally religious Individuals who are personally secular but maintain ties to religion for cultural or familial reasons. Religion has historically served as a carrier of cultural tradition, and celebrating those traditions (foods, clothing styles, etc.) can be a way of affirming a particular cultural identity. This is a common pattern among immigrant groups especially those for whom religion is closely tied to a particular ethnicity (e.g., Jews, Catholics). People who are culturally religious are often marginal affiliates.

Marginal affiliates Individuals who affiliate with organized religion but limit attendance to holidays and rites of passage.

Millennial generation A person who reaches adulthood in the twenty-first century. The term derives from "millennium," which refers to a thousand-year period, and the end of the twentieth century constituted the beginning of another millennium. Some scholars divide people into age-cohorts based on the year people were born. The Pew Research Center, for example, considers anyone born between 1981 and 1996 (ages twenty-three to thirty-eight in 2019) a millennial, and anyone born from 1997 onward is part of a new generation often designated postmillennial or Generation Z.

Nones A term used for individuals who say they have no religious affiliation. The term comes from survey research asking respondents to identify their religious preference or affiliation. The term is problematic because it labels people based on what they lack. The reason people have no preference or affiliation varies, so the term obscures a wide variety of worldviews.

Secular Secularity refers to nonreligion or the quality of being nonreligious, so it can only be understood in reference to religion. Since scholars do not agree on what religion is or what it means to be religious, there are varying definitions of secularity.

List of Contributors

Ryan T. Cragun is Professor of Sociology at University of Tampa, USA.

Mathieu Colin is a PhD candidate at the University of Montreal, Canada.

Luke Galen is Professor of Psychology at Grand Valley State University, USA.

Ariela Keysar, a demographer, is Senior Fellow at the Public Policy and Law Program at Trinity College, USA.

Christel Manning is Professor of Religious Studies at Sacred Heart University, USA.

Amanda Schutz is Research Area Specialist at the University of Michigan, USA.

Jonathan Simmons is a Sociologist and Graduate Writing Specialist at the University of Alberta, Canada.

Jesse M. Smith is Associate Professor of Sociology at Western Michigan University, USA.

David Speed is an Associate Professer at the University of New Brunswick, Saint John, Canada.

Daniel Swann is Visiting Assistant Professor at Goucher College, USA.

Joel Thiessen is Professor of Sociology at Ambrose University, Canada.

Caitlin Trombley is a Postdoctoral Research Fellow at New York University, USA.

Sarah Wilkins-Laflamme is Assistant Professor of Sociology at the University of Waterloo, Canada.

Index

Abbot, D. M. 18
accommodation 85, 155
accountability 198, 206
activism
    political grievances and 159–60
    politics of 160–2
affirmative secularity 9–10, 196
age and generation 34–5
agnosticism 5–6, 34, 48, 121, 127–8, 195
alternative approach 204
Amarasingam, A. 162
American atheists (AA) 10, 70, 83–4, 87, 92, 124, 130, 180, 182
American Civil Liberties Union (ACLU) 92
American Humanist Association (AHA) 18–19, 55–7, 84–5, 87, 99, 130, 160, 199, 204
American Religious Identification Survey (ARIS) 30–3, 37
Americans United for Separation of Church and State 18–19
Anti-Discrimination Support Network 17
apostasy 7
apostate 7
asceticism 136
Asian American atheists 125–7
atheism 5–6, 70, 182, 196. *See also* New Atheism
    and feminism 163
    in Mexico 127–8
    workplace discrimination 52
Atheist Alliance International (AAI) 160
Atheist Awakening (Cimino and Smith) 82
Atheist Community of the University of Ottawa (ACUO) 70
atheists 5–10, 12, 14–21, 30–4, 48–53, 55, 63, 67–8, 70–1, 75, 107–8, 112, 158–9, 171, 174, 182–4, 196, 201.
    See also black atheists
    in Canada 130–1
    identity 48, 50, 70, 101, 125, 130, 145
authoritarianism 142–3

Baird, J. 88–9
Batson, C. D. 145
Beaman, L. 75
Becker, P. E. 108
belief 44
Berger, P. 14
Bethke, J. 195–6
black atheists 105, 120–1
    history of 121–4
    in the United States 124–5
black nonreligion 120–1, 123, 125
Blankholm, J. 103
Block, T. 87
Bradley, R. E. 52
Brewster, M. E. 162
Bush, G. W. 89–90

Cameron, C. 121
Campbell, C. 7
Camp Quest 85
Canada 17, 75–6
    atheists in 130–1
    history 64–6
    left-leaning 72–5
    less antagonistic 70–2
    minority atheists in 131
    minority nonreligion in 128–30
    nonreligion/nonreligious 128–30
    population 9, 69
    racial/ethnic minorities 130
    religious nones in 64–7
    secularism in 67–70, 85–9
Canadian Election Studies (CES) 73
Carroll County School Board 54–5
case study 101
    Houston (*see* Houston)
    The Satanic Temple (TST) 89–94
census 8, 29
Center for Inquiry (CFI) 57, 85, 88
Centre for Inquiry Canada (CFIC) 87–9

Christianity 44, 47, 51–2, 54, 56, 64–5, 73–4, 83, 92–3, 118, 121, 123–4, 128
Cimino, R. 82
coherency 183
Cole v. Webster Parish School Board 53–4
collective identity 160, 163
communal secularity 20
confrontation 85
consensual sex 176
consequentialism 137
conservative 158
conventional approach 203–4
Council for Secular Humanism (CSH) 85, 160
Cragun, R. T. 7, 9, 81, 112
culturally religious 158, 195
curvilinear relationship 183

Dawkins, R. 160
deep equality 75–6
Democratic Party 65, 157–8
demographer 29
demographics 29, 40
   age and generation 34–5
   education 38
   gender 33–4
   marital status 37–8
   race/ethnicity 36–7
deontology 137
Dilmaghani, M. 182
discrimination 51–2
   education and 53–5
   nonreligious 51–2, 55–6
   public 55–6
   workplace 52–3
divorce 202
Doe, M. 93–4
Douglas, T. 65
Downy, M. 17

ecological fallacy 144
Edgell, P. 51
education 38
   and discrimination 53–5
Employment Equity Act 129
establishment clause 91–2
Ethical Culture movement 19
ethnicity 36–7
evangelical
   Christians 71, 74, 102
   heathens 17

Evangelicalism 65, 70, 75, 201
events 103–4

Fazzino, L. L. 81
fear of death 13
feminism 163
Fiddes, J. 88
Fischer, C. S. 15
Four Horsemen 85
Fowler, K. 182–3
Freedom From Religion Foundation (FFRF) 56, 84, 94, 99, 124, 163
free exercise clause 91
Freethought Association of Canada 88
Frost, J. 20, 110

Galen, L. W. 45–6, 81
García, A. 103
Gaylor, A. N. 84
gender 33–4
generalist organization 107
generalized results 181
General Social Survey (GSS) 32–3
geography 17, 39
Gervais, W. 16
godless congregation 105–7, 109–10
Godless Revival 20, 107
God question 45, 48
Golden Rule 198, 206
goth 112
Gould, F. J. 84
Greaves, L. 89, 93
Grief Beyond Belief 57
grievances 159–60, 161, 163

Hammer, J. H. 7, 52–3
Harrison, H. 123–4
Henderson, B. 93
Hispanic and Latinx Americans 125–6, 131
Holden, J. 56
Holyoke, G. J. 6, 197
homophily 74–5
Houston 101–3
   church-like 110
   competition 107
   conflict 107–9
   coordination 106–7
   events 103–4
   identities 104–5
   ideological disagreement 109–10
   Oasis 106, 108–9, 113

organizational forms 105–6
practical reasons 109
stigma 111–12
Hout, M. 15
Hughes, L. 123
humanism 6, 46
Humanist Association of Canada (HAC) 19, 86–7
Hurston, Z. N. 122–3
Huxley, T. 5

identities 104–5
identity conflict 108
ideological disagreement 109–10
inactive believers 69
inactive nonbelievers 68
indifferent 200–1
informed sex 176
in-groups and out-groups 71
intermarriage 202
intersectional 124, 127, 131–2
involved believers 69
involved seculars 68–9
irreligion 6–7

Jarry, M. 89

King, M. L. Jr. 124
Kurtz, P. 85, 88

La Révolution tranquille (the Quiet Revolution) 86
Latinos 36–7, 40
LaVey, A. 89
LeDrew, S. 46
Lee, L. 3, 48
left-leaning 72–5, 109, 157
LGBTQ community 48–9
LGBTQ National Coming Out Day 49
liberal 158
local secular community 101–2
events 103–4
Houston, Texas 102–3
identities 104–5
organizational forms 105–6
local secular organizations 99–106, 109–10, 113
local secular participation 109
church-like 110
ideological disagreement 109–10
practical reasons 109
stigma 111–12

Manning, C. 201, 203
marginal affiliates 195–6, 198
marginalization 153, 159–60
marital status 37–8
McClure, A. I. 201
meaning making in life 56–8
metaethics 137–8
Mexico 131
atheism and agnosticism in 127–8
nonreligious in 8–9, 18, 21, 101, 120
millennial generation 35, 194
Millennial Trends Survey (MTS) 68, 71
minority
atheists 131
nonreligion 128–30
Mollen, D. 18
Monsiváis, C. 128
Moral Foundations Theory 135–6
morality 16, 44, 48, 51, 57, 83, 135–8, 141, 143, 145–7
Morgentaler, H. 87
multiculturalism 65, 74, 161

National Day of Reason 49
national secular organizations 82, 86, 99–100, 107, 112, 124
negative familial responses 50
New Atheism 82, 85, 87–8, 152, 161
politics of 160–2
nonbeliever 47
nones 7–9, 39–40, 171–6, 178–80, 194–7
composition of 31–2
religious 64–70, 72–6
non-providers 205–6
Nonreligion and Secularity Research Network 2
nonreligion/nonreligious 9–10, 12–15, 44–7, 153
Canada 128–30
communities 18–20
defined 3–5, 30
deleterious effects 181–2
discrimination 51–2, 55–6
and health 178–82
label 47–50
Mexico 8–9, 18, 21, 101, 120
politics of 156–8
prejudice and 16–18
and the public sphere 153–6
and religious 146
research on 8–9, 20–2

salutary effects 179–81
socialization 66
United States 21, 30–5, 45–9, 51–2, 57–8
null results 178–9

O'Hair, M. 83–4, 87, 130
Oklahoma Capitol Preservation Commission 93
Oklahoma Ten Commandments monument 92–4
oppression 51, 124
organizational forms 105–6
outsourcing 204

parochialism 137
Pasquale, F. L. 45–6, 81
passive secularity 196
personal choice 198
Pew Religious Landscape Surveys 30, 32–3
Pew Research Center 39
philosophical secularism 199
plausibility structures 14
politics/political 153
    grievances 159–60
    of New Atheism 160–2
    of nonreligion 156–8
    secularism 18–19
    tensions and conflicts 162–4
polysecularity 20
prejudice 16–19, 57, 105, 196–7
prescriptions 175–8
privilege 51, 66, 105, 162
problem of death 13
progressive 158
proscriptions 175–8
prosociality 139–41
    situations 145–6
psychological spirituality 48
public discrimination 55–6
public sphere 81–3, 89–92, 153–6, 159, 161

Quack, J. 4
Quebec 86

race 36–7
racial and ethnic minority 104, 118, 120–1, 125–7, 130–2
Randolph, P. 121–4
rational choice theory 12–13

religion 30
religion/spirituality (R/S) 171–3, 177–8, 182–4
    health relationship 173–4
    sexual debut 176
    social support 175
religious
    economies model 12–13
    engagement paradox 144
    exiting 7
    nones 64–70, 72–6, 152
Religious Landscape Survey 35
Richter, C. L. 20
Ritze, M. 92
Roman 71–2
Russell, B. 5

Satanic Ritual Abuse 90
The Satanic School of Romanticism 89–90
Satanism 89–91, 93
Scheitle, C. P. 18
Schulzke, M. 161
Second World War 65
secular 67–70, 199
secularism 6, 8, 81, 197
    in Canada 67–70, 85–9
    defined 197
    meaning and values 196–7
    philosophical 199
    political 18–19
    in the United States 82–5, 89–91
secularity 12–15
    definition 3–5, 194–6
    research on 8–9, 20–2
secularization 1–2, 12–14, 35, 37, 40, 65–6, 82, 86
secular organizations 5–6, 18–21, 81–2, 84–6, 99, 105, 199, 204
    local 99–106, 109–10, 113
    national 82, 86, 99–100, 107, 112, 124
secular parenting 194, 198, 203
    alternative approach 204
    conventional approach 203–4
    family structure 201–3
    impact of 206–8
    indifferent 200–1
    location 201
    non-providers 205–6
    outsourcing 204
    self-providers 205
secular worldviews 198–201

self-providers 205
Sherkat, D. E. 30
Sherman, M. 87
Shook, J. 20
Silverman, D. 84
Smith, C. 44–6, 82
Smith, J. M. 9, 20
social stigma 18, 21, 48, 51, 65–6, 71, 196
social support 175
sociocultural influences 143–4
specialist organizations 107
Speed, D. 180, 182–3
spiritual but not religious (SBNR) 69, 199–200, 203
stages of decline 66, 69
stereotypes 145–6
Steward, A. 121
stigma 111–12
Sunday Assembly 19–20, 68, 106–7, 141, 204, 207
Sunday service 106

Taves, A. 15
theism 44–6, 50
   coming out 46
   pervasiveness of 44
   questioning 44–5
   rejecting 45–6
The Satanic Temple (TST) 89–94
third variable problem 139

three Bs 30
Tomlins, S. 64, 70
Toronto Humanist Association 88
Toronto Secular Alliance 88
Trottier, J. 88–9

unchurched 48
Unitarian Universalist Association (UUA) 204
The United States
   black atheists in 124–5
   nonreligious in 21, 30–5, 45–9, 51–2, 57–8
   population 9, 29, 69
   secularism in 82–5, 89–91
US Census 29

value misalignment 15
Volokh, E. 56

Wallace, M. 52
Wesselhoft, P. 93
Wilkins-Laflamme, S. 68
Wolf, G. 160
workplace discrimination 52–3
World Values Survey (WVS) 8, 31
worldview 139–41, 144, 147, 204
Wright, A. H. 52

Zimmerman, K. J. 18, 49–50
Zuckerman, P. 45–6, 81, 207